W0246918

PENGUIN BOOKS
OF CRICKET, GUINNESS AND GANDHI

Vinay Lal teaches history at the University of California, Los Angeles. He writes widely on Indian history, the popular and public culture òf India, the Indian diaspora, global politics, and the politics of knowledge systems. His most recent books include *Empire of Knowledge: Culture and Plurality in the Global Economy* (Pluto Press, 2002); *The History of History: Politics and Scholarship in Modern India* (Oxford University Press, 2003), *Introducing Hinduism* (Icon Books, 2005), and (co-edited with Ashis Nandy) *The Future of Knowledge and Culture: A Dictionary for the Twenty-first Century* (Penguin, 2005).

Of Cricket, Guinness and Gandhi

Essays on Indian History and Culture

Vinay Lal

PENGUIN BOOKS

An imprint of Penguin Random House

PENGUIN BOOKS

USA | Canada | UK | Ireland | Australia
New Zealand | India | South Africa | China | Singapore

Penguin Books is part of the Penguin Random House group of companies
whose addresses can be found at global.penguinrandomhouse.com

Published by Penguin Random House India Pvt. Ltd
4th Floor, Capital Tower 1, MG Road,
Gurugram 122 002, Haryana, India

Penguin
Random House
India

First published by Seagull Books Private Limited 2003
First published in paperback by Penguin Books India in association with
Seagull Books 2005

Copyright © Seagull Books 2003, 2005

All rights reserved

10 9 8 7 6 5 4 3 2

ISBN 9780144000050

Typeset in Perpetua by Mantra Virtual Services, New Delhi
Printed at Repro India Limited

This book is sold subject to the condition that it shall not, by way of trade
or otherwise, be lent, resold, hired out, or otherwise circulated without the
publisher's prior consent in any form of binding or cover other than that in
which it is published and without a similar condition including this condition
being imposed on the subsequent purchaser.

www.penguin.co.in

This is a legitimate digitally printed version of the book and therefore might not
have certain extra finishing on the cover.

For my mother Shanno Devi
and my father Kishori Lal
with whom matters Indian I have been
discussing for nearly two decades

Contents

III

GANDHIAN HERMENEUTICS/HERMENEUTIC GANDHIISM

IV

THE CATEGORIES OF KNOWLEDGE:
A CIVILIZATIONAL PERSPECTIVE ON INDIA

ACKNOWLEDGEMENTS

The essays in this volume have been several years in the making. All of them, though previously published, have now been revised, some to a very substantial degree. Many friends—Ashis Nandy, Bernard Cohn, Ziauddin Sardar, I. K. Shukla, and Dipesh Chakrabarty, among others—have encouraged me to collect some of my essays in a volume, and I am grateful to them for making me persevere in this enterprise. I am grateful as well to Anjum Katyal and Naveen Kishore of Seagull Books for the enthusiasm with which they embraced this book.

Chapter I was previously published under the same title in *Suitcase* 1, nos. 1-2 (1995):60-73, and was first delivered as a seminar paper at the University of California, Santa Barbara, at the invitation of Mark Juergensmeyer. Chapter VII also first appeared in *Suitcase* 3, nos. 1-2 (1998):60-73, under the title of 'The Hijras of India: Gender-Bending and the Cultural Politics of Sexuality.' A longer version of the essay on Hijras was published as 'Not This, Not That: The Hijras of India and the Cultural Politics of Sexuality', *Social Text*, no. 61 [Vol. 17, no. 4] (Winter 1999):119-40; the views it adumbrates were first tested out at the Annual Conference on South Asia held at the University of California, Berkeley, 14-15 February 1998, and I am grateful to Professors Barbara Metcalf, Frank Korom, and Robert Goldman for their remarks. *Suitcase*, published by graduate students in the Departments of English and Comparative Literature at UCLA, had a short but brilliant life, and it has since ceased to exist; it is, as far as I am aware, entirely unavailable in India. It embodied in some respects those principles of criticism and dissent which my book champions.

Chapter II was first published as 'The Impossibility of the Outsider in the Modern Hindi Film', in *The Secret Politics of Our Desires: Innocence, Culpability, and Indian Popular Cinema*, ed. Ashis Nandy (London: Zed Press and Delhi: Oxford University Press, 1998), pp. 228-59. Chapter IV was published in the Australian journal *South Asia* (New Series) as 'The Security Fantasies of the Indian Nation-State: Black Cat Commandos, Gunmen, and Other Terrors', Vol. 20, no. 2 (December 1997):103-38.

The two essays on Gandhi have travelled a greater distance than most of the other essays. The essay on Gandhi and ecology was delivered in 1998 as the Second Joseph Asanbe Memorial Lecture on Multiculturalism at Austin Peay State University in Clarksville, Tennessee, and I am grateful to the members of the Asanbe Lecture committee for bestowing this honour on me. Edward Goldsmith was deeply appreciative of the ideas expressed in the essay, though he is not entirely in agreement with my critique of deep ecology; nevertheless, we entered into a lively correspondence. My friends Kalpana Das and Robert Vachon at the Intercultural Institute of Montreal, then published it in their superb but little-known journal *Interculture*, which has been one of the principal voices of informed dissent in the last two decades. They even arranged for its translation into French, and published it as 'Au-Dela de L'Ecologie Profonde: Gandhi et La vision Ecologique de La Vie', *Interculture*, no. 137 October 1999):37-60. A slightly different version of the article also appeared recently as 'Gandhi and the Ecological Vision of Life: Thinking Beyond Deep Ecology', *Environmental Ethics* 22, no. 2 (Summer 2000):149-68. The two anonymous reviewers for *Environmental Ethics* provided useful suggestions, and I thank them for their careful reading of the essay. The other essay, which forms Chapter V, has been published as 'Nakedness, Non-violence, and Brahmacharya: Gandhi's Experiments in Celibate Sexuality', *Journal of the History of Sexuality* 9, nos. 1-2 (January-April 2000):105-136.

The remaining two essays in this book, which form Chapters III and VIII, have appeared in earlier versions in the journal *Humanscape*, published from Mumbai. I am grateful to Jayesh Shah and Hutokshi Doctor for giving me this forum, though it is no exaggeration to suggest that activists, human rights advocates, and scholars all over India should be thankful that *Humanscape*, which is still in relative infancy, has so far successfully resisted pressures to turn trendy, commercial, and smart, and remains seriously devoted to many issues that most periodicals, popular and scholarly alike, are loath to address. The germ of the essay on India's nuclear pretensions (and much worse) is to be found in an opinion-editorial piece of around 350 words entitled 'Coming Out From Gandhi's Shadow', *Los Angeles*

Times (19 May 1998), also published as 'Modern India Blows Up Its Bridges Back to Gandhi', *Salt Lake Tribune* (24 May 1998), Commentary Pages. To the best of my knowledge, it was the first critical piece on India's nuclear explosions by an Indian in any major American newspaper, and it is with some sadness that I recall the vituperative and even ferocious response it evoked from many Non-Resident Indians. One respondent, describing herself as 'very proud Indian Woman, a research physicist,' thought fit to lecture me on Indian history, to wit: 'Do you think nonviolence would have worked in the era of Mongols [sic] like Aurangzeb, or the reign of Hitler? You are indescribably naive (stupid in plain language) if you believe that Nonviolence is going to preserve and protect Indian culture and India from the dangers it faces in the likes of Muslim Fundamentalists of Pakistan, and China's expansionist vision. Instead of using your education and position to educate the US public regarding the history of torture and devastation of India by Muslim Invaders, you have degraded us by using words like "effeminacy" and "eunuchs" '. Another writer, also a woman and a history graduate, sent me an email accusing me of ingratiating myself among white American academics: 'You perhaps think you have proved your credentials as a "liberal-intellectual" who can critique his country and thus suck up to the white media and colleagues to extract tenureship. But all you have established is your sycophancy and ignorance of the reality of the US and it's [sic] establishments which have always excoriated your birth country. You need only go to Canada and the UK to see the esteem Indians are held in.' These responses, and other like ones, furnish the most compelling testimony to the necessity for framing dissenting frameworks of knowledge.

Permission to include material from previous essays is gratefully acknowledged.

I would, finally, like to thank my student and friend, Mark Mairot, for his extensive help with newspaper research for the essay on security fantasies, and am grateful to various graduate students—Mitch Numark, Ashok Hegde, Ben Marshke—who have helped me with library work at other times. Wendy Belcher gave me a demonstration of her superb editorial skills by carefully looking over the essay on hijras in its earliest incarnation when it appeared in *Suitcase*.

This book is for my parents, Shanno Devi and Kishori Lal, who—

unlike many Indian middle-class families—never attempted to persuade me that only the careers of a doctor, engineer, scientist, chartered accountant, investment banker, and the like are worthy of respect or calculated to give one an acceptable standard of living. The immense pressures placed on the students of Indian descent whom I have encountered on the campus of the University of California, Los Angeles, over the course of the last eight years, suggest to me that middle-class Indian-Americans from professional families who seek to study the softer social sciences and the humanities must still be prepared in many cases to face the determined opposition of their families, and I am immensely glad that my parents, who luckily had none of the advantages of having studied in an university located in the bastion of liberal democracy, were more enlightened in this respect.

INTRODUCTION

The eight essays that comprise this book offer a dissenting, futurist, and hermeneutic perspective on Indian civilization. Over the course of the last two decades, the study of Indian culture, politics, and society has been very considerably enlivened by the numerous intellectual trajectories, among them postcolonial theory, feminism, subaltern studies, and post-structuralism, which together are encapsulated under the term 'cultural studies'. In a bibliographic study published five years earlier, I had enumerated the contours of South Asian cultural studies, and suggested that much promising work had been done in India, and by scholars of Indian studies abroad, in such diverse areas as women's studies, the sociology of science, subaltern history, and the study of media and popular culture. However, it has been transparent for a number of years that South Asian cultural studies could go the way of cultural studies in the British and especially American academy, rapidly denuded of its political content and acquiring a mechanistic and formalist interpretive framework. Consequently, I had then argued that intellectual production in India would not have distinct characteristics, or political salience, unless it was prepared to enter into a conversation with the traditions of marginalized people, local forms of knowledge, and the non-modern (though by no means necessarily 'traditional'), antihistoricist, mythic, vernacular, and pluralist elements of Indian civilization. At the same time, South Asian cultural studies would have to embrace the task, to quote from my earlier work, of engendering 'post-modern and non-modern alternatives to the dominant official discourse of the scientific, managerial, modern nation-state.'

The present volume can be described as taking up the challenge I had then proposed, though its moorings—of which the essays provide many hints—are in spiritual, political, and cultural traditions, and intellectual practices, that are not frequently encountered in works that commonly fall under the rubric of cultural studies. My engagement with the problematics of 'Orientalism' and its critique is a case in point. In the twenty-five years since the work of Foucault first came to be known in the Anglo-American world and Edward Said published *Orientalism* (1978), the critique of 'colonialism and its forms of knowledge' has been the bedrock of much work in cultural studies. Numerous variations on the thesis of Orientalism have been introduced; finer distinctions have been offered about the relationship between colonialism and the forms of representation; and 'resistance' surfaced almost immediately as the missing element in Said's analysis. Said's admirers and detractors, as well as those who seek to strike a balance, have been locked in battle: there are those who think that Said had a rather monolithic conception of colonialism and a highly textualist approach when he himself derided the textualism of Orientalism, while others have argued that Said's work opened up new questions about the discursive forms of colonialism. But the more interesting question is how far the thesis of Orientalism may have led astray even the most nuanced critics of colonialism's framework of knowledge, as evidenced by the unfortunate and frequently encountered suggestion that Mohandas Gandhi's vision of India was ironically 'Orientalist'. Such an interpretation merely takes Gandhi as a text to be read like anything else, and betrays a profound unease with Gandhi's ahistoricism and his radical enactment of dissent. Consequently, the moorings of this current work are not substantively in the tradition of the work that, over the last two decades, has derived from Said and other notable practitioners of colonial discourse analysis.

Since this book does not take as its brief the idea that recourse to 'theory' demands an overt engagement with those schools of critical thought which, for all their apparent deviance from older orthodoxies, have acquired immense respectability in the academy, the reader will seldom encounter any direct discussion of the contemporary intellectual trajectories which the subjects of the essays might have seemed to evoke. Though cultural studies has introduced the 'holy trinity' of race, gender, and ethnicity into recent discussions of politics, history, and culture, and helped to pose certain vital questions about the constitution of nations, the political and narrative strategies of texts, the voices in which history speaks to us, and the politics of representation, it seldom steps outside the frame of knowledge established by the various academic disciplines. This recent interpretive work offers us rearrangements of the pictures within the frame, but it is loath to dispense with the frame; it has broadened our notion of the 'subjects' of history, but it understands ahistoricism only as primitivism or as an aspect of the pre-historical; it has a more expansive conception of what can reasonably pass for art, but it seeks to place the Bengali patua or scroll painting in the frame that once held the Picasso: the frame does not only confer respectability, it brings new objects into the arena of study and also makes them available as commodities. Whether in its incarnation as postcolonial theory, women's history, self-reflexive anthropology—one of the numerous academic variants of the fever of apology gripping the white, liberal male—or the less Eurocentric 'world history' that is increasingly being embraced on university campuses in the United States and increasingly Britain as well, cultural studies appears as the ecumenical enterprise of late modernity.

But just how dedicated is cultural studies to the ecological survival of plurality? Just how wide is its interpretive frame and what is its vision of dissent? The recent work on India, and more broadly on colonialism, offers some cues. Subaltern history has doubtless made many advances upon previous work in Indian history, but its incapacity to deal with religion is all too evident. A certain awkwardness with respect to religion afflicts much of the secular Indian intelligentsia, and it is notable that those who purport to be religious-minded, such as the adherents of Hindutva ideology, are just as uncomfortable with Hinduism. The Hindutvavadis derive their teachings from Veer Savarkar, who was eminently secular: he had only disdain for that fuzzy, unbounded, multi-pronged, and largely unregulated religion called Hinduism. The secularists, it is true, have no interest in creating the conditions that would lead to a Hindu nation-state, but nonetheless they share with their putative opposites a similar indifference to matters of faith. Cultural studies, in whatever shape or form, is spectacularly devoid of religious or even spiritual and—as shall become clear—civilizational moorings.

Or consider the case of Indian cinema. For many years Marxist critics behaved as though Ritwik Ghatak was the only filmmaker at work in India, though on occasion the head was turned in acknowledgment towards Mrinal Sen or the early films of Shyam Benegal, and even now the critical corpus on Ghatak they have produced probably exceeds their writings devoted to the vast popular Hindi cinema. Now that cultural studies has made it agreeable, indeed sexy, to study popular films, whether produced in Hindi, Tamil, or other Indian languages, a body of academic work is beginning to emerge on 'Bollywood'. The tenor of much of this work, however, can be suitably judged by the work of those who write for the *Journal of Arts and Ideas*: their idea of film criticism is shaped almost entirely by formalistic film analysis, the film theory that had developed in relation to European and American cinema, and by the tenets of postcolonial theory, which behooves us to consider the politics of inclusion and exclusion in the constitution of nations. Thus the work of these film critics, dwelling as well on the more artistic side of commercial cinema, has revolved around a handful of films such as *Roja*, *Bombay*, and *Border*, and delivered no more than the predictable observations that these films are insidious attempts to insert the ideology of the (Hindu) nation-state into the fabric of Indian society or that the Muslim in India invariably remains short-changed.

If the most substantial achievements of cultural studies practitioners, most particularly postcolonial theorists, appear to pertain to work on colonialism, even here it is remarkable how far they have remained indifferent, if not hostile, to Gandhi. It has become routine for these theorists to lionize Fanon, but Gandhi leaves them cold. Yet it is Gandhi who had a far-reaching critique of modernity, industrial civilization, the culture of waste and excess, the fetishization of science, instrumental rationality, and regimes of violence, and it is Gandhi who in so many ways has shown himself to be the most prescient figure of the late twentieth century. But non-violence has never been too sexy, and if the habits (in Churchill's notorious description) of a 'half-naked seditious fakir' rankled British viceroys and their political masters back home, they are perhaps only slightly less offensive to the sensibilities of postcolonial critics for whom dissent is largely a matter of aesthetics, and sometimes little more than the fond imagination that their rumblings from the seat of the American academy will be enough to change the world. Gandhi had, moreover, not even remotely anything to do with psychoanalysis, and it is generally supposed that he was much less sophisticated than Fanon, lacking intellectual rigour and psychological insight. It has become something of a cliché to say that Gandhi was no systematic thinker; he never penned any 'treatises' as such. Indeed, by the common consent of many intellectuals, he was 'a man of action', not a thinker. He was supremely indifferent to 'art' and the finer things of life; he never even watched a movie, and his religiosity, unadorned prose, singular lack of political oratory, and sartorial presence, all make him an acute embarrassment even to those critics and scholars who might otherwise have been expected to embrace him. Said himself offered, in *Culture and Imperialism*, an oddly pedagogic guide to, as it were, the anti-colonial masterworks of the South, and though Gandhi must by any standard be deemed one of the founders of anti-colonial resistance, he receives barely a passing mention.

The chapters of this book, then, point to a somewhat different kind of politics of knowledge, of which I furnish no explicit statement, though I hope that the sensibility which informs this politics is more than adequately on display in these essays—a politics that defies the models of defiance put forth by the academy, dissents from normalizing forms of knowledge, points to the monoculturalism of globalization and sets up competing universalisms from what are taken to be particularisms, and argues for an ecological plurality of knowledges. This collection of essays should also be construed, if I may somewhat immodestly put forth this suggestion, as an attempt to help in establishing a tradition of modern Indian criticism in English, of whom there are only a handful of practitioners—such as Ashis Nandy, Rustom Bharucha, Shiv Visvanathan, and T. G. Vaidyanathan—in India today. Subaltern historians, as I have suggested before, work largely within the parameters of history, just as the chosen field of enquiry for postcolonial critics is mainly literature (though film is increasingly falling into their ambit). The enterprise of criticism, however, is often not congruent with the tasks of scholarship. Criticism requires a different sensibility and inhabits a different space: it is associated with self-reflexivity, transdisciplinarity, a wide engagement with the world, an ability to adopt a canvas that is simultaneously large and small, and a passion for commentary.

The book is divided into four parts. Section I, on 'Public and Popular Culture', opens with an essay that explores the passion which drives Indians to unusual achievements that would earn them a place in the *Guinness Book of Records*. In a world where achievement is increasingly measured by records and numbers, it is not unexceptional to find that Indians should be attempting to emulate the West, even if it is possible to do so only by playing out the very Orientalist stereotypes generated under colonialism. It has been suggested that a long period of tutelage under colonial powers induced an extraordinary inferiority complex among Indians, and certainly nowhere is this more evident than in the public soul-searching that accompanies every Olympic Games, when Indian athletes, representing a nation with a population that today stands at one billion, return home empty-handed. (In the last two Olympic games, India each time won one bronze medal.) There is an immense anxiety among the middle classes at these visible demonstrations of Indian failure, and more than a mere suggestion that Indians lack manliness, the drive to succeed (unless it be at computers or other cerebral games), and, most significantly, what (borrowing from America) is called the 'killer instinct'. This essay, an exploration of the political and cultural contours of the Indian obsession with the *Guinness Book*, also offers some oppositional readings. I argue, for instance, that in some respects Indian record-holders can also be viewed as resisting narratives of development and modernization: what is quite transparent from many of the records is the disutility of these 'achievements'. Modernity was doubtless embraced by many segments of the population, but it is also countered at every turn; and, as a more complex narrative of 'statistics' and 'numbers' in the Indian cultural imaginary suggests, the modern is for many Indians merely a particular insignia of the non-modern.

The second essay moves to a consideration of that remarkable manifestation of popular culture, the commercial Hindi film. In sociological literature, 'Bollywood' is an expression of fantasy, the poor person's form of escapism from a life of hard labour and drudgery. From the standpoint of the new generation of film scholars, who are well-versed in postcolonial theory, the popular Hindi film, particularly in the last few years, betrays an anxiety about nation-making; and they have argued that many filmmakers have perforce adopted the mandate of the state, setting into place firm ideas about what counts for membership in the nation. I argue, quite to the contrary, that the Hindi film is uniquely structured in the mythos of Indian civilization, and that we must take seriously the remark that the Hindi film director, Manmohan Desai, who made many 'blockbusters', offered about his own films when queried by a reporter: 'All my films are really about the Mahabharata.' The particular thesis that I offer is yet bolder: the Hindi film has no real outsider, no significant Other. It has villains, to be sure, but even its villains are likely to be rakshasas (demons, who are scarcely subject to the same rules of morality and conduct that bind human beings), or figures of comedy and caricature. Their villainy is so obviously exaggerated—consider the remark by the corrupt Deputy Inspector-General of Police in the film *Badal* (2000) that for a sum of Rs 10 crores he would even kill his own mother—as to have no indexical value to the world of crime in India. The argument is pursued by a close reading of four films, *Deewar* ('The Wall', 1975), *Shakti* ('Strength', 1982), *Gardish* ('Days of Dust', 1993), and *Khalnayak* ('The Villain', 1993). Though much maligned and ridiculed, the commercial Hindi film has so far remained 'loyal' to the imperatives of Indian civilization; but as the idea of India as a nation-state begins to take precedence over the idea of India as a civilization, Indian cinema will perhaps become hospitable to the idea of the Other, just as the cultural pluralism and accommodation that have shaped India begin to become imperilled.

The note on which I conclude my essay on the popular Hindi film serves as a point of entry into the next set of two essays on 'Politics and the Culture of the Indian State' that comprise Section II of this book. Here the framework is furnished by the dialectical and dialogic opposition of India as a civilization and India as a nation-state. As a civilization, India has an enviable history—part of that history, stretching back to some 4,000 years, and perhaps more, was to remain indifferent to historical productions and to the historical sensibility. Civilizations are resilient, even more so than cultures: they have room within them for competing narratives, they can absorb resistance, and they create the conditions for the ecological survival of plurality—plurality not merely as a policy of the state, or as an occasion for the celebration of diversity, but as the fibre of being. As a nation-state, India is slightly more than 50 years old, and its bark is much worse than its bite. Though middle-class Indians, especially, entertain visions of India as a great power, and gladly cite any American authority—from Henry Kissinger and Bill Clinton to the newly created tycoons of Silicon Valley—who has at any time consented to describe India as an emerging power, as a nation-state India has scarcely had a role to play in world politics, and the various international organizations of which it has been a key player, such as NAM (Non-Aligned Movement), the Commonwealth, and the G-77, have been of very little consequence. India as a civilization never forecloses conversation with its other, more modern, self, though its confidence has greatly eroded with the recognition that civilizational values do not have much purchasing power in the modern market-place; by contrast, the nation-state of India has increasingly sought to disassociate itself from what it takes to be its non-modern and embarrassing civilizational self.

Nowhere was the contrast between these two selves of India more apparent than when the Hindu nationalist government of India decided, in May 1998, to turn the country into a declared nuclear state. In the corridors of the Indian Foreign and Defense Ministries, it had never been doubted that the United States took China seriously only when the Communist country openly went nuclear, and when the Bharatiya Janata Party (BJP) took power, it wholeheartedly embraced the view that India would not achieve any recognition as a political entity until it could stake a claim as a 'great power': its civilizational achievements were not enough to earn India the respect of the world. As I suggest, though most commentators pointed to the domestic compulsions of the BJP, the increasing hostility between India and Pakistan, the diminished importance of Russia, the arrogance of the United States, and other similar political considerations in an endeavour to explain why the BJP desired to gain admittance for India into the debased nuclear club, we might perhaps acquire a more enhanced understanding of the Indian anxiety about recognition by turning to the cultural politics of sexuality, the fear of Gandhi, and the modern desire for what I would characterize as 'mistaken clarity'. It is an open secret that India long had the power to become a nuclear state, but the Indian Defence Minister, George Fernandes, expressed rather well the sentiments of the hawks when he stated that the government desired to remove the haze of 'ambiguity' surrounding India's nuclear status. The world was to know that it could no longer walk all over India. Not less telling is the reported observation of Bal Thackeray, the leader of the militant Shiv Sena party who has openly instigated violence against Muslims, upon first hearing of India's nuclear tests: 'We have shown them [Pakistan's Muslims] that we are not hijras (eunuchs).' Over 200 years ago, the British were to caricature the Indians as an effeminate people, and following their brutal suppression of the Indian rebellion of 1857-58, they went so far as to institutionalize a policy that divided Indians into 'martial' and 'non-martial' races; and ever since, the Hindu male has thought of the meat-eating Muslim as more manly and virile, a member of a race of conquerors. Gandhi, with his advocacy of non-violence, appeared to furnish flesh to the stereotype of the Hindu male, and his assassin was not speaking in jest when he charged Gandhi with the heinous crime of having 'emasculated' the nation and contaminated it with his womanly and superstitious habits of spinning and fasting. It is in this context that I describe India's nuclear tests of 1998 as a second assassination of Gandhi, as a renewed attempt to embed India in an intensely masculine and realpolitik vision of the nation-state.

This same politics of the nation-state, and an embarrassment at being seen as 'soft' and 'woolly-headed', manifests itself as an obsession with security for politicians. In the fourth chapter, 'The Security Fantasies of the Indian Nation-State', I explore the manner in which the state violently intrudes upon the private lives of Indian citizens, ironically in the name of furnishing them and the country's political leaders with security. This essay begins, then, with a consideration of Mahatma Gandhi's repudiation of personal security, and traces the eventual emergence of a security apparatus in independent India that, in the name of combating terrorism, has created new forms of terror for Indian citizens. In this shift, we can witness as well the hardening of the Indian nation-state, and the attempted Indian emulation of Israel, the United States, and other no-nonsense states which are presumed to have given the right signals to terrorists about zero tolerance for terrorism. Yet, the Indian nation-state constantly betrays its other, civilizational self: much of the security apparatus, including the Special Protection Group, presents something of a parody of what is described as 'tight security'.

I have called the third section of this book, also comprised of two chapters, 'Gandhian Hermeneutics'. The official deification of Gandhi as the 'Father of the Nation', accompanied by a scarcely disguised contempt for Gandhi's emphatic repudiation of industrial civilization, realpolitik, instrumental rationality, and 'big science', as well as the manner in which Gandhi's largely self-appointed disciples have rendered him into a colourless figure exemplifying only piety, stern discipline, religious brotherhood, and devotion to the nation, have together succeeded in taking the politics out of Gandhi. If the idea was—and I use this word with deliberation—to emasculate Gandhi, the successive governments over the course of the last five decades have good cause to congratulate themselves, none as much as the present militantly Hindu government. Ironically, as I have suggested earlier, the belaboured attempts of the last few years to remove the spectre of Gandhi may have had the effect of resuscitating the interest in Gandhi. Indian Marxists, who never failed to deride Gandhi for his alleged support of 'bourgeois' institutions and Hindu social practices, have suddenly discovered in Gandhi a martyr for the cause of religious harmony and a genuine upholder of India's ecumenical traditions. This reassessment of Gandhi has emanated not from any genuine conviction that Gandhi was an astute critic of modernity, but rather from having witnessed the ascendancy of militant Hinduism: Gandhi now appears as a palatably 'soft' figure, doubtless too enthused by religion but at least an exemplar of religious catholicity. Gandhi now seems curiously 'relevant'.

My endeavour, in the two essays on Gandhi, is not to make Gandhi relevant to our times, which would be a rather pedestrian exercise, but to suggest some interpretive moves and epistemological arguments that make us aware of Gandhi as a figure of immensely radical dissent and extraordinary political daring. Chapter V takes as its subject Gandhi's experiments in—what would strike most people as an oxymoron— 'celibate sexuality'; more particularly, the intent is to offer an interpretation, and perhaps even a defence, of a practice that Gandhi resorted to in the last few years of his life, namely of going to bed naked with one or more naked young women. Not even his most vociferous critics have ever insinuated that this 'experiment', as Gandhi termed it, entailed sexual intercourse, or any other overt form of sex; indeed, Gandhi took a vow of celibacy in his late 30s, and for the remaining 40 years of his life he appears never to have wavered even remotely from this vow. Yet this experiment was undertaken at a time when Gandhi was taken by many people in India and abroad to be a saint; he was at the helm of his moral influence, and his action was calculated to earn him the opprobrium, as indeed it did, even of many of his close friends and associates. I suggest an interpretive framework which begins with an elaboration of Gandhi's experiment and a consideration of his ideas about sexuality and brahmacharya (celibacy, the striving towards Godhead). I then move to a discussion of Gandhi's relations with women, the passionate intensity of his platonic relations, and the ease with which he comported with women; this narrative is complemented by an account of the long history of his abhorrence for, and disavowal of, sex. I then ground my discussion in Indian views about androgyny and the sexual exercises of renunciates, as well as parables about the lives of Krishna and the late nineteenth-century saint, Ramakrishna. The thrust of this discussion is to suggest that Gandhi at times endeavoured to be a woman, and was taken by many of his women associates to be one: he saw women as better practitioners of ahimsa (non-violence), and thought, not incorrectly, that they were likely to understand that one could abjure sex and yet be the most consummate practitioner of sexuality. I suggest as well, though perhaps incidentally, that Gandhi put forth an alternative model of anthropological research, one that sought to liberate anthropology from the stain which it has carried ever since its inception, namely the demarcation of those who study from those who are studied. Gandhi was that anthropological subject who turned himself into the object of anthropological enquiry.

In this respect as in many others, Gandhi was a player of infinite games; he played not merely within the boundaries, but with the boundaries; he did not merely rearrange the elements within the frame, he stepped outside it altogether. The essay that comprises Chapter VI moves the discussion to the realm of ecology. Gandhi was not an environmentalist, as that term is commonly understood, and yet he was profoundly ecological in every aspect of his thinking and conduct. I suggest, after reviewing the most dominant strands of radical ecology in the West—eco-feminism, social ecology, and deep ecology—that Gandhi went far beyond these; he is much deeper than deep ecology. Gandhi was devoted to animals, but it is doubtful that he would have found the practice of keeping pets admirable; similarly, though he chided many for plucking flowers from trees, it is very unlikely that he would have supported the idea of setting aside large tracts of land as 'wilderness' or 'conservation' areas. Gandhi's embrace of the ecological view of life is best seen in his advocacy of 'needs' rather than 'wants', in his deep commitment to recycling at least three decades before it started becoming institutionalized in some parts of the world, and in the brevity of his enormous writings (running to 100 volumes). His entire life, I submit, constitutes an ecological treatise.

The final section, though it is of a piece with the rest of the volume, offers a civilizational perspective on India from a yet different standpoint. One essay invites the reader to consider the place of the ubiquitous hijras, the purported 'third sex', in Indian culture; the other engages with India's rivalry with Pakistan, particularly over cricket. In Chapter VII, I consider the numerous attempts to categorize the hijras: they are variously referred to in the literature as eunuchs, transvestites, homosexuals, bisexuals, hermaphrodites, androgynes, transsexuals, and gynemimetics, or as sexually anomalous beings who are intersexed, transgendered, or castrated. None of these terms is entirely inaccurate; none does justice to the complexities of their identity. Traversing a large range of historical, anthropological, epic, and mythological literature, and rejecting the arguments which seek to describe them as disguised homosexuals, castrated and effeminate men, at best as a 'third sex', I suggest that they are neither male nor female; neither non-male nor non-female; equally, they may well be both male and female, non-male and non-female. They stand thus for what I call a 'hijra politics of knowledge', for a specific tolerance of ambiguity and liminality that has marked Indian culture. The hijras defy the paradigms of classification and enumeration which are dominant in modern knowledge systems; their lifestyle choices are deeply transgressive, not easily assimilable to models of gay politics or queer theory, or the forms of transgendering and transsexual behaviour which have become the common stuff of recent studies on sexuality. Indeed, the hijras are among the last few dissenters of our times, those who have defied the very models of defiance.

The final essay was occasioned by the cricket World Cup which was being contested as Pakistan and India were waging a war over the Himalayan heights at Kargil. In one of the earlier, qualifying matches, India defeated Pakistan, and to many Indians and Pakistanis, the decisive match of the World Cup had been fought. Nonetheless, Pakistan did reach the finals, where it was thrashed by Australia. Returning to India from Osaka the day after the finals, I was apprised of the fact that Pakistan's humiliation had produced much jubilation in India, as though India itself had inflicted another loss on Pakistan, and that sweets had been distributed on the streets of Delhi to celebrate Pakistan's defeat. Thus the essay, 'The Bittersweet Sweets of Modernity', begins with a reflection about the culture of sweets, and the changing indexicality of sweets in the culture of South Asia. Alongside changes in the political culture of the Indian state, the practice of passing out sweets also appears to have undergone immense changes over the course of the last two decades. Doubtless, some people who had suffered the loss of family members and property during the dislocations and violence that accompanied the Partition of India were jubilant when they heard of the assassination of Mahatma Gandhi, whom they imagined to be responsible for the calamitous events of that time, but it is most substantially in the 1980s that the culture of sweets first began to take on new contours. Now, as is suggested by the distribution of sweets following India's nuclear explosions in 1998, and Pakistan's defeat in the World Cup a year later, social practices once rooted in the principle of inclusiveness have been debased to the point where they are a sign of boundary formation.

I

PUBLIC AND POPULAR CULTURE

One

INDIANS AND THE *GUINNESS BOOK OF RECORDS:*
THE CONTOURS OF A NATIONAL OBSESSION

Buddhist texts commonly tell a story where a holy man (sometimes the Buddha himself), seated at a crossroads, is faced with a difficult decision. The holy man sees a man run by him; moments later, another man, or group of men, come running by, and enquire of him if he knows which road the first man has taken. In the interpretive traditions surrounding this story, the holy man or the Buddha is faced with an intersecting array of considerations, and at least three choices are evidently available to him. He can choose to tell the truth, with the possible consequence of endangering the life of the man who ran by him; he can choose to tell a lie, and perhaps save the life of this man, but at the price of violating an indispensable injunction of the ethical life, the obligation to remain bound by the truth; or he can choose to remain silent. This parable speaks to us about the difficulties of adhering to the life of truth, about the conflicting interpretations of truth and falsehood, and about the virtues of stillness and equanimity; it also says something about energy, and about the dialectic of rest and motion; and yet again we can also read it as a homily on the contingent nature of all systems of knowledge, on the ambiguous necessity of choosing between interpretations, and on the difficulties of deriving the meaning of meaning itself.

    Whatever the holy man's eventual choice, the compilers of the *Guinness Book of Records* appear to have had no difficulty in locating the meaning of another story involving a seated man. For a good many years, the *Guinness Book* accredited an Indian holy man with the world record for remaining seated for the longest period of time. The entry notes that 'the silent Indian fakir Mastram Bapu ('contented father') remained on the same spot by the roadside in the village of Chitra for 22 years from 1960-82.'[1] It would seem quite logical that this record should be held by an Indian. The fakir has been, for some centuries, an iconic figure in popular representations of India, and Westerners have, over the years, flocked to India to learn something of the ascetic and meditative practices of Indian holy men. In colonial writings, the hot climate of India was seen as inducing a stupor in its natives, making them indolent and averse to a life of action; and a stationary and seated man would have been the most apposite icon of a static country—impervious to the passage of time and the attraction of places—where men were quite content with the simplest of human needs, fulfilled with a minimal expenditure of energy. By the twin processes of condensation and iteration, this image is then captured in the entry in the *Guinness Book*, which also imposes its own categories of knowledge. Thus the editors must have thought that there was nothing ironic in placing the entry under the caption 'Camping out'. Indians know nothing of camping, and the practice of pitching tents or placing stakes in the great outdoors remains a largely Anglo phenomenon, common to the great American, Australian, and Canadian expanses of wilderness or sparsely inhabited land. There is yet a more supreme irony, one that Henry David Thoreau, who wrote of the world and stayed in the woods around Walden Pond, whose water he thought had mingled with that of the Ganga, would most certainly have relished: in having stayed at one spot for a good part of his life, Mastram Bapu had nonetheless managed to arrive, propelling himself into the pages of what the West calls 'history'.

    The peculiar achievement of Mastram Bapu is only one of many such stories. News bits about Indians finding a place in the *Guinness Book of Records* have become staple items in Indian newspapers, whether published in India or abroad, over the last ten to fifteen years. Though Indians hold only a small fraction of the tens of thousands of records of human achievement, endurance, prowess, ingenuity, and foibles, lavish attention is bestowed by Indian print and visual media upon each Indian triumph, and there is every indication that Indians today are scrambling, with resounding success, to have their names etched, in howsoever bizarre a manner, in the annals of fame. Most of the records for which Indians are included in the *Guinness Book* were set in the last ten years, in the immediate aftermath of the Rajiv Gandhi 'era', and according to the London headquarters of the *Guinness Book*, at least one tenth of all mail they receive is from India, mainly from people seeking to receive acknowledgment of some record that they have set.[2] Indians who have been admitted into the pages of the *Guinness Book* also belong to the World Record Holder Club of India, and the President of this club changed his name from Harprakash Rishi to Guinness Rishi.[3] What explains this compulsion Indians apparently feel to find a place in the *Guinness Book*? Must one point to fragile egos and a feeling of inferiority in comparison to Anglo-Saxon culture, or can one evoke, as has one writer, the notion of a fetish for records? Or is there perhaps, in the narrative of Indians' enchantment with achieving records, something that can be inferred about the manner in which configurations of masculinity, femininity, eccentricity, competitiveness, sportsmanship, and 'Indianness', all shaped by the experience of colonialism and modernity, have contributed to the shaping of contemporary Indian middle-class public culture?

While these records are to most people a matter of some curiosity, they would also appear to be nothing short of trivia. The authors of those assaults upon the 'canon' that were common in the 1980s and early 1990s, while denouncing with good reason the grand narratives of Enlightenment rationality,[4] or questioning the place of foundational categories in interpretive critical theory, or—less subtly—substituting the works of women and men of colour for the writings of white males grounded largely if not exclusively in European traditions of enquiry and intellectual practices, have nonetheless retained a fairly conventional sense of what constitutes 'material' for the purposes of intellectual enquiry and political argumentation. The place of gossip, rumours, and anecdotes in the construction of narratives, and in the creation of a cultural politics of resistance, is beginning to be explored,[5] and in allowing the *Guinness Book* to be a refracting medium, particularly for certain positions on modernity,

I am doing no more than extending the meaning of the 'canon'. Let us recall that the word canon, which has an extraordinarily rich history, largely forgotten in current debates, meant in the first instance a yardstick, standard, rule, or model; only later did it acquire some other meanings, such as the notion of a 'list', which is indeed one of the meanings inherent in the idea that there exists a grand canon of literary works. Rules, much like records, exist to be stretched, indeed broken, and there are also, needless to say, rules for establishing records. If I appear to be enshrining trivia, by constituting the *Guinness Book* as my central text, I do so with the encouragement of a not inconsiderable authority, Walter Benjamin: 'Method of this work: literary montage. I need say nothing. Only show. I won't steal anything valuable or appropriate any witty turns of phrase. But the trivia, the trash: this, I don't want to take stock of, but let it come into its own in the only way possible: use it.'[6]

To speak of records is, for the most part, to speak of numbers. Take, for example, the record for needle threading. The 1992 *Guinness Book* noted that the record for the number of times that a strand of cotton thread had been threaded through a number 13 needle (eye 0.5 in. x 0.16 in.) in two hours was 7,238, set by Brajesh Shrivastava on 12 December 1990 in Bhopal, a city notorious for the record number of dead left behind by a gas leak in a Union Carbide plant in 1984; however, this record was not to last long, as his fellow countryman, Om Prakash Singh, a clerk at a bank in Allahabad, threaded a needle 20,675 times in the same amount of time before a live audience on 25 July 1993.[7] The former gentleman, having been deprived of his world record, was to demonstrate his tenacity, and his will to fame, by the mere expedient of setting a record in an altogether different domain: as the *Guinness Book* for 1995 states, Shrivastava holds the record for having created the largest hand-painted wooden fan in the world, nearly eighteen and a half-feet-tall. Shrivastava, who appears to have nursed lifelong ambitions to appear in the *Guinness Book*, first made his way into the *Limca Book of Records*,[8] which largely whets the appetites of those Indians who are not manly, bold, or lucky enough to make it to Guinness' compilation of world records, but can nonetheless satisfy themselves with the thought that they hold some record in India, with numerous records for microwriting, such as writing 61,800 characters, which cannot be read by the naked eye, on three-fourth space on one side of a postcard. This sort of record would seem to appeal to Indians: according to the *Guinness Book*, the record for 'minuscule writing' is held by Surendra Apharya of Jaipur, who wrote 1,314 characters on a single grain of rice on 28 February 1991 (*GB* 1992:457).

If there is, then, a fetish for records, it is in the first instance a propensity towards numbers. As in any other civilization, numbers have played a fecund role in the shaping of Indian culture, but it is arguable that the Indian imagination is particularly drawn to taxonomies, numerology, and the sheer play to which numbers lend themselves. The Hindu Puranas contain the most complex concatenations of numbers, and numbers have been critical to such enterprises as divination, ritual sacrifice, literary compositions, construction of genealogies, cosmogony, and astrology. The *Kama Sutra*, the well-known Indian guide to love-making, is precise about the number of sexual positions during copulation, and a recent cartoon history of the world mocks this 'Hindu thoroughness' by showing a couple engaging in intercourse, while the man, whose one hand holds a book, expostulates: 'O.K. Position #133.'[9] Similarly, the *Atharva Veda* notes that 53 kinds of sorceries are possible (with dice), or that there are 101 varieties of death.[10] The Hindu use of numbers, or rather playfulness with them, filled the English with exasperation, and James Mill pointed to Hindu numbers—such as the 1,555,200,000,000 years during which the Creator was incubating, or the 17,064,000 years during which the Creator transformed itself from 'neuter to masculine, for the purpose of creating worlds'—as a sign of the 'rude and imperfect state' of the Hindu mind.[11] Hegel, like most other 'great' European philosophers, was without a clue as to how Indian texts might be read, and could only consider 'large numbers' in 'Hindoo writings' as having 'a quite arbitrary origin.' If certain kings were said to have reigned 70,000 years, and Brahma is said to have lived 20,000 years, one had to presuppose that the 'numbers in question, therefore, have not the value and rational meaning which we attach to them.'[12]

Memory, too, has a hand in this nexus of records, numbers, and statistics, and what has not been adequately realized, much less studied, is how numbers function as mnemonic devices. Competitions lasting over days, even weeks, in which pandits recite entire texts—such as the Ramayana and the Bhagavat Purana—from memory, or recite passages from sacred texts picked for them randomly, are quite common. It is a similar facility with memory,[13] and the resort to those mnemonic strategies by which cultures (and not mere texts) have been preserved and transmitted may help to account for the fact that the most extraordinary 'human computer' in the world has been an Indian, Shakuntala Devi. When she was given two 13-digit numbers (7,686,369,774,870 and 2,465,099,745,779) to multiply, Shakuntala Devi, who apparently became known at the age of eight as 'a living wonder',[14] did so accurately within 28 seconds; and she has repeatedly performed such feats. 'Some experts on calculating prodigies refuse to give credence to Mrs Devi', states the *Guinness Book*, 'on the grounds that her achievements are so vastly superior to the calculating feats of any other investigated prodigy that the authentication must have been defective' (*GB* 1992:176). It is not an accident that India is today one of the principal countries for research in statistics, and that her statisticians are renowned the world over.

   That those numbers which Hegel and James Mill derided may not have been without 'meaning', or that they followed a cultural logic impervious to an instrumental rationality, would not have occurred to European commentators on Indian culture and 'experts' on Indian knowledge systems. This form of indulgence in, and engagement with, numbers owed something to what we might call a cultural cosmology, whereas the present-day obsession with numbers among many Indians has, *in part*, a rather different locus. Ian Hacking, the historian of science, has noted that in the 1830s and 1840s England was engulfed by a 'sheer fetishism for numbers': bodies were furiously counted, and statistics were accumulated on everything, from railway mileage and the total number of lashes administered in a year to all habitual offenders, to the number of drunkards and lunatics contained in prisons and asylums.[15] Where numbers were at one time an occasion for men and women to give expression to their ludic tendencies, even rendering themselves ludicrous, in the nineteenth century numbers acquired a restraining function. The colonial rulers in India were to follow suit: in the nineteenth century, the state began to acquire enumerative functions, and this obsession with statistics, which was to constitute one of the central features of the colonial sociology of knowledge, was conveyed in such practices as the census, anthropometry, criminal statistics, and numerous other classificatory, investigative, disciplinary, and repressive procedures.[16] This avalanche of numbers was to be described by Foucault as 'biopower'; an entire administrative and regulatory machinery, harnessed to the body, was to come into place.[17] It is useful to recall that the word 'statistics' is etymologically related to the word 'state'; and statistics would henceforth do the work of the state.

If we appear to be at great remove from the quest for records, we might return then to the relation between records and numbers. The modernizing Indian middle classes are never so happy as when India's achievements are honoured, when her sportsmen and sportswomen are lauded, and when she is recognized as a nation on the move. If it should take nuclear explosions to push India out of its supposed inertia, and into the realm of nations that *do* matter, these Indians are well prepared—as I argue elsewhere in this book at much greater length—to undertake such political adventurism. It is these same elements, to whom Mastram Bapu would be an anathema, who have been pressing for India's admission into the Security Council, on the supposed ground that India's might and importance as a nation ought to be recognized, but they are oblivious to the fact that the United States, the leading power in the world, has rendered the United Nations into a highly disreputable body which is increasingly seen as serving its interests rather than the welfare of all humankind. No country is loath to surrender its monopoly over power when other, more effective and thorough, avenues for wielding power have been found; and if India does make its way into the Security Council, to the great delight of its elites, it shall be a Security Council for whose decisions the United States will have little or no use. It is the political and economic elite in India who remind us that India stands third in the strength of its scientific manpower, that it is a member of the 'Nuclear Club', that its software engineers have conquered (so to speak) the heights of Silicon Valley, and that it is the only Third World nation to join a few of the post-industrial countries as an exporter of satellite and rocket technology.[18]

Sadly, India is also the country that holds the world record for the largest child labour force in the world, the largest number of illiterates, the largest number of people suffering from malnutrition, the largest exploited force of tribal people, the largest population of lepers and the blind: the list is almost infinitely long with respect to these shortcomings.

However, these gross forms of exploitation are viewed as deplorably necessary, or as shortcomings of an earlier era; the elite are prepared to believe that a price has to be paid for 'development', and that some of these problems will disappear over time. However, what cannot so easily be tolerated, especially when the country is making a bid to be considered a strong and important member of the world community, is the shockingly poor performance of Indian sportsmen and sportswomen. There is no greater lamentation that fills the Indian papers than the continued inability of India's sporting hopes to haul home a few trophies and medals, and that humiliation is aggravated when the smallest nations, which cannot possibly have any pretension to being a major player in world politics, and which in the view of Indian elites can even less lay claim to the enormously complex and rich history of a civilizational entity like India, are shown to have better and more manly athletes. In the 1992 Olympics, India failed to win a single medal, not even a bronze, and there was much soul-searching and agonizing in middle-class homes and organs of middle-class opinion; in the 1996 Olympics, it scarcely did better: Leander Paes brought home a bronze medal in men's tennis, when the sport, that year, had been boycotted by the greater majority of the major men players. 'The rot in Indian sports continues', wrote one commentator in the *Hindustan Times* (4 August 1996), though Paes himself was congratulated for having brought 'glory' to the country. 'Paes does India Proud', screamed one newspaper headline, while in California a major Indian community newspaper described Paes' bronze as having ended India's Olympic medal 'drought'.[19] That India has nearly every year a great many other droughts, which ruin the lives of millions and lead to their dislocation, is of less import to those who are accustomed to viewing triumphs in beauty contests and Olympic games as the true measure of a nation's greatness.

The anguished breast-beating following the debacle after every Olympics leads to much media speculation about the causes for India's failure in sporting events. It is commonly alleged that politicians intervene in the conduct of sports, making it impossible for true sportsmen to flourish; one hears of the country's disinclination to invest in its sports programme, and thus in its youth. Sporting programmes, like everything else in the country, are described as having been victimized by corrupt and nefarious practices. In a word, India's youth had never had much of a sporting chance. Never mind that Indian youth are not able to accomplish much in sports, at least the country can claim the distinction of having the oldest athlete in the world, Baba Joginder Singh, who competed in the Indian National Athletics Meet for Veterans at the comparatively young age of 105 and struck gold in discus throwing.[20] Perhaps India's medal chances should be left to its elderly citizens; they might at least restore some dignity to India's athletic ambitions.

Had India's Herculean disaster at successive Olympics stood in singular isolation, it might have been less sinister, considering that athletes who compete in the Olympics are often groomed for competition since their infancy, but more recent sporting events have only confirmed that Indian sports and athletics are in a bad way. At the 1994 Asian Games in Hiroshima, where India was competing not only with Japan, China, and South Korea, the sporting giants of the continent, but with Macau, Turkmenistan, Brunei, Myanmar, and Tajikistan, not countries whose presence in the mental cartography of most people is overwhelming, India could only manage to finish eighth in the medal tally. India won four golds compared to 137 won by China. Of India's four gold medals, two were won in tennis, one in *kabbadi*, a game that is played only in South Asia, and one in pistol shooting. 'A Notch Better, India Still Falls Far Behind' is what *India-West*, the principal organ of Indian opinion in California, had to say about India's performance.[21]

The medal for shooting makes one pause. Three weeks before the Asian Games, at the Commonwealth Games, where India's competitors included Britain, Australia, and Canada, India's small tally of six gold, eleven silver, and seven bronze—occasioning a remark from one major newspaper that there had been 'a lot of concern over the poor performance of the Indian contingent'—included four medals won by just one sportsman, Jaspal Rana. The subject of India's poor showing was important enough to merit an editorial, significantly entitled, 'Shooting, the saving grace.'[22] One might be forgiven for thinking that the writer of the editorial is a card-carrying member of that fanatical and constitutionally-blessed American organization known as the National Rifle Association. It is particularly ironical that India should be winning virtually its only medals in shooting and weightlifting. Throughout nearly the last one hundred years of colonial rule, India was governed by the Arms Act, which forbade Indians from owning arms or weapons. Very few Indians know how to handle a gun; the vast majority have never even seen one; and those imbecilic debates that are carried out in the United States over the most trivial measures to limit gun ownership would be incomprehensible to Indians, as indeed they are to most people elsewhere in the world. In the British colonial sociology of knowledge, the Indian could not be manly; his effeminacy was supposedly apparent in his diet, apparel, and behaviour, and his inability to confront the Englishman. In the characterization of Robert Orme, who penned an essay in 1770 on the 'effeminacy of the inhabitants of Hindustan', an Englishman had merely to brandish a stick and the Indian would be sent flying.[23] A gun was scarcely to be expected in the hands of an Indian; nor was the Indian known for flexing his muscles through the practice of weight-lifting, which is scarcely to say that there are no Indian traditions of body-building.

A certain anxiety, first generated during the colonial period, and subsequently aggravated by the process of nation-building, over masculinity and the manliness of a people, no less of a nation, must also account to a great degree for the quest among Indians to have their names etched in the *Guinness Book*. Part of the ethos of manliness consists simply in gaining recognition, in being acknowledged as supreme in one's chosen field of endeavour. One long-lasting effect of colonialism has been that the Indian continues to look up to the white European male, who confers recognition upon inferiors, and who has established the standard that the Indian (like other formerly colonized people) must meet. That is the canonical truth, the 'kanoon' of this world. Anthony Parakal of Bombay, who engineered his way into the *Guinness Book* by having the largest number (3,700) of published letters to an editor, was catapulted into the pages of *Time*, which devoted a full page to him, and he has been interviewed and photographed by other American publications.[24] Such recognition, which is unquestionably a mark of 'achievement', does not come easily to Indians. the *Guinness Book* is there to remind them that such recognition is possible and desirable, and the editor of the *Guinness Book* has himself gone on record as saying: 'We at the *Guinness Book of Records* greatly value the interest shown by Indians in our book and respect their zeal in trying to better world record targets in a wide range of subjects.'[25]

It appears to matter little to some Indians themselves that the records they have set exemplify, in minute detail, the Orientalist constructions of India. Speaking of effeminacy, it is notable that the record for needle-threading is held by an Indian man, in a country where stitching at home is invariably deemed to be a woman's job. The *Guinness Book* also notes that the record for 'the longest duration in a typing marathon on a manual machine', 142 hours 50 minutes, was set by an Indian man from 25-31 July 1990: he hit 916,000 strokes (*GB* 1992:530). Perseverance at a typewriter is scarcely the most persuasive demonstration of manliness, or of the ability of Indians to excel, or be taken seriously as a modernizing people, and in India, as women continue to join the work force in large numbers, jobs requiring typing are almost exclusively the preserve of women.[26] It is perfectly apposite that the record for minuscule writing and letter-writing should be held by Indians: writing was construed by India's colonizers as something quite feminine, the task of men being to rule, govern, and administer. (India's colonial rulers did leave behind voluminous records and would appear to have displayed a penchant for the written record: when the men wrote, however, they recorded 'minutes' and 'memoranda', and these forms of adjudicative and prescriptive writing would have been distinguished from more frivolous engagements with the pen.) The large statue of John Lawrence, the 'saviour of the Punjab' and the Viceroy of India, that stood in Lahore and that was the target of a satyagraha campaign in the 1920s by the people of Lahore seeking to have it removed, bore the inscription, 'Will you be governed by the sword or the pen?', though the countenance and demeanour of Lawrence belied the force of the interrogative.[27] English officials in India had no anxiety that nationalist-minded effeminate Bengalis would ever pose a threat to their sovereignty: 'the Baboodom of Lower Bengal', exclaimed Bulwer-Lytton, the Viceroy of India in 1878-79, 'though disloyal, is fortunately cowardly and its only revolver is its ink bottle; which though dirty, is not dangerous.'[28]

When the Indian was not seen as lazy, dirty, a lying cheat, and effeminate, he was construed as being bizarre and eccentric, bound to peculiar customs, wild in his looks, wholly obsequious to authority. Here, again, Indians whose names are enshrined in the *Guinness Book* would appear to endorse this representation. Much was written in colonial days about the 'Hindu Juggernaut', and of fanatical believers who would allow themselves to be crushed under the wheels of the chariot at the Jagannath festival in Puri. In 1994, over a period of eight months, the sadhu Lotan Babu rolled his body nearly 2,486 miles, or an average of six-seven miles a day, from Ratlam to Jammu by way of rendering homage to Vaishno Devi (*GB* 2000:77). In a similar vein, during a period of fifteen months ending on 9 March 1985, Jagdish Chander crawled 870 miles, apparently 'to propitiate his favorite Hindu goddess, Mata' (*GB* 1992:526; *GB* 2000:70). Students of Indian history might recall that the notorious General Dyer, perpetrator of the Jallianwala Bagh massacre and of the even more infamous 'crawling order', which required Indians to crawl on a particular street where an Englishwoman had been assaulted, when asked to explain his conduct, replied that some 'Indians like to crawl'.[29] It may be poetic justice that the record for the longest continuous crawl is held by an Englishman, who traversed 28.5 miles in a mere nine and a-half-hours. To be eccentric is, literally, to be off-centred, or to be peculiarly balanced: so showed N. Ravi of Sathyamangalam City, who stood on one foot for a record 34 hours. As the *Guinness Book* states plainly, 'The disengaged foot may not be rested on the standing foot nor may any object be used for support or balance' (*GB* 1992:186). Not to be outdone, his countryman Girish Sharma bettered this record ten years later by nearly 22 hours.[30] India's yogis and rishis have long been viewed as capable of the most bizarre or absurd acts, and Swami Maujgiri Maharaj of Shahjahanpur, Uttar Pradesh, took it upon himself to engage in the most unusual form of penance by continuously standing for 17 years, thereby establishing a world record that no one is likely to break too soon. 'When sleeping', adds the *Guinness Book* for the benefit of those left somewhat mystified, 'he would lean against a plank' (*GB* 1992:186). Hindus will apparently do anything as a gesture of their devotion to God: this, in the event, appears to be the explanation furnished by Amar Bharti for having kept his right hand raised for a period of 26 years (*GB* 2000:71).

Numerous other records of this kind are held by Indians. Thus far I have suggested that the quest for records by Indians must be viewed not only in relation to their absorption in, and engagement with, numbers but also in relation to anxieties about masculinity, modernity, and the nation-state. It is not accidental that virtually all of the records were set in the last 20 years, and most of these in the last 10 to 15 years. In late 1984, following the assassination of his mother, Rajiv Gandhi assumed the office of the

Prime Minister of India. Himself a rather young man, quite unlike many of India's geriatric politicians, Rajiv Gandhi gravitated towards the youth, and made known his commitment to making India a strong, modern nation-state. It is perfectly apposite that '*Mera Bharat Mahan*'—which may be read as 'My India is Great', or 'May My India Be Great', should have become the slogan most closely associated with him,[31] and that Rajiv Gandhi became known as the man eager to usher India into the twenty-first century, the iconic representation of which was fittingly a train, which supposedly first propelled India into modernity, and which today serves as the reminder of a greatness that India can achieve if it can retain the political integrity of its borders. It is in Rajiv Gandhi's time that the Indian Railways inaugurated its most prestigious train, the Shatabdi (literally, a century) Express, as though to suggest that India would, under his leadership, be well positioned at the beginning of the next century (and millennium), an ancient civilization once again poised to leave its impress upon the minds of men and women. The youth were extolled to excel at sports; the artistic community was urged to bring home honours; and Indian scientists were encouraged in the belief that their endeavours would be suitably rewarded. Telecommunications might well be in a complete shambles, but Rajiv Gandhi's technological adviser, Sam Pitroda, could quite blithely speak of cellular phones as though the day when they would be in every Indian home, howsoever humble, was just around the corner.

In such a climate of opinion, it is no surprise that, amidst fortune-hunters, Indians seeking records should also have found a place under the sun. It is worth bearing in mind, however, that the project of modernity has never received the endorsement of all Indians, and that even a greater number of Indians do not think of the nation-state as the inevitable and 'natural' culmination of history. Nor are those Indians who fancy themselves as members of the modernizing elite unequivocally pleased about Indian achievements of the sort that are celebrated in the *Guinness Book*; indeed, they are quite embarrassed, and occasionally angry, that Indians should be recognized for endeavours that, in their view, only reinforce Orientalist representations of Indians as exotic, effeminate, and custom-bound. Nothing fills Indian elites, who are eager to invite foreign capital into the country, and crave for the acceptance of India as a tourist mecca, with greater dread than the thought that India might be construed as backward.

(I might note, incidentally, that the world record for 'backwards running' is held by Arvind Pandya of India: he covered the distance between Los Angeles and New York City in this fashion in 107 days, from 18 August to 3 December 1984, just at the time that Rajiv Gandhi was starting to give his painfully monotonous speeches on taking India forward [*GB* 1992: 785]. These elites cannot but feel that most Indian achievements are not 'real'; the real, and the capacity to grasp the real, lies only in the West.[32]

The freakish activities that leave Indian elites disturbed represent, I would submit, a counter-hegemonic force to modern orthodoxies about development, production, competition, and modernity. The competitive spirit, we have been told, brings out the best in human beings, and encourages people to excel. The narrative of the 'competitive spirit' usually counterpoised to the stagnation and decay of the East, 'vegetating in the teeth of time' (in Marx's memorable phrase), has a long history in the West. The story of one element in that narrative is the story of capital, self-aggrandizement, and the greed that drove the West to acquire colonies and markets overseas; the other element is encapsulated in the phrase 'cultural capital', though I use it here less in Bourdieu's sense, and more to suggest that narratives of the like of 'competitive spirit' are used to engender pride in the nation, refurbish the ever fragile masculinity of the male of the species, and promote a cultural ethos that thrives on such notions as a purported individualism and self-improvement. It is this 'spirit' of competition that has contributed to the restlessness, anomie, and anxiety of Indian youth, and to those riots and disturbances over positions and privileges that have been witnessed in India from time to time, and which seemed to reach their apogee in 1990 when several young men took to self-immolation in protest against the stated policy of the government to implement a plan for increased educational and employment opportunities for the disadvantaged.

It is precisely the narrative of competition and triumph, which modernity has claimed as its very own, that is being defied, and there is no better way of defying this narrative than by seeming to emulate it, and even giving it one's most profound homage. If the 'competitive spirit', which stands behind the quest for records, leads to the drive to excel, or to raise productivity, why not do so by setting records in activities, appearances, and achievements where the *disutility* is all too apparent? What could be the point in growing the longest fingernails in the world, as has Shridhar Chillal of Pune, whose five nails on his left hand together measured 205 inches—so long indeed that his nails must generate their own political (and undoubtedly gendered) economy?[33] Chillal would appear to have made himself quite useless: one cannot be certain how he prevents his manicured hands from being grazed by objects, how he dresses himself, or how he attends to his other daily needs. Similarly, what might be the point in growing the longest moustache in the world? Kalyan Ramji Sain of Sundargarh had grown, by July 1993, a moustache measuring 133.5 inches (*GB* 2000:261); one of his illustrious predecessors, a life convict in a New Delhi jail by the name of Karma Ram Bheel, received the permission of the prison governor to keep his moustache untrimmed, which by 1979 had grown to 7 feet 10 inches (*GB* 1992:169). He too generated his own political economy: we do not know how many prison personnel were assigned to help him in keeping his moustache groomed, or in preventing his fellow prisoners from tampering with so seductive an appendage to a man's body. Moreover, as the *Guinness Book* states, Bheel used 'mustard, oil, butter and cream to keep it in trim', and no doubt a number of cows were tethered by the jail to service this man's appetite and ambition in a city that, much to the chagrin of its residents, faced chronic butter and milk shortages on a frequent basis throughout the 1970s and early 1980s.

Butter is not the only item that is in short supply, or that is unusually expensive: for the size of Indian cities, there are relatively few petrol pumps, and petrol prices are almost *exorbitant*. Nonetheless, in the city of Poona, renowned (or so think its residents) for martial valour, a number of its men, among them Harprakash [later Guinness] Rishi, could think of no better way of entering into the *Guinness Book* than by keeping a motor scooter in nonstop motion for 1,001 hours, covering a distance of 49,831 miles at Traffic Park between 22 April and 3 June 1990 (*GB* 1992:371). Though Guinness Rishi's immersion in the world of the *Guinness Book* is self-evident, it can be better gauged by the fact that he appears to hold the world record for the 'longest will (104,567 words, 489 pages)'; the 'shortest valid will' in the world, comprised of 2 words in Hindi, was written in the name of Bimla Rishi, who—a reasonable inference—is related to Guinness Rishi.[34] Evidently, too, Guinness Rishi has a great deal of time on his hands. Many of the *Guinness Book*'s Indian heroes appear quite insistent on leaving their imprint on the economy—predecessors, perhaps, of the Indian CEOs, venture capitalists, and computing 'geniuses' whose names are now encountered in the *Wall Street Journal*—much as they are interested in acquiring cultural capital. Often these two objectives are sought to be achieved by the attainment of a single record: no other interpretation so readily comes to mind in explaining why the former Tamil Nadu Chief Minister Jayalalitha presided over a wedding where 5,004 couples tied the knot and 500,000 guests helped in raising the cost of the whole affair to $2 million. Her colleague, AIADMK [All-India Anna Dravida Munnetra Kazhagham] party leader M. Chinnaswamy, reportedly said: 'Our rivals are green with envy at our achievement, which should find a place in the *Guinness Book of World Records*.'[35] Not only do Indians marry early, they marry in style, and why not? Marriages, according to an old saying, are made in heaven, and one Indian would seem to be quite set on proving this right. An Indian businessman based in Dubai, one newspaper has reported, recently chartered an Air India Airbus so that he could have his son conduct the marriage nuptials with his fiancée in the presence of a Sikh priest at a height of 20,000 feet above ground. According to the report, 'Popley senior said he hopes the couple, bonded just a tad below heaven, will wing their way into the *Guinness Book of Records*.'[36]

If the *Guinness Book* is the poor Indian's medium for acquiring cultural capital, for the nouveau riche their entry into the book of fame, and the book of numbers, is rendered possible by conspicuous consumption. In either case, modernity is at once both emulated and defied, honoured and parodied, celebrated and mocked; if the scientific spirit and the competitive ethos appear to be enshrined, it is unequivocally clear that the achievements which have enabled Indians (in the most clichéd phrase of the times) 'to make history' scarcely rebound to the credit of the nation-state, or do modernity proud. It is the same ambivalence towards modernity, the ethos of development and the achievements of science, that can be witnessed in the photograph that appeared in many Indian newspapers and magazines during the outbreak of plague in Surat in the mid 1990s, showing a man holding a dead rat in his naked hand, his mouth covered by a small piece of gauze! Modernity in India is luckily an unfinished business, and the increasing triumph of Indians in entering the Guinness Hall of Fame simultaneously enacts a deification and defilement of modernity. If the

Indian obsession with the *Guinness Book* is construed as constituting irrefutable evidence of Indians' feelings of inferiority or their emulation of the 'achieving races', and their commitment to modernity and the nation-state, perhaps one should also begin to view the records set by them as markers of the resilience of a complex civilization against the homogenizing and deleterious effects of modernity. Resistance in an era of globalization and totalization will perforce enact both homage and parody.

Notes

1. Donald McFarlan ed., *Guinness Book of Records 1992* (New York: Bantam Books, 1992), p. 311. All references to the *Guinness Book*, including parenthetical references in the text (in the form of *GB*), are to the 1992, 1995, and 2000 editions.

2. Private communication from Peter Matthews, Editor of the *Guinness Book of Records*, London, 13 April 1995. A brief unsigned article in the *Chicago Tribune* of 6 May 1993, entitled 'A peculiar fetish with records', states that nearly 'one-fifth of all *Guinness* mail to its London headquarters is from India'.

3. Anon., 'A peculiar fetish with records', *Chicago Tribune* (6 May 1993). My email inquiries to Guinness Rishi, who lives in Delhi, have gone unanswered, but Mr Rishi's own website is not uninteresting. Among other things, he collects editions of the *Guinness Book*, of which he may well have one of the largest private collections. The membership roster of the Guinness Book World Record Breakers' Club is available at <www.recordholders.org/en/members.html> [accessed 12 November 2000].

4. We might recall here Benjamin's aphorism: 'There is no document of civilization which is not at the same time a document of barbarism.' See Walter Benjamin, 'Theses on the Philosophy of History' in Hannah Arendt ed., *Illuminations* (New York: Schocken Books, 1969), p. 256.

5. The literature on rumours is now quite rich. For two very different works in which rumour appears as the principal analytical category, see Ranajit Guha, *Elementary Aspects of Peasant Insurgency in Colonial India* (New Delhi: Oxford University Press, 1983), and Patricia A. Turner, *I Heard It Through the Grapevine: Rumour in African-American Culture* (Berkeley, California: University of California Press, 1994). On anecdotes, see Joel Fineman, 'Fiction and Fiction: The History of the Anecdote', in H. Aram Veeser ed., *The New Historicism* (New York and London: Routledge, 1989), pp. 49-76.

6. Walter Benjamin, '[Theoretics of Knowledge; Theory of Progress]', *The*

Philosophical Forum 15, nos. 1-2 (Fall-Winter 1983-84), p. 5.

7.   *GB* 1992:528; 'Needle Threading Record', *India-West* (15 July 1994), p. 14. The new record appears in the 1995 edition of the *Guinness Book*.

8.   The *Guinness Book* is named after Guinness Stout, the largest-selling alcoholic beverage in Ireland; Limca, as Indians know, is the name of a soft drink.

9.   Larry Gonick, *The Cartoon History of the Universe II,* vol. 8-13 (reprint ed., Mansfield, Ohio: Main Street Books, 1994), p. 38. I am grateful to my friend, Bernard Morrow of Baltimore, for drawing my attention to this work.

10. Maurice Bloomfield, tr., 'Hymns of the Atharva-Veda', *Sacred Books of the East*, 42 volumes (Oxford: Oxford University Press, 1897; reprint ed., Delhi: Motilal Banarsidass, 1964), vol. II, p. 38 and vol. XIX, p. 2.

11. James Mill in Horace Hayman Wilson ed., *History of British India* (London: James Madden & Co., 1840), vol. 1, pp. 335-36.

12. G.W. F. Hegel, *The Philosophy of History*, J. Sibree tr. (reprint ed., New York: Dover Books, 1956), p. 163.

13. I cannot here explore the relations between orality and memory. But the Indian facility with numbers extends to matters beyond numbers. A six-year old Indian girl living in California earned a place on the Tonight Show on 31 May 1998 because she is known to be able to spell any word, forwards and backwards, after having glanced at it only once, and similarly she can recite any whole number. See Viji Sundaram, 'Six-Year-Old Can Spell Any Word Backwards and Forwards', *India-West* (13 September 1996), p. B13.

14. See: http://www.ebhasin.com/shakuntaladevi/cp.htm

15. Ian Hacking, 'How Should We Do the History of Statistics', *Ideology and Consciousness*, no. 8 (Spring 1981), pp.15-26. See also Hugh Kenner, *The Counterfeiters* (Bloomington, Indiana: Indiana University Press, 1968), pp. 104-114, 143-55.

16. I have written about this elsewhere: see my chapter on 'The Epistemological Imperatives of the Colonial State', in 'Committees of Inquiry and Discourses of "Law and Order" in Twentieth-Century British India,' Ph.D. Dissertation, 2 vols. (University of Chicago, 1992), vol. 1, pp. 27-90, and my critical introduction to M. Pauparao Naidu, *History of Railway Thieves* (reprint ed., Gurgaon, Haryana: Vintage Books, 1996). See also Arjun Appadurai, 'Number in the Colonial Imagination', in Carol A. Breckenridge and Peter van der Veer eds., *Orientalism and the Post-Colonial Predicament* (Philadelphia: University of Pennsylvania Press, 1993).

17. See Ian Hacking, 'Biopower and the Avalanche of Printed Numbers', *Humanities in Society* 5, nos. 3 and 4 (Summer and Fall 1982), pp. 279-95.

18. See, for example, Viji Sundaram, 'Agreements Boost India into Global Space

Market', *India-West* (10 February 1995), sec. A, p. 1.

19. Viji Sundaram, 'Paes' Bronze Medal Ends Drought in Olympics', *India-West* (9 August 1996), Sec. A, p. 1. In the 2000 games, India once more had to be content with a single bronze, only its third individual medal in the entire history of the Olympics. This bronze was won by the weightlifter Karnam Malleswari in the women's 69 kg. category: once again a 'drought' had been ended, and she was suitably feted.

20. *GuinnessWorld Records 2000: Millennium Edition* (New York: Bantam, 2000), p. 87.

21. Issue of 21 October 1994, Sec. C, p. 91. The writer glumly added: 'The failure of the Indian sports system to provide a counter to improving continental standards stood pronounced as the last vestiges of its past domination in athletics were wiped off the record books at the games.' It is extraordinary that the past, when India's medals came in a trickle, should now—when at present the country is witnessing a virtual drought—fondly be remembered (remembered both as recalled and as re-masculinized) as a time when India dominated athletics! The only domination that any Indian can remember in 'athletics' is that of P.T. Usha, who won a number of gold medals at the Asian Games in women's races. Long before her time there was Milkha Singh, but the present generation of Indians know little of him.

22. *The Pioneer* (31 September 1994), p. 8.

23. Robert Orme, *Historical Fragments of the Mogul Empire, of the Morattoes, and of the English Concerns in Indostan from theYear MDCLIX* (London: W. Wingrave, 1785; reprint ed., New Delhi: Associated Publishing House, 1974), pp. 58-62.

24. 'Bombay letter-writer pens his way into Guinness Book', *Pioneer* (30 July 1993), p. 1.

25. Private communication from the editor, Peter Matthews, 13 April 1995.

26. Students at what are termed 'typing colleges', which are to be seen not only in the cities but in large towns as well, are largely if not exclusively women. The computer is making inroads into India and may well render the typewriter obsolete in a decade or so, but the computer keyboard is modelled after that of the typewriter. It is worth emphasizing that while both men and women are to be found in computer-related jobs, new entrants into jobs where typing on a typewriter is required are invariably women.

The brothers Abhishek and Anurag Jain have competed worldwide in various typing competitions, and the former now holds the world record for striking 6,736 strokes in 10 minutes, or 135 words per minute, with only seven errors. Anurag was a silver medallist in 1996. Abhishek practices on the typewriter three-four hours every day, but prepares himself for a major championship by setting himself a rigorous schedule of eight hours of practice for three months. According to one news item, 'His name appeared in the Hindi version of the *Guinness Book of World Records* as the youngest and fastest world typewriting champion. However, he regrets that his achievement does not feature in the English version.' See 'Typing Prodigy Wins Top Place in World Meet', *India-West* (26 July 1996), sec. B, p. 8. Editions of the *Guinness Book* in Malayalam, Tamil, Telugu, and Kannada were introduced in the 1980s.

27.   I have written about this in 'The Political Signification of Public Monuments: The Lawrence Statue Satyagraha, 1921-25', unpublished paper, 1995.

28.   Cited by Anil Seal, *The Emergence of Indian Nationalism*: *Competition and Collaboration in the Later Nineteenth Century* (Cambridge: Cambridge University Press, 1971), p. 141.

29.   See Vinay Lal, 'The Incident of the "Crawling Lane": Women and the Punjab Disturbances of 1919', *Genders*, no. 16 (Spring 1993), pp. 35-60.

30.   Mark C. Young ed., *Guinness Book of Records 1995* (New York: Facts on File, 1995). A fellow South Asian from Sri Lanka improved upon the record in 1997, engaging in this particular balancing act for 76 hours 40 minutes (*GB* 2000: 72).

31.   'Mahan' is most accurately rendered as 'strong' or 'powerful', but here should be understood as 'great', great in the sense of 'this great country', or 'our great civilization'. Indira Gandhi's slogan was 'Garibi Hatao' ('Wipe out poverty'): whatever her authoritarianism, pretensions to socialism and egalitarianism were critical to her idiom, but Rajiv Gandhi dispensed with such pretensions for the most part.

32.   It was in quest of a 'real' record that Salauddin (Saloo) Choudhury and his wife Neena, of Calcutta, went around the world in an Indian Contessa Classic in 69 days, 19 hours and 5 minutes, thereby setting a record. 'Many Indians see freakish activities as the only way to get into the book', Choudhury told an interviewer. 'I broke that pattern by trying to set a real record' (see 'A peculiar fetish with records', *Chicago Tribune* [6 May 1993]). Salauddin Choudhury then became involved in a controversy which lasted over several years, and finally led to a resolution which must have pleased him. His record of going around the world, set in 1989, did not appear in the *Guinness Book* until 1991. When the record was broken by an English team, which covered 26,078 miles in 39 days 23 hours 35 minutes, the Choudhurys again broke the record, improving upon the British record by 3 hours and 20 minutes. Though they completed their second journey on 17 December 1991, their world record did not appear in the *Guinness Book* until the 1994 edition. Choudhury has alleged that the Guinness Publishing Company was unwilling to concede his record because

of 'racial prejudice and the ego of the Anglo-Saxon race', but this charge is predictably denied by Peter Matthews, then the editor at the *Guinness Book* offices in London: 'If he's alleging there was a deliberate attempt to do something against him, that's wrong'. Ibid.

In late 1993, Choudhury successfully sought an injunction in the District Court in Calcutta preventing the Guinness Publishing Company from selling the *Guinness Book*, either in English or in Indian language editions, anywhere in India. The Guinness Publishing Company appealed against the injunction. Mr Matthews, in a letter to me, has stated: 'We entirely and completely reject Mr Choudhury's allegations and it is very curious indeed that he has twice appeared in the *Guinness Book of Records* and yet he takes action against us.' Noting the interest of Indians in the *Guinness Book*, and the zeal with which they have been trying to improve upon the records, Mr Matthews adds: 'It is therefore very sad that the activities of one man should prevent them from currently being able to purchase a copy of the *Guinness Book of Records* in India' (private communication, 13 April 1995).

But, then, the proverbial happy ending: Choudhury appears to have prevailed in his battle with the *Guinness Book* people, and the Millennium Edition states that the 'record for the first and fastest circumnavigation of the world by car, under the rules applicable in 1989 and 1991, embracing more than an equator's length of driving (24,901.41 road miles), is held by Mohammed Salahuddin Choudhury and his wife, Neena, of Calcutta, India' (*GB* 2000:12).

33. The 1992 *Guinness Book* states 181 inches; the figure of 205 inches is from the 1995 edition. Measurements taken on 25 February 1995 yielded a total of 226 inches. Chillal last cut the fingernails on his left hand in 1952. I am grateful for this information, and for updates, to Ms Amanda Brooks, Corresponding Editor with the *Guinness Book*, letter (with enclosures) of 29 March 1995. On 10 July 1998, Chillal appeared on *Guinness World Records: Primetime*, and measurements taken that day of the fingernails of his left hand indicated a length of a little more than 242 inches (*GB* 2000:260,500).

34. See http://www.recordholders.org/en/members.html

35. P. V. Krishnamoorthy, 'Jaya Blesses over 5,000 Couples at Mass Wedding', *India-West* (16 Feb. 1996), sec. A, p. 14.

36. 'Match Made in Heavens', *India-West* (21 October 1994), sec. A, p.13. This account itself relies on reports appearing in the *Times of India* and *Hindustan Times*.

Two

THE NEAR IMPOSSIBILITY OF THE OUTSIDER, OR THE
SIGNIFICANT OTHER IN THE MODERN HINDI FILM

I

For a number of decades now, India has laid claim to the largest film
industry in the world. Like many other observations about Indian cinema,
particularly popular Hindi films, this is something of a cliché, since a large
number of Hindi films are never completed, and the revenues generated
by Hollywood far exceed the total earnings of the Hindi film. Only a
minuscule number of Hindi films do well at the box office. There are, as
well, many Indian cinemas, though this is seldom recognized outside India.
To film connoisseurs and aesthetes, Indian cinema may be synonymous
with the names of Ritwik Ghatak, Satyajit Ray, and Mrinal Sen, or a number
of other directors—Adoor Gopalakrishnan, Shyam Benegal, Kumar
Shahani, to name a few—whose films appear in film festivals,[1] or are
otherwise thought to be deserving of the attention of serious film scholars
and critics. However, this so-called 'art' cinema, which owes a great deal to
traditions of humanism, social realism, and the cinematic conventions
associated with European (and less often American) cinema, is dwarfed by
the less high-brow films that are popular with the masses, and which play
to packed houses in gigantic cinema halls throughout the length and
breadth of India. These popular films, some of them immensely long,
were once informally divided into two categories, 'mythological' and

'social',[2] although at another level they all appear to belong to a genre more commonly associated with American cinema, the 'musical'.[3] The 'mythological' has nearly vanished, for reasons that I will hint at in the course of this chapter; what remains is the film which is centred around problems of contemporary living, the loss of innocence, the triumph of 'good' over 'evil', the nature of human communities, the problem of 'law and order', adolescent love, the contaminated nature of politics, the corruption of social institutions, the demands of patriotism, and the onerous presence of the nation-state in modern life.

On the one hand, a strong set of 'family resemblances' characterize many of these films: for instance, the family hardly ever appears whole— if one parent of the hero is present, the other is long since dead, while just the reverse explains the family situation of the heroine; or the film will feature two or even three brothers, often torn away from each other at birth or in early childhood, and unable to recognize each other in adulthood—and circumstances take them along different and violently conflicting trajectories in life.[4] Numerous other characters are seen as orphans: thus films begin with families encountered in midstream, having already gone through the travails of life. The revenge motif often dominates: the hero is bound to avenge the murder of his wife, or punish the beasts who have outraged the modesty of his sister, while the 'villain' cannot countenance his humiliation by the hero in a court of law or the public square. Or, just as often, the enormous chasm between the social standing of the hero and the heroine may prevent the union that they both so ardently desire, and that can only be achieved after an unmentionable tragedy is barely avoided.[5] One could, in fact, speak quite easily (after Vladimir Propp) of a morphology of Hindi films: there is a limited cast of characters, and they exist in relation to each other in a prescribed number of social relations: all the elements combine to yield a certain number of well-defined plots.[6] As the folktale allows variations within limits, so the cast of characters within the Hindi film stays within certain parameters. Thus, to take one example, the doctor, whose advent in the Hindi film serves as a barometer to the emergence of a middle-class sensibility increasingly torn from its moorings in indigenous systems of medicine and forms of treatment, is a mainstay of the Hindi film, but the psychiatrist, until quite recently, was never present in the popular Hindi film.[7]

On the other hand, popular Hindi films are held together by certain conventions of narrative, storytelling, and ambience, among which two very pronounced ones are the stylized fight and the song-and-dance sequences. Though these conventions may now be operative at a different lexical and semantic plane, as the prolonged fight in (say) the film *Gardish* suggests, where the narrative provides complex readings of the nature of stratification, authority, and masculinity in Indian society, certain characteristics have helped to maintain the identity of the Hindi film. The fight with fists, though the villain will grab a deadly implement at an opportune moment, for unlike the hero he is not sworn to sportsmanship, is masterminded by the 'fight' or 'stunt master', which alone highlights the importance of the fist fight in the Hindi film. For a race of men whom the colonizers thought of as effete, unable to protect their own women, and who are constantly reminded of their physical incapacities by their failure to win medals at international sporting events, the fist fight is an assertion by the Hindu male of his masculinity, and a demonstration of his ability to protect his women-folk. The fist fight does a whole lot of good: it provides the man with the self-assurance of his physical prowess, which the heroine might put into question with some deliberate remark; it puts the villain away; and it provides an assurance to the woman that her modesty will be honoured. Lately, with the emergence of the AK-47, which has become a mere extension of the long hand of evil, one might have expected the fist fight to altogether disappear; on the contrary, and not unexpectedly, the fist fight remains, because when technology itself comes to the aid of violence, the fist must even more singularly mark an authentic masculinity and dignity of self. He who is armed with intelligence, virtue, and tenacity need not have any other arms. In *Gardish*, this point is ironically and thus forcefully established by having the anti-heroic hero (who is mistaken for the villain) appear in the fight dressed like a middle-class college boy making his way to the offices of a large business firm for his first interview, a book tucked underneath his arm. Now, in an adaptation of the convention of the fist fight, the well-placed and powerfully delivered fist does not merely keep the pretty girl out of harm's way, it even does the work of the nation-state, as in the film *Krantikshetra* ('The Field of Revolution', 1995) where the Sikh college boy delivers a 'Hindustani mukka' to the terrorist who is an enemy to the nation.[8]

By far the most unique characteristic of the popular Hindi film is the song-and-dance sequence, which remains indispensable to many high-brow Hindi films as well. In the old convention, either the hero or the heroine could break out into song, but the song-and-dance sequence, which involves a principal singer who takes to the stage or the floor against the backdrop of a large ensemble of women (and sometimes men) clad in village or ethnic costumes, took place largely in the field, such as at harvest time, or in the wedding hall, or at the palatial residence of the international smuggler and local mafia boss cloaked in the garb of respectability. The song served as a telescoped narrative, often signalling the flowering of romance or the separation of lovers, or served as a vehicle for conveying existential dilemmas and the cruel power of fate; at times it provided the point of transition between two moments in the plot. The song-and-dance retains all these features, but the narrative style and choreographic traditions in which it is embedded point to the emergence of a new cultural politics, the advent of a middle-class consciousness notable for its aggrandizing spirit, the gradual erosion of the transcendent from everyday affairs, and most evidently a matrix of action and behaviour in which style acquires a life of its own, mechanistic movements predominate over more wayward and uncertain gestures, and machismo replaces the older and softer virtue of restraint. Whereas in the older song-and-dance sequence the women were likely to form themselves into circles, the choreography of the modern collective dance dictates that the field of movement be constituted into squares or other rigid geometric patterns; and where previously the erotic had an element in it of the coy and the tentative gesture, today it has elements of rank sexuality, brutish pride, and vulgarity. Naked feet adorned by anklets have been replaced with high leather boots dancing to the tunes of Indian rap, and the pelvic thrust suggests the hunger of a newly unleashed sexuality, the vengeance of the flesh too long dominated by the language of the spirit. In the theatre of sexuality, as in other spheres of life, the Indian adventure with 'globalization' is on display. Nonetheless, the song-and-dance sequence remains an integral part of the Hindi film, and it retains, as it has in the past, strong links with other narrative elements of the Hindi film.

The continuity of certain narrative and aesthetic traditions, and the visible retention of what I have termed 'family resemblances', may help to

explain the longevity of the popular Hindi film and its resounding success
in India and among Indian communities in the diaspora. The long run that
the popular Hindi cinema has enjoyed is usually described as an aspect of
the films' 'escapist' tendencies. In the conventional sociological view,
poverty, drudgery, and a life of unrelenting labour are the lot of the Indian
masses; the Hindi film offers relief from the tediousness of an impoverished
life, just as it holds out the hope, howsoever remote, of a glimmering and
resplendent future. As one critic, writing in a 'serious' film journal asked,
'Is it [the cinema] not meant merely to provide a temporary and vicarious
catharsis from the rigours of urban poverty?'[9] If the poverty of the hero or
the heroine underscores the grim reality of the slum, the obscene opulence
of the Other is a striking suggestion of the beyond. We least desire to see
on the silver screen that which we encounter daily, and in the naive
sociological view, though the popular Hindi film may be born in the slum,
it lives in the bellies of India's urban spaces, and finds its orgasmic and
ecstatic fulfillment in the pleasure domes of the rich. The argument about
the inherent 'escapism' of commercial cinema similarly seeks to account
for the failure of the 'art' cinema by its chosen formula: having seen enough
poverty in their lives, can Indian audiences be expected to queue up for it
and thus shatter those utopian expectations by which we all live? The
Hindi film allows us to dream, and if we are free to dream, that is no small
freedom.

A more sophisticated explanation for the success of the commercial
Hindi cinema, as I have suggested, would take into account the narrative
conventions and aesthetic norms of popular films. It is even possible to
extend this argument and view the Hindi film as the 'Kaliyuga avatara of
Sanskrit drama', as a representation of the ancient Indian theatrical tradition
for our times.[10] Thus *Satyam, Shivam, Sundaram* (Love Truth Beauty, 1978)
could be viewed as a modern rendering of the *Shakuntala* of Kalidasa and,
in a more general way, the Hindi film could be described as a cinematic
enactment of the theory and structure of action sketched out in the
Natyashastra.[11] The more philosophical aspect of this argument would locate
the Hindi film within what Ashis Nandy has described as the 'language of
continuity', one of the languages 'which often hide[s] the implicit native
theories of oppression in many non-Western traditions.' Whereas Western
intellectual traditions construe continuity 'as only a special case of change',

in Indic traditions the language of continuity, which assumes that 'all changes can be seen, discussed or analysed as aspects of deeper continuities', occupies a predominant place.[12] Change, in other words, is only a special case of continuity—and this is best exemplified in the Hindi film.

It is unarguably clear that the Hindi film, whatever view one might hold about its narrative traditions, is deeply embedded in certain mythic structures which have defined the contours of Indian civilization. The doyen of commercial Hindi cinema, the late Manmohan Desai, claimed that all his films were inspired by the Mahabharata, and on occasion everything in the Hindi film, from the archetypal figure of the mother to the anti-heroic hero, appears to belong to the deep recesses of the Indian past. But I wish to advance and elaborate upon another argument which appears to explain the underlying philosophical assumption of the Hindi film, and suggests why the Hindi commercial cinema has such an enduring popularity among the masses. As I will endeavour to argue, the Hindi film almost altogether denies, and certainly until very recently did wholly deny, the possibility of any significant Other, and in this respect it remains uniquely true to the genius of Indian civilization, of which the most characteristic specimens are undoubtedly the Puranas. There has never been any true outsider in the commercial Hindi film, although as the demands of the Indian nation continue to supersede the ethos of Indian civilization, and the boundaries of inclusivity continue to shrink, the outsider will finally, to put it ironically, have found a place in Indian society. If and when the popular Hindi film shows a keen awareness of the outsider, and gives the notion of the Other an ontological sanctity, we shall have irreversible proof that in India, as in the underdeveloped West, the nation-state is enshrined in the hearts of women and men, and that the project of modernity has, in this most resilient of civilizations, found a hospitable home.

II

It would be useful, in the first instance, to disembed my argument from the matrix in which it might reasonably but nonetheless mistakenly be placed. In the study of Indian society and culture, Indological and Orientalist views have long prevailed though subject, over the course of the last two decades, to more or less rigorous examination.[13] Certain tropes determined the contours of colonial discourse on India: thus, in addition to the 'crafty

Brahman' and the 'effeminate Hindu', one could also speak of the 'martial races', the 'valiant Rajput', the 'fanatic Muslim', the 'scheming bania', the 'noble Pathan', and of course the 'Oriental despot'. On the Indological view, India can moreover be encapsulated through certain categories or essences, among which can be numbered caste and the 'village community'.[14] Most significantly, the individual was said to be present nowhere in India, for Indian society was dominated by collectivities. As the *Economist*, then and now a respected journal of Tory opinion, put it in dramatic fashion at the conclusion of the Swadeshi movement in Bengal, 'Whatever may be the political atom in India, it is certainly not the individual of Western democratic theory, but the community of some sort.'[15] A large constellation of ideas contributed to the shaping of this argument. Francois Bernier, and following him Thomas Munro, Karl Marx, and Sir Henry Sumner Maine, to mention only a few of the more notable individuals who so generously aided in securing a permanent home for error, somehow reached the conclusion that the idea of private property was entirely foreign to the Indian. Property was owned only in common, a rather retrograde thing. Large enough as India was, it had no room for the individual ownership of property, with one singular exception: the Oriental despot, presiding at the top of the apex, had it within his power to deprive any person of his property, and the life and limb of each subject were at his disposal. The Oriental despot, who took as his personal fiefdom an entire society congregated into communities——'divided', as Maine put it, 'into a vast number of independent, self-acting, organized social groups——trading, manufacturing, cultivating'[16]——provided a telling example of the fact that the sole individual in India could only exist as a degraded form of the noble individual of the West. When the despot could appropriate everything at his will, and rule by whim, one could not speak of the individual, and much less could one speak of the individual assertion of rights.

In the communalist reading of Indian history, the notion of communities was inherited from Indological discourse, and these communities were now said to be constituted largely on the basis of religious identity. If caste was the principal nodal point for the colonial sociology of the second half of the nineteenth century, religion in the form of a rigid differentiation between Hindus, Muslims, and Sikhs was to provide the main focus for colonial investigations of Indian society in the twentieth century. This should not obscure the fact that, in the colonial view, Hinduism remained the quintessential religion of India, for Hinduism's metaphysics and religious practices were easily placed alongside the sociological view, whose components I have already sketched briefly, to form a holistic picture of India. As the Oriental despot demanded complete submission, to the point where the individual was not a feasible entity, so Hinduism, at least in its pristine form, was associated with the teaching that the aim of one's life is absorption into the Absolute. How the *advaita* of Shankaracharya came to be held as *the* philosophy of India is another story, but it suffices to note that, in the view of such Indological scholars as Max Mueller, the entire teachings of Indian philosophy were sought to be compressed in such formulae as *tat tvam asi*, 'thou art that', signifying the merger of the atman with the brahman, the individual soul with the universal soul. Along with Buddhism, the 'pure form of Hinduism'—as if the originary moment of Hinduism could be accessed—was viewed as advocating the extinction of the self, the loss of individual identity, the surrender to the Absolute. The 'individual' existed only to forget herself or himself.

The political structures, religious beliefs, philosophical systems, caste system, and socio-economic patterns of living in India all appeared to militate against the idea of the individual. Drawing upon this foundation, the French anthropologist, Louis Dumont, was to provide a systematic analysis of Indian society, part of his endeavour being to show that in such a society the individual, and more particularly the outsider, cannot have a place. Distinguishing between hierarchy and social stratification, Dumont sought to argue, through a structural analysis of caste, that hierarchy is the organizing principle of Indian society. Dumont viewed caste through the lens of religion: in the 'purely structural universe' that is India, it is the 'whole which governs the parts', and it is 'religion which provides the view of the whole'; 'ranking will thus be religious in nature.'[17] Caste allotted everyone, howsoever humble or great, a place in Indian society; its influence was inescapable, and its omnipresence was justly recognized. 'A sect cannot survive on Indian soil if it denies caste', wrote Dumont, 'and it has long been recognized that Buddha himself, if he transcended caste, did not attack or reform it.'[18]

As Dumont was to recognize, he had to be able to account for another characteristic feature of Indian society, the yogi or world renouncer. In the figure of the yogi, Indian society appears to have an outsider, a significant Other, someone who cannot be consumed by caste. But in what respect is the renouncer really an outsider? His very act of renunciation is predicated on the existence of the caste system, and that seems to establish, at the very least, that caste reigns supreme, both as a lived reality and as an aspect of the mind. The effect of renunciation must, ironically, be to strengthen the caste system. Dumont further noted that the yogi is bound by rules; renunciation is not an unhampered freedom, and renunciation creates its own burdens and obligations. The renunciation of the world by a man who has already raised a family, and whose hair are now turning white, is a matter of convention, and he can expect to receive accolades because of the dutiful manner in which he has discharged his duties. When the renunciation of the world is undertaken in youth, not in the manner prescribed by the shastras, but because the yogi is possessed of profound spiritual insight, there too the action is blessed: in either case, we are not speaking of the outsider who cannot be accommodated, someone who cannot stand within the charmed circumference of what a society might stipulate as its *Lakshmanrekha*. Such an outsider is not the exception to the rule; he is a seeming exception, and in India there is no escape. Going far beyond Dumont, we might even say: Where the outsider is not banished, where the outsider exists to remind others of those values of transcendence of which we become oblivious owing to the impositions of daily life, there the outsider has become an insider. Such an outsider, far from being the significant Other, that Other in whom we invest the evil that we recognize within us, is nothing but our true Self; that outsider is our own mutilated, spat-out Self.

As I have argued, the Indological view insists that Indian society is characterized and dominated by collectivities, the individual being particular to societies in the West. Where there is no individual, there can be no outsider, unless we are all outsiders in the metaphysical sense, biding our time on earth, living this life as though it were a sojourn from which we must return to an earlier point of origin. In Dumont's version of the hard truth about India, caste is bound to dictate the life of every Indian, assigning him or her a place in that multitudinous society, and its influence is all the more pronounced precisely when it is sought to be denied. The political effects of such readings are there to be seen, in the history of colonialism as much as in the barbaric attempts by the West to impose yet another new international order; just as evident is the tyranny of the sociological method, which would make a complex civilization hostage to the categories of an impoverished social science discourse, and would seek to transmute the rich confusions of an ancient and pluralistic culture into a purportedly seamless, error-free account bound by no strictures other than those routinely placed upon intellectuals in the academy.

While seeking to disassociate myself entirely from the intellectual practices, ideology, and political repercussions of Indological discourse, I would nonetheless maintain that the popular Hindi film has never displayed, at least until very recently, any sense of the outsider or the significant Other. The Hindi film has more than its fair share of villains, and of these some are demonic, but for that reason all the more assimilable to rakshasas, the creatures of mythology rather than of history. A preponderant number of the villains are of the run-of-the-mill variety, mere camp followers, easily dispatched into a state of unconsciousness by the fighting skills of the hero or other principal protagonist, and with no particular investment in the life of crime. They are of no consequence, a point that the Hindi film makes by almost invariably introducing, into what appears to be a bloody fight, indeed a struggle unto death, a ludicrously comic element. One of the 'bad men' will be struck on the head with a saucepan, another will be diverted from the performance of his nefarious activities by some silly trick or the other.[19] On account of this, and for the more ponderous reason that no civilization is without its Others, I wish to underscore *significant* in 'the significant Other' of the title of this chapter.

Who, then, might the significant Other or outsider be? In pursuance of this query, we must take a particularly close look at the principal figure of antagonism in the Hindi film. In a film such as *Deewar* about which I shall have a great deal more to say in due course, though Shashi Kapoor represents the forces of 'law and order', it is clearly Amitabh Bachchan, who takes to a life of crime and easy living, who elicits our sympathy. There may well be an argument of broader psychological scope that one could make at this juncture, not particular to India, namely that villains are generally more attractive than heroes, for somehow we suspect that the greater majority of villains were not born as such, but were turned by the dint of circumstances into criminals, social misfits, and figures of alienation. Still, the Indian handling of this ubiquitous theme also draws upon a different set of ethical and socio-cultural considerations. Amitabh could have been the significant Other, but the ethos of inclusivity upon which the film relies draws him into our moral universe. He may even begin his adult life by being an outsider, but even his attachment to the life of crime is tentative, as though the fruits of his actions are of little consequence to him. The 'evil' in him has no ontological life, and it is for that reason that though he may be an outsider to his own kith and kin, and to the social institutions around him, his remoteness is never a complete hindrance to the formulation of human relationships. Through certain modes of cultural accommodation, not yet lost to a civilization reeling under the impact of modernity, a relentless materialism, and the vociferous demands of a nation-state that believes itself to be besieged by forces of terror and instability, he is incorporated into the human community.[20] He is never truly the figure in whom evil resides, and he is never irredeemable, for that would render him into an outsider, strange and alien, repository of an Otherness.

Although my point could be pressed further by arguing at a level of generality, I will draw mainly upon four films, and occasionally stray into other films. All four films—*Deewar* (1975), *Shakti* (1982), *Khalnayak* (1993), and *Gardish* (1993)—belong to the mainstream of the commercial cinema: *Deewar* was until then one of its most marked successes, and *Gardish* alone did not receive box-office acclaim. *Deewar* is recognized as the film that established Amitabh Bachchan as one of the most formidable stars in Indian film history, and in *Shakti* Amitabh was paired with another stalwart of the film industry, Dilip Kumar. *Deewar* also has the distinction of helping to inaugurate what is usually termed as the 'angry young man' phase of Hindi films, and in fact the film is usually seen as an instance of the celebration of the outsider, the very opposite of the argument which I shall be deriving in my reading. Moving to the 1990s, *Khalnayak* ('The Villain') then had the effect of further consolidating the reputation of Sanjay Dutt, the most highly paid star of Hindi films at that time, while *Gardish* featured Jackie Schroff, another major presence in the film world. *Khalnayak* had a very successful run, bolstered no doubt by the inclusion of a song, 'Chholi Ke Peeche Kya Hai?', that was to gain considerable notoriety. The limited success of *Gardish*, as I will suggest, has something to do with the complexity of its narrative structures, the confusions it creates in the mind of the viewer about the protagonist, and the fact that it comes perilously close to having a significant Other.

III

In *Deewar* the family of four (but not the ideal four of family planning programmes) is, at the outset, practically reduced to three. The father, who leads the workers of a mill on strike in quest for higher wages and better working conditions, is confronted with a cruel choice by a desperate and ruthless management. His wife and two young sons are taken hostage, and under duress he signs, in his capacity as representative of the workers, certain papers whereby the workers relinquish their demands, forsake their right to strike, and agree to work under conditions laid down by the management. Having saved the lives of his family members, he also betrays the trust reposed in him by the workers, and his life is made miserable by the town dwellers. In utter shame, he flees the town, leaving the family to fend for itself and bear the people's fury.[21] One day, Vijay (Amitabh Bachchan), the elder brother, is accosted by a group of townspeople, and when he returns home that day, bruised and beaten, his arm is shown to have been tattooed with the words, 'Your father is a thief'. These words are furrowed deeply not merely into his arm, but into his mind as well, and the constant memory of that burning insult never leaves Vijay. Hounded by their near and distant neighbours, the family leaves town, and like countless others they arrive in the city of dreams, to spend their days on the footpaths of Bombay. The mother finds work as a labourer, and gradually Vijay takes to shining shoes, for on two meagre salaries Ravi (Shashi Kapoor), Vijay's younger brother, can be sent to school. Thus the two brothers take two different paths, a point highlighted by Vijay's adamant refusal to step inside the temple, stopping short at its entrance, though Ravi, the dutiful son that he is, cheerfully accompanies his mother inside. It is the destiny of sensitive people, one might say, to live on the threshold and be marked by liminality: only those whose self-assurance extends to a rather neat distinction between 'good' and 'evil' enter the sanctum sanctorum of the temple.

Years have elapsed, and Vijay is now a labourer at the docks. A masterfully orchestrated fight with the local mafia, who consider it their right to extort protection money from every worker at the docks, earns

Vijay a fearsome reputation, and another underworld don, played by Iftikhar, invites Vijay to join his business. Before long, Vijay is in possession of millions, and his mother and brother are now moved to a palatial mansion. Bombay must, after all, remain the city of hopes and desires. But long before the two brothers had been set on different paths, and as fate would have it, Vijay's unemployed brother is commissioned into the police and entrusted with the task of finding evidence that would implicate Iftikhar and his associates with smuggling and other illicit operations. Duty compels: brother is pitted against brother. Once Ravi learns that his own brother is leading a life of crime, the two cannot stay under one roof; Ravi leaves, and takes their mother along with him to his humble abode. The film winds its way to the foregone conclusion: a search warrant is issued in Vijay's name, and a chase through the city streets leaves Vijay, wounded by a bullet from his brother's revolver, dead—but not before he collapses into his mother's arms, where he can at long last find the eternal sleep of those who know they are wanted. It is, as some would maintain, the return to the womb and to the ocean of eternal sleep.

It has been argued that 'the Amitabh persona is the quintessential outsider of the ghetto', and the narrative I have offered would so far appear to corroborate that reading. K. Chandrasekhar, from whose article I have quoted, further argues that Amitabh, whether in *Deewar*, *Shakti*, or indeed almost any of his other films, 'longs to belong, to find security, to be spared the turmoil of survival in the ruthless city. He hankers for his roots, he yearns to put the clock back to the epoch when all human society was pastoral.' Vijay merely has 'the lumpen desire to belong'.[22] Quite to the contrary, the difficulty with Amitabh is precisely that he belongs, and in this respect the Hindi film never entirely attains the rank of tragedy. To begin with, Amitabh is never completely shunned by others: in Iftikhar, the father figure is reincarnated and the family rendered whole,[23] and in Parveen Babi, who makes her entry into the film as a night club hostess (of loose morals), and makes her departure as a repentant woman fully cognizant of the glorious virtues of motherhood and wifehood, he finds a female companion who gives him that hearing which others would deny him. But the restoration of the 'natal' family is aborted, for Iftikhar is taken under arrest,[24] while Amitabh is prevented from starting his own family by the violent elimination of Parveen Babi, whose repentance cannot obfuscate the fact that her attempt to tie the knot with Amitabh and thus acquire respectability constitutes a threat to the social order which alone can stipulate the rules under which marriages can be tolerated, much less sanctified.

Iftikhar and Parveen Babi are, nonetheless, minor figures, and so we must take recourse to a stronger argument, turning to the mother (played, here and elsewhere, by Nirupa Roy, who—alongside Rakhee—appears to have cornered the trademark on this role in Hindi films) as the pivotal axis around whom the plot and, in particular, my argument must revolve. The figure of the mother, as perhaps every student of the popular Hindi film is aware, is central to the commercial cinema. At a very general level, this is easily explained by the importance attached to fecundity in India from the days of antiquity, while it is also possible to argue that Indian civilization has always had a substratum of matriarchy, certainly antecedent to the patriarchy which is far more characteristic of Indian society today. On another view, no more important or poignant relationship exists in Indian society than that between mother and son,[25] and the Hindi film best exemplifies the significance of this nexus. Chandrasekhar's argument, as it appears in his article 'The Amitabh Persona', adopts this viewpoint; as he says, Amitabh's films embody a 'uterine world-view', and the fury of the 'angry young man' abates 'the moment the umbilical cord is restored.' 'In the Indian context,' he adds, 'the sole irreproachable ideological thesis one can defend is love of the mother.'[26] Vijay's only desire in *Deewar* is to restore the state of original bliss that existed before he was parted from his mother, and towards the end of the film, as Vijay is bleeding to death, he states that his only desire is to enjoy, in the lap of his mother, that profound sleep of contentment which he has missed since she left him. The Hindi film, then, enacts for the Indian male a double return to the source: seated in the dark chambers of the movie theatre, we all descend into the darkness of the womb, but for the Indian male that darkness is like a wellspring of light, and the womb that place where our sleep is always undisturbed and calm. A film such as *Deewar*, to extend the argument further, represents the regression of the male into a state of childhood, an attempt to reinstate the primacy of the umbilical stage.

I want to argue, however, that the critical place of the mother in *Deewar* (and the Hindi film more generally) owes considerably more to the fact that she is the force that prevents Vijay from becoming an outsider, a significant Other. As is quite transparent, both Vijay and Ravi vie for her affection and attention, and when the manner in which Vijay is making his living becomes known to her, and she seems determined to leave the mansion he had brought for her, his only defence is that he has done everything in her interest. ('*Maine jo kuch bhi kiya, tere liye kiya.*') Indeed, it is to avenge her humiliation that he has purchased for her a skyscraper, which was built with the sweat of her labour: a magnanimous notion of the 'gift', though I cannot pursue that reading here.[27] (Clearly, she belongs to him, much as the building belongs to him.) But this argument does not prevail, and it is even possible to interpret her resistance to his claims as resistance to the presumed fact of ownership; mother and Ravi leave. In what is perhaps the most famous scene of the film, Vijay arranges a rendezvous with Ravi, and attempts to persuade him that he should arrange to get himself transferred to another police station, as the mafia is hungry for his blood. Back and forth goes the argument; finally, being quite at the end of his patience, Vijay says: 'I have a bungalow, a car, wealth, good clothes to wear. What do you have? What do you have besides a measly job, a uniform, a mere roof over your head?' This is a dramatic moment, for by this time it has been established what is at stake; and thus Ravi can look Vijay squarely in the face, and say with immense pride: 'Mother. I have mother.' ('*Ma. Mere pas Ma hai.*') Thunder roars; lightning strikes: when mother is so honoured, even the gods must bow down and render obeisance. The silence itself is thunderous.

The victory has been clinched, but only seemingly so. What attenuates the 'victory' is the peculiar fact that when Ravi speaks, he speaks not only as the brother of Vijay, and as the one whose abode she shares, but that he also speaks in the voice of patriarchy, as the defender of the family and the social order, and also as the reincarnated husband, with all the 'rights' that accrue to the husband. When she stands by Ravi, she is only reaffirming the extraordinary hold that the social order has over us, and helping to restore the family; she is not making a choice between her two sons, though in fact, as she admits at some point, she has always loved Vijay more than Ravi. In one respect, Ravi is quite incapable of having an unencumbered human relationship, for he must bear the burden of the social institutions around him, as well as the anthropological burden of kinship: thus he never addresses Vijay as Vijay, but always as bhai. Social institutions and mores speak through Ravi. Vijay's relationship with his mother is not constrained by duty or form, and it is a sign of the strength of that relationship that he locates her at the centre of his moral—rather than social—universe. It is at the risk of being captured by Ravi that he attempts to visit his mother at the hospital; more tellingly, when her life is hanging in the balance, he takes the unthinkable step of going to the mandir and asking God, though scarcely in a voice of reverence, for her life. We recall that it is at the temple steps that the two brothers, in their adolescence, already seemed to be veering towards two different paths, and that Vijay seemed marked as the loner, as the outsider; but now, if it has not been established before, it becomes indubitably clear that he, too, must be drawn into the circle of inclusivity.

Far from being a film about the outsider, *Deewar* is about the impossibility of being one. In the Hindi film, the end is where we start from, a point that is reinforced by *Shakti*, a slightly later film. Here the police officer (Ashwini Kumar, played by Dilip Kumar) is the father of Amitabh (Vijay in this film also), and—as in most Hindi films—he is a man of strict moral code, bound beyond everything else to the performance of his duty, incapable of being corrupted. Ashwini's moral resolve and fierce combativity make him an altogether unpalatable figure for J. K. (Amrish Puri), a man who runs illicit liquor shops and a large smuggling business, and who now resolves upon kidnapping Vijay as the only way of breaking Ashwini's will and having his principal associate released from jail. Vijay is taken hostage, and J. K. places a call to Ashwini, saying that he must have his answer in half an hour. Looking across at Vijay, J. K. says: 'We shall soon find out how much your father loves you.'[28] But Ashwini avers that he shall not compromise his duty in order to save the life of his son: 'I know my son's life is in your hands at this time. You can kill him. Do what you want with him, but I won't dishonour my obligations.' Unknown to him, this message, as it comes across the machine, is heard by his son in captivity, who will henceforth, for the rest of his life, labour under the illusion that his life has no meaning to his own father. Vijay little realizes that his father's love for him and his duty as a police officer are not mutually exclusive, nor is he cognizant of the fact that, in having prolonged the negotiation, Ashwini has gained the time he needed to have the phone call traced. Before Ashwini and his men can arrive at J. K.'s hideout, Vijay has given his captors the slip, and that day, as he is chased down narrow alleys, his life is saved by Narang (Kulbushan Kharbanda), who will himself become a mafia don one day and the employer of a grateful Vijay.

As in *Deewar*, so in *Shakti*, Vijay undoubtedly has the sense of being abandoned. Where in *Deewar* the words, 'Your father is a thief', were burnt into his flesh, in *Shakti* the refrain of those words, 'You can kill him', leave an indelible impress on Vijay's mind. If ever language, and an act of 'misreading', dictated the course of a man's life, such is Vijay's life. As he returns from school one day, kicking a can lying on the street, we see him transformed—through a match cut—to a lanky young man, aimlessly adrift. The match cut signifies not merely the empty passage of time, but also the alteration of states of mind: thus, through this match cut, we are confronted with the possibility that Vijay's transformation into an outsider is now virtually complete. The conversation that then takes place between him and Roma (Smita Patil), a woman whose modesty he has prevented from being outraged by some goons with whom she was travelling on a train, appears to confirm this:

> VIJAY: Won't your folks at home be anxious [at your
>   being late]?
> ROMA: If there were folks at home, they would have
>   been—I live alone.
> VIJAY: You live alone? Aren't you afraid?
> ROMA: When I'm alone, then there is only me. And
>   what is there to fear from oneself?
> VIJAY: The only person I'm afraid of is myself.
> ROMA: Do you also live on your own?
> VIJAY: Well, one can be alone even while living with
>   others.

If in the existential sense one recognizes oneself and knows oneself as an outsider, then that perhaps defines Vijay's state. But no such claim about Vijay, in the ontological or even sociological sense, is advanced; and indeed from here the entire movement of the film will be to draw Vijay into the realm of the human community. As in *Deewar*, Vijay falls into a relationship with Roma, and if the relationship with Parveen Babi was first abrogated with her death, in *Shakti* it will terminate with Vijay's own death. The brutal fact that such relationships cannot be sanctified through the act of marriage, because they are violative of the social codes instituted by sanctimonious patriarchs, does by no means render Vijay into an outsider; rather, it is suggestive of the fact that his incorporation will have to take a different route. Those morphological elements which determined the structure of *Deewar* are present in *Shakti* as well, which means that the figure of the mother will be critical, except that in *Shakti* she cannot be an altogether successful source of mediation between her husband and her son. At one point, having been admonished by his father for leading the life of an idler and worse, Vijay quite sternly tells his mother: 'I have no need for lectures.' She replies, 'Yes, you seem to need no one. Not even me', whereupon he is quick to respond: 'I need you very much.' ('*Mujhe tumhari bahut zaroorat hai.*') Here, and elsewhere, the son is no outsider to the mother, but nonetheless the relationship between mother and son is not entirely on the same footing as in *Deewar,* for a mechanical application of the formula will satisfy neither Vijay nor the viewer.

It is his father with whom Vijay must settle his relationship if he is not to become the outsider that he appears to be, and accordingly the film moves towards that resolution. Ashwini has made J. K.'s life miserable, his illegal operations have been largely shut down, and J. K. must now flee the country, but before doing so he resolves upon terminating Ashwini's life. The bullets intended for Ashwini find their target in his wife instead: that death, too, was necessary, for as the film has suggested all along, no rapprochement between father and son is possible as long as she is alive, not that she aimed at being a hindrance to the achievement of that objective. Some matters can only be settled between fathers and sons. At this point, with the death of Sheetal, Vijay's incorporation into the human community is complete, for father and son can now mourn in common. That much Ashwini realizes: whatever his son may be, he is fully cognizant of the fact that Vijay feels that loss deeply, and Vijay too is brought to an awareness of the loss suffered by his father. This obviates the necessity for a more formal reconciliation, but the plot must move to its end dialectically. Now is not the time for contemplation, but for action, and this can signal nothing else but a violent end to the life, at the hands of Vijay, of J. K., who it transpires is the same man who had abducted him years ago. But Ashwini is a senior police officer, and duty reigns supreme: he chases Vijay across the length of the airport, and his reluctant bullet eventually finds its mark. There everything is revealed, and the 'misreading' is set straight; as Vijay dies in his father's lap, it is with the reassurance that his incorporation into the family fold, and into his father's inner life, is now complete.

IV

The Hindi film, I have been arguing, has almost no notion of the outsider or the significant Other. I will dare more, and venture to add that the Hindi film, until recently, has had little conception of the villain that we could take seriously. In the school of advaita, villainy can have no place, for when man commits an error or does some wrong, he does so from ignorance. We need not apply such a magnanimous reading to the Hindi film, but it appears to me that the concept of the villain has been taken for granted. At the lowest level, as I have already stated, we get 'bad men' en masse, but these nameless goons have no life of their own, leaving no impression whatsoever on the mind of the viewer. They can scarcely remind us of the dark side of the institutions of state or society, or even the dark side of ourselves. At a far more impressionable level, we have villains such as Samant and Dawad in *Deewar*, J. K. and Narang in *Shakti*, or Robert and Ajit in *Yaadon Ki Baarat* ('Procession of Memories', 1973). Their 'villainy', however, is easily put into question. Robert, an international smuggler who flies out of India on private jets, is an altogether improbable figure; Ajit, along those lines, is quite comical, and indeed Ajit jokes, which have always been vastly popular in Delhi, have become a staple of Indian parties, even in the diaspora. As villains, Robert, Ajit, and their ilk are rather unbelievable; and indeed it is in its depiction of villainy that the Hindi film, which in any case cannot be accommodated within some social realist framework, completely abandons any pretensions to the real. More compelling, in this respect, are the likes of Dawad, Samant, J. K., and Narang, but they are curiously handicapped in their attempts to be full-blooded villains on account of being overshadowed by men such as Vijay. Nor can the Dawads of this world, who rule by decree and by the gun, and are garbed in respectability, deceive us. They may tend to the violent extreme in their behavior, as with J. K. in *Deewar*, but they do not have the moral courage that we require of villains as well. They, too, must remain minor players on the stage, for they do not strike a chord of ambivalence within us. Amitabh, on his part, though he is drawn into the life of crime, must always be redeemed, and his villainy as such is easily forgotten, which is why he—rather than the unambiguously moral figure, whether it be Ravi in *Deewar*, Ashwini in *Shakti*, or Ram Sinha in *Khalnayak*—remains the pole of attraction for the viewer.

The outsider, then, continues to elude us. A reasonably recent film, *Khalnayak*, provides the most compelling evidence for my argument. The film opens with the shot of a mother, Aarti (Nirupa Roy), pining for the return of her son, Balu, whose photograph she has placed amidst the pages of her Ramayana, and who became enmeshed in the world of crime over six years ago. An elderly man, a fellow villager, says in harsh yet imploring tones that she should forget him, for he will not return. What is the use, he asks, of keeping the picture of Ravana in the Ramayana?[29] A son who has entered the world of crime cannot return from it; and what can one say of a son who killed his own father and who stole her husband from her? When he has declared her dead as well, which Balu does while offering testimony before the court, has he not turned himself into a beast, into a veritable outsider to the human community? 'A mean bastard who has transformed his living mother into a dead one', says the old man to Aarti, 'such a person should be forgotten.' 'But how can I forget', she implores him, 'he is my son.'[30] Thus, as the film establishes Balu as the outsider, the absolute Other, from the outset, it works simultaneously to unravel that impression; and henceforth the film will move dialectically between the two positions.

'*Nayak nahi, khalnayak hai tu*'. The son of a poor but honest father, with small prospects in life to lift himself from the conditions under which he is born and raised, and unable to find employment, Balu is easy prey for the evil genius, Roshi Mahanta, under whose influence he readily murders his own father. But, if there are laws of compensation at work in the universe, for every *khalnayak* there must always be a *nayak* as well, and so he appears in the figure of the upright police officer, Ram Kumar Sinha. Balu is caught at the site of the murder by Ram, and the court sentences him to twenty years in prison, but is there a jail that can hold Balu? A battle, at once physical, psychological, and verbal, ensues between Balu and Ram: just as Balu with overweening pride can characterize himself as a *khalnayak*, Ram is unwilling to admit that there is ever any human being who cannot be persuaded to see the light of truth and reason. Balu, in Ram's view, is not a free agent; he is the pawn of foreign powers who are determined upon destroying India. 'Your boss', Ram tells Balu, 'is a rakshasa'—but that man whom Ram describes as a rakshasa, Balu is inclined to see as his guru. It is in the name of this guru, and in the name of his mother (now 'resurrected'), that Balu swears to escape from prison.

And so he does—to be hauled back into jail, eventually, as a convoluted consequence of the efforts of Ganga, Ram's consort and a policewoman. Disguising herself as a nautch girl, a courtesan of sorts, Ganga is under the impression that she has won his confidence, although a later scene reveals that he has known her true identity all along. Though Balu lusts after Ganga, he does not violate her, a sure sign that the *khalnayak* who can take the life of his own father and ruthlessly gun down other political opponents of his guru, is nonetheless a *nayak* who keeps his conduct within certain parameters. Once her identity is known, she is purposefully retained as a hostage, as a guarantee to a safe passage. It is from this point onwards that the film takes an extraordinary, and from the point of view of my argument, a significant turn. Balu slowly becomes attracted to Ganga, little realizing that she is already committed to Ram, his inveterate foe; Ganga, on the other hand, while filled with revulsion at him, gradually comes to the realization that within him there are the seeds of a good man, the sprinkling of 'good Indian blood'. As she puts it to him, 'Within every *khalnayak* some *nayak* is hidden. Even Ravana had some of the virtues of a *nayak*'. Ravana, we are reminded, is not the Satan of Christian traditions; Ravana is certainly not the Other in whom we invest all evil. Balu is not so easily persuaded, and there is a certain pride with which he can assert his own villainy. 'Man can become an animal', he responds, 'but do you know of an animal that can become a man? I've come too far along to get on the right path now.' Balu's claim to Otherness, to being an outsider, is contradicted by his admission that there is a 'right path', a path that he is not following.

The woman who came as his death has now come, as Balu imagines, as his life. As he prepares to place the mangalsutra, the icon of wifely devotion, or (as in the feminist reading) the symbol of woman's enslavement, around her neck, she makes it known that she belongs to someone else. Just then the police appear and surround Balu's hideout, and Ganga, though seeking only to save Balu from certain death, unwittingly becomes the instrument of his escape. As she states in her defence, she saw him 'turning into a man', and was not prepared to see him killed by the police: what she finds wholly unacceptable is the supposition that Balu must be construed only as an outsider, the repository of irredeemable evil, and that such outsiders are to be dealt with by the machinery of death. Violence, particularly when its end is extermination, can only subsist on the sign of the Other; and that violence which the State is on the verge of unleashing upon Balu, fed by the stream of vengeance, threatens to extinguish the flame of self-realization that Ganga, erstwhile the ocean of life, has lit within Balu. For this offence against the state, for the crime of having aided and abetted a criminal, and for the greater crime of having betrayed the oath and principles of her profession, she is taken into custody and put on trial.

The legal quagmire in which Ganga has placed herself is the least of her difficulties, for the force of rumour and public opinion induces a greater trauma. The 'whole world' *(sari janta)* gossips about Ganga's infidelity, for is it not possible that during her 'captivity' under Balu, she entered into an amorous relationship with him? 'Ram's Sita went to Ravana', says the public, and if the Ram of the Satya Yuga ('the age of truth') could renounce his Sita at the word of a mere washerman, then why should not a common mortal like Ram Sinha sacrifice his now tainted beloved? Caught in Balu's love-nest, has not Ganga committed treachery against her country and compromised her colleagues in the police force? 'Now the entire country', the newspapers report, 'is calling her a *desh-drohi*, "an enemy of the country"'. Such is the stigma attached to her name, suggests one newspaper, that even Ram Sinha is unable to erase that mark against her name, and like his namesake, the Ram who presided over the destinies of Bharat, he is thinking of sacrificing her: 'The crux of the matter is that today's Sita cohabited with Ravana and demeaned Ram.'[31]

Khalnayak, then, as I have been suggesting, must be viewed as performing an interpretation of the Ramayana. While I do not wish to pursue that line of argumentation much further, as it takes us far beyond the parameters of this chapter, it is critical to note that the film does not accept a conventional reading of the Ramayana story. The story of Sita's banishment has always been a difficult moment, not only for the devotees of Ram, but for Indian civilization itself. If Ram could banish and outlaw his chaste wife owing to the demands of a public inclined to think of Sita as having been defiled by her long captivity, what kind of example can he—the noble and just king, the devout husband, the very incarnation of the Gods—be said to have created for his subjects? Is not the effect of Ram's banishment of Sita to render her into an outsider to civilized society, the Other of his conscience? Must not standards of morality appear to be altogether shifting and arbitrary if Ram can place Sita outside the framework of an inclusive morality? As Ramachandra Gandhi has so poignantly observed in a recent work, the story of Sita's banishment can, in fact, be located within a framework where Sita is not rendered into the Other. For their repeated violation of the ecological order, as when Ram takes the life of Mareech, or when Ram shoots dead one of a pair of curlew birds engaged in love-play, Ram and Sita too must enact, by way of atonement and compensation, and by mutual consent, the pain of separation; and this story, when placed into the hands of patriarchs and chauvinists, becomes 'distorted into the sexist banishment of Sita by Rama for suspected infidelity in Lanka.'[32]

If Sita can be recovered, if she is not the outsider that she appears to be, the recuperation of Ganga in *Khalnayak* might well be expected. Once Balu finds that he has been 'spurned' by her, that he cannot win her love, he returns to the path of villainy—but this return, as the film establishes, is only imaginary. His stated ambition, as Balu declares before his guru, Roshi Mahanta, the corrupter of youth and the sworn foe of India but a shadowy presence in the film, is 'to become the world's worst man'. Yet the *nayak* in him has triumphed over the *khalnayak*, his real self has established its lordship over his ignorant self, and he will eventually locate himself within an inclusionary polity, and render himself subject to the laws of the community. Thus, towards the end of the film, as Ganga is sentenced to seven years imprisonment for aiding and abetting a dangerous criminal, and Balu appears to be ensconced as the new head of the empire of evil, he appears suddenly in court and bares forth the truth. But, before an audience to whom the word of a notorious criminal is not worth much, what can he do to persuade them that the account he is about to render of Ganga's captivity—an account that Ravana was prevented from giving to the citizens of Ayodhya—merits belief? Though he cannot swear by the Gita, the Bible, or the Quran, he is prepared to swear by his mother—for she is his book. The Sita that he has known, Balu tells the court, is *pavitra*, pure, and in every drop of her blood there is Ram. Seeking the penalty due to him, Balu pleads that this Sita must not be separated from her Ram. With an ending that one has come to expect of Hindi films, Ram and Sita are finally together, and Balu, having separated the ephemeral within him from that which is enduring, is drawn back into the arms of the human community.

V

Balu could not be rendered into the Other. In an extraordinarily suggestive and curious scene, Balu's mother wanders into a church, with the expectation that she might find her son there. But he is nowhere to be seen; there is only the padre, and high up on the wall, a painting of Christ. 'Whom are you looking for?' inquires the padre, and she replies, 'For my son.' 'What does he look like', he asks, and she points most innocently to the painting of Christ: in the long hair and the somewhat unkempt beard, there is a keen resemblance. Man, said Emerson, is nothing but God in ruins. The happy ending of *Khalnayak*, and dozens of other films of recent years, should not obscure the fact that the Hindi film has come perilously close to an acceptance of the Other or the outsider. The nation-state has always made heavy demands of its subjects, but now, as the spectre of terrorism—by which is meant principally the secessionist movements in the Punjab, the North-East, and Kashmir—has loomed large, it demands an unflinching loyalty: if one is not with the nation, then one is against it. An unflinching commitment to the cultural and political integrity of the nation becomes the requirement of the day, and *Khalnayak* is indubitably an enactment of that loyalty. In the shot that opens the film, the national flag flutters in the wind; the camera then cuts to railway tracks and a running train; and finally the face of Nirupa Roy, the mother of Balu, appears on the screen. The tricolour is the quintessential icon of the political unity of India, of the sanctity of its borders, while the figure of the mother points to the matriarchal roots of Indian civilization, and the sanctity of the idea of motherhood across India. The political and cultural unity of India is maintained through the railways, the lifeline of India, a demonstration of the transparency of borders within the country. As if to reinforce the political integrity of India's borders, the closing shot of the film is again of the tricolour, and throughout the film, the national flag serves as a reminder of the duty we owe to the state, besides evoking in us the loyalty that we ordinarily reserve for our mother. In tandem with the thrust towards political unity for which the film stands, *Khalnayak* also makes a less obvious plea for the cultural and spiritual union of India. If Ram stands for the Vaishnavite strand of Indian culture, Ganga—the consort of Shiva, otherwise known as Ganga-dhara, the upholder of the river Ganga— signifies Saivism. Thus the wedding of Ram and Ganga, which must perforce be inevitable, is nothing less than the cultural union of India.

If we are to read *Khalnayak* as a cinematic plea for the preservation of India's political and cultural unity, we are also invited, as it seems, to view the terrorist as the Other—the absolute repository of evil, the signification of unassimilability—and as the implacable foe of the nation. With the terrorist, the significant Other appears to have finally arrived, and to have asserted its presence in the life of the Hindi film. However, as I have already suggested, this reading cannot be sustained, even though no more plausible construction of the Other is possible in the Indian context today, unless it be the construction of the Muslim. In a film such as *Krantikshetra*, where the plot involves the takeover of a private college by a 'dreaded terrorist' (in the language of Doordarshan) in an attempt to secure from jail the release of his convicted brother, the task of freeing the students from the clutches of the terrorists is entrusted to Major Khan. As the film suggests, the vision of India's cultural unity has never excluded the Muslims, and Hindu-Muslim unity, through the naive figure of the 'good Muslim',[33] is in fact critical to the preservation of the nation's integrity. Moreover, even the terrorists appear as comical figures: one does not for a moment imagine that they will triumph, and the anxieties of hard-nosed functionaries of state, who are wont to think of India as especially victimized by supposedly ruthless terrorists, appear somewhat misplaced (see Chapter III). So poignant an event as the assassination of Rajiv Gandhi, engineered by a woman who had a bomb strapped to her body, and who went up to the Prime Minister to place a garland around his neck, is parodied in *Krantikshetra*: thus the amusement of a number of the kids consists in placing dynamite-filled garlands around the necks of figures of authority, and it is with this contraption that a number of the terrorists become the laughing stock of the audience. Those who are under the illusion of being honoured are in fact humbled, but that is a mode of rendering them subject to the human community.

There is nothing comical, by way of contrast, about Roshi Mahanta in *Khalnayak*, though he has a seductive style of speech, and has a charming way of eliminating his rivals or unreliable sycophants. '*Hota hai, chalta hai, duniya hai*', says he while stabbing to death one of his bearers whose ineptitude leads to Balu's arrest as he is about to flee after having shot his father.[34] The corrupter of youth, the foe of the family, the nemesis of the nation, the personification of evil in every respect: Roshi, the force behind Balu, is all this and yet he remains a secondary figure. Unlike the traditional mafia boss or head of an international smuggling ring who takes an inordinate interest in women, and has his body pumped full of bullets while he is having his fill (somewhat like Samant in *Deewar*), Roshi displays no interest in women. He has the concentrated powers of attention that we would associate with a yogi, much as Ravana did, and it is with single-minded devotion that he pursues the path of evil. Roshi Mahanta, as I would submit, is not so much an evil man, for then we could legitimately speak of his demonization, of his status as the Other, as a demon. From the standpoint of Ram Kumar Sinha, the battle is never for his soul, for Roshi belongs truly in the realm of the mythological. By mythological I do not here mean a form which allows for cultural pluralism, but rather in the sense of being outside the conventional history of humankind. Roshi has neither any history nor any family; his antecedents remain entirely unknown. As a character, he impresses upon us not as the Other, but as the possibility of an Other, and that unfulfilled possibility is represented by Balu. Roshi points, I might add, to the contradictory reasons why the mythological has largely vanished as a genre of the Hindi film. The mythological, here understood as a form of cultural pluralism, as an open-ended form which shifts between the gods and humans, finds itself oppressed by the cultural logic of the nation-state and nationalism; on the other hand, the element of the mythological has made its way into the mainstream Hindi film, and appears always as a reminder of the imperative to keep the circle of inclusion open.

As I have thus far argued, the figure of the terrorist, with which the commercial Hindi film appears to have an increasing interest, has come dangerously close to providing us with a formulation of the Other. Still, that line of irreversibility has not been crossed, though that becomes a more real possibility with the increasing encroachment of modernity, and with the increasing assent to the idea of India as a nation-state among India's modernizers. It is no surprise that, with the emergence over the last ten years of a large middle class in both India and Pakistan, for whom the trappings of a modernizing nation-state have a consummate attraction, that rapprochement between the two countries has become treacherously difficult. Jingoism must have its enemies, and the day may not be far when in India, as in America, the yellow ribbons will fly from tree-tops and poles not merely to pray for the safe return of the boys back home, but to celebrate the complete decimation of the 'enemy'. Already the colonial past has been subjected to some fervently nationalistic readings, as the wholly unsympathetic (but altogether minor) figure of the British General in *1942, A Love Story* (1995), so amply demonstrates. If he is the Other there, he is still a figure belonging to the past and thus of little consequence, though that does not obviate the more pressing query as to whether he might not already be an iconic figure for an Otherness that henceforth will not be so distant. As the idea of India as a nation-state takes precedence, the idea of India as a civilization will become imperilled, and the cultural pluralism and accommodation of that civilization will most likely become, as they have already to some degree, the first victims of that nefarious development. The commercial Hindi film, a much ridiculed and maligned art form, has so far remained loyal to the wellsprings of Indian civilization, and it remains to be seen whether it will become a hostage to the nation-state, and thus become a hospitable home to the idea of the Other.

Filmography

Deewar (The Wall, 1975), with Amitabh Bachchan, Shashi Kapoor, Nirupa Roy, and Parveen Babi

Gardish (Days of Dust, 1993), with Jackie Shroff, Amrish Puri, Asrani, and Billa Jilani

Khalnayak (Villain, 1993), with Sanjay Dutt, Madhuri Dixit, Nirupa Roy, and Roshi Mahanta

Shakti (Strength, 1982), with Dilip Kumar, Amitabh Bachchan, Rakhee, Smita Patil, Amrish Puri, and Kulbushan Kharbanda

Yaadon Ki Baraat (Procession of Memories, 1973), with Dharmendra, Vijay Arora, Zeenat Aman, Ajit, and Tariq

Notes

1. One could easily add to this list of Indian directors who are believed to have adhered to some notion of 'acceptable' aesthetic standards a number of other names, such as Guru Dutt and Bimal Roy, but this history is necessarily outside the purview of this paper.

2. Today, commercial Hindi films are more likely to be divided into 'action films' and 'romantic films'; the two are not mutually exclusive categories, and almost all films of one category have elements of the other.

3. I use the word 'musical' advisedly, and in a rather colloquial way, for as a genre the American 'musical' has certain formal elements which are lacking in its Indian counterpart.

4. The tale of two brothers at odds with each other found its classic statement in *Deewar*, discussed elsewhere in this chapter. Ashis Nandy has discussed doubles, and implicitly 'family resemblances', in popular Hindi films. See his 'An Intelligent Critic's Guide to Indian Cinema', published in *Deep Focus* in 3 parts: vol. 1, no. 1 (December 1987), pp. 68-72; vol. 1, no. 2 (June 1988), pp. 53-60; and vol. 1, no. 3 (November 1988), pp. 58-61.

5. Two immensely popular films with this motif are *Bobby* (1973) and *Maine Pyar Kiya* (I Have Fallen in Love, 1989).

6. The obvious reference is to the classic study by Vladimir Propp, *Morphology of the Folktale* (2nd rev. ed., 1968; reprint ed., Austin, Texas: University of Texas Press, 1975). I do not, in invoking Propp, mean to convey my endorsement of the structuralist view, and indeed, in the following pages, I shall be taking exception to the most structuralist work in the anthropology of India, *Homo Hierarchicus* (see section 2).

7. It is quite probable that mental illnesses are vastly under-reported or otherwise unaccounted for in Indian society. Even allowing for that, it nonetheless seems quite probable that the incidence of mental illnesses in India is not as high as it is in the countries of the West. The breakdown of the family, the loss of community, the atomistic life of the individual, and the stresses of modern, urban living have all been mentioned as likely reasons for both the high incidence of mental illnesses, and the greater number of visits to psychiatrists, in countries such as the United States. It has also been argued that in India a stigma is attached to the visit to a psychiatrist. Cultural notions of what constitutes 'mental illness' are also bound to vary, to put the matter mildly, for what is really at stake is the ontological, epistemological, and personological notion of the 'self'. While I cannot join the debate on these issues here, there appears to me to be a particularly noteworthy aspect to the figure of the

doctor in the Hindi film to which no one has yet drawn attention. Despite the emergence of the medical profession, and the esteem in which the doctor is held by the lettered and the unlettered alike, every Indian remains his or her own doctor. For instance, though no study has been made of how many Indians practice homoeopathic medicine in their homes, often dispensing medicine to family members and friends, the number is undoubtedly a very large one. The doctor can be a friendly figure, an adjunct to the family home, and despite the fact that medical training today entails a great deal of specialization, the doctor in the Hindi film is seldom a remote figure, a picture of detached 'expertise'. Unlike in the West, where 'expertise' compels extraordinary respect, the Indian is almost never awed by 'expertise'. As one has one's milkman and family tailor, so one has one's neighbourhood doctor. But to the figure of the psychiatrist there must invariably be attached the notion of 'expertise', and that 'expertise' is at an extremity that renders the psychiatrist into an unattractive figure. The tension between the doctor and the psychiatrist is the dialectic between the 'soft' and the 'hard', the folk and the classical, which is mirrored through the narratives of the Hindi film itself.

8.   It is not insignificant, given the history of Sikh separatism, that the 'Hindustani *mukka*' is aimed at the terrorist seeking to destroy India, by a Sikh student. The Sikh, to prove his loyalty to the nation, must make amends and give lie to his supposed infidelity; moreover, by transforming the Other into the terrorist, where only a few years ago every Sikh was liable to be so named, the Other is not merely not confronted, but a false impression is sought to be created that the 'Punjab problem', as it used to be called, stands resolved.

9.   K. Chandrasekhar, 'The Amitabh Persona: An Interpretation', *Deep Focus* 1, no. 3 (November 1988), p. 57.

10.   M. C. Byrski, 'Bombay *Philum*—The Kaliyuga Avatara of Sanskrit Drama', *Pushpanjali* 4 (November 1980), pp. 111-18.

11.   Ibid., pp. 117-18.

12.   Ashis Nandy, 'Cultural Frames for Social Transformation: A Credo', *Alternatives* 12, no. 1 (January 1987), p. 118.

13.   For a detailed representation and critique of the Indological view, see Ronald Inden, *Imagining India* (Oxford: Basil Blackwell, 1990).

14.   The ethnographic record, by which I mean travelogues, official compilations of Indian castes and tribes, histories by scholar-administrator types, and the entire array of colonial record-keeping, tells the story of the Orientalist construction of India in massive and intricate detail. On the question of the effeminacy of the Hindu, the *locus classicus* is Robert Orme, 'On the Effeminacy of the Inhabitants of Indostan', in *Historical Fragments of the Mogul Empire, of the*

Morattoes, and of the English Concerns in Indostan from theYear MDCLIX (London: W. Wingrave, 1785; reprint ed., New Delhi: Associated Publishing House, 1974); likewise, on Oriental Despotism, see Alexander Dow, 'A Dissertation on the Origin and Nature of Despotism in Hindostan', in *The History of Hindostan*, 3 vols. (London: S. Beckert & P.A. de Hondt, 1770; reprint ed., Delhi: Today & Tomorrow's Printers & Publishers; 1973), vol. 3. Many of the tropes found in writings on India are common to writings on other colonized societies as well; on the 'lazy native', for example, a compelling analysis is provided by Syed Hussein Alatas, *The Myth of the Lazy Native* (London: Frank Cass, 1975). Though his material is drawn from Malaysia under British rule, it could just as easily have come from British India. For a more detailed discussion of what I have elsewhere characterized as the 'epistemological imperatives of the colonial state in British India', the reader is referred to my unpublished Ph.D. dissertation, *Committees of Inquiry and Discourses of 'Law and Order' in Twentieth-Century British India* (Chicago: University of Chicago, 1992), vol. 1, Chapter 1, as well as to Bernard C. Cohn, *Colonialism and Its Forms of Knowledge* (Princeton: Princeton University Press, 1996).

15. *Economist* (London), 27 February 1909, quoted in Bipan Chandra, *Communalism in Modern India* (Delhi: Vikas Publishing House, 1984), p.26.

16. Sir Henry Sumner Maine, *Village Communities in the East and West* (new ed., London: John Murray, 1890), p. 57.

17. Louis Dumont, in Mark Sainsbury, Louis Dumont, and Basia Gulati tr., *Homo Hierarchicus: The Caste System and Its Implications* (rev. English edition, Chicago and London: The University of Chicago Press, 1980), pp. 43-44, 66.

18. Dumont, 'World Renunciation in Indian Religions', Appendix B, ibid., p. 269. This appendix originally appeared in *Contributions to Indian Sociology* 4 (1960), pp. 33-62.

19. Thousands of instances of the comic element in the fight could be furnished, and the reader who has some familiarity with the Hindi film will instantly recognize this narrative element, which appears in the most recent productions as well. In *Krantikshetra*, a film released in the late summer of 1994, a terrorist takes over a private college. In the long, drawn-out fight that takes place at the very end, one episode involves two college boys who spread Fevicol on the floor, with the consequence that one of the goons who comes by at that moment finds his feet stuck to the ground, and thus is rendered into a laughable figure rather than the henchman of a dreaded terrorist that he is.

20. The most notable example of this is Balu in *Khalnayak*; the film is discussed in section 4 of this chapter.

21. The character of the father, Anand-babu, suggests that the Hindi film, in a

manner of speaking, does conceive of the possibility of the outsider, but only
in its minor characters. Anand-babu becomes a vagrant, leading his life in
trains, travelling aimlessly from one town to another, all this being suggested
through one or two brief episodes. But in at least two respects he is not the
outsider that he seems to be. His fate remains unknown to his family; but his
wife, in any case, lives on the assumption that he is very much alive: he has not
become an outsider to her. She understands that if he 'betrayed' the workers,
he did so only to save her life and that of their children, and no man can be said
to have done evil if the action is performed under compulsion. He may have
been disowned by the world, and even by one of his sons, but not by her. More
compelling still is another episode. In a scene towards nearly the end of the
film, Ravi, Vijay's brother who is now a policeman, is informed that a dead
body has been found on a train, and it is suggested that the body be disposed
of as 'unclaimed'. A search through the dead man's belongings reveals a
photograph, and it so transpires that he is none other than Anand-babu. As
Ravi says, 'Let not anyone say that this corpse is unclaimed. I will claim it.'
Even in death, Anand-babu cannot become an outsider.

22.   Chandrasekhar, 'The Amitabh Persona', pp. 54-55.
23.   Cf. Madhava Prasad, 'Escape from Childhood: The Development of Hero in
      Popular Cinema', *Deep Focus* 1, no. 1 (December 1987), pp. 29-32.
24.   I am taking the least complicated view of this matter, for the reappearance of
      the father-figure is not critical to my own argument. But I should note here
      that Iftikhar, who places Vijay in charge of his business fortunes, making him
      the virtual inheritor of his vast empire, is not the only father-figure, for in Ravi,
      the upholder of the social order, the custodian of law, and the protector of the
      family and its honour, the father is re-born. It is thus in two respects that the
      restoration of the family is rendered impossible: Iftikhar is eliminated, and
      Vijay and Ravi separate.
25.   See Sudhir Kakkar, *The Inner World: A Psychoanalytic Study of Childhood and Society
      in India* (Delhi: Oxford University Press, 1978). True, a view less sensitive to
      cultural particularities holds that everywhere sons are attracted to mothers,
      and daughters to fathers, but the centrality of the couple—exemplified most
      clearly in the husband-wife nexus—to Western social institutions can scarcely
      be questioned.
26.   Chandrasekhar, 'The Amitabh Persona', pp. 56-57.
27.   Vijay stops short of revealing this to his mother.
28.   '*Abhi pata chal jaiga ki tumhara baap tumse kitni mohabbat karta hai.*'
29.   The reference to Balu as Ravana may appear to render him into the 'Other',
      but the thrust of the entire film is to deny such a reading. Moreover, it is only

on an exceedingly partial and uninformed reading of the Ramayana that one can unambiguously construe Ravana as the villain, or as irredeemably wicked. As in many Indian tales of powerful kings who do evil, Ravana displays such extraordinary qualities—for example, *tapasya* and devotion to Sita—as to leave the Gods impressed; more significantly, there are many traditions of the Ramayana, and in some Ravana emerges as the hero. See Paula Richman, ed., *Many Ramayanas*: *The Diversity of a Narrative Tradition in South Asia* (Berkeley: University of California Press, 1991).

30. When confronted by a man who reveals that his mother is alive, Balu's response is, 'I make any old woman my mother. I'm an orphan.'

31. '*Saransh yah hai ki aaj ki Sita Ravana ke pas rahi aur Ram ko badnam kiya*'.

32. Ramchandra Gandhi, *Sita's Kitchen: A Testimony of Faith and Inquiry* (New Delhi: Penguin Books, 1992), pp. 21, 51; see also Vinay Lal, 'Advaita's Waterloo', review-article on *Sita's Kitchen*, in *Social Scientist* 21, nos. 5 and 6 (May-June 1993), pp. 82-89, pp. 87-88.

Once the story of Sita's banishment had become enshrined by patriarchs as the decisive interpretation, other readings of the story were rendered difficult. The late Professor A. K. Ramanujan, one of my teachers at the University of Chicago, once mentioned that in a certain version of the Ramayana, Sita is described as telling Ram, 'In all other versions of the story I am banished, so how can it be otherwise in this version?' Ananthamurthy has related a variant of this story: here Sita insists on accompanying Ram into the forest and adds the observation, 'In all other versions of the story I accompanied you, why should it be otherwise now.' [Personal communication, Delhi, December 1995.]

33. The 'good Muslim' is a difficult figure in the Hindi film, for his very goodness can be construed as a sign of Otherness, as a sign of the emptying out of his humanity. By way of analogy, one can think of the construction of woman as goddess, mother, and whore. But this will require an extended argument, which I cannot take up here.

34. 'It happens, everything goes, that's the world.' What is rather interesting is that Roshi is being shaved when this macabre scene of killing takes place. In the Hindi film, the boss who plays for high stakes, such as Roshi Mahanta, often appears at his worst while he is being shaved: one wonders whether the touch of flint upon flesh lends itself to some psychoanalytic interpretation. In the film *Gardish*, to which I have referred before, the local leader of the working classes (a figure comparable to Anand-babu in *Deewar*) is summoned into the presence of Billa Jilani, the fearsome *goonda* before whom the police tremble, and summarily given orders to desist from standing for office. These orders are

issued while Jilla is being shaved; and while Jilla will be shown in more frightening scenes, as when he burns alive this man, the scene where he is being shaved is chilling precisely because it is an omen of things to come, and the audience recognizes it as such. The iconic image of the *goonda* being shaved while he causes others to tremble (or worse) may owe something to the genre of the Western, although that should not preclude us from pursuing the barely concealed association between killing and cleansing.

II

POLITICS AND THE INDIAN STATE

Three

NOW ARE WE MEN, NOT EUNUCHS?
REFLECTIONS ON THE NUCLEAR EXPLOSION

As India marked the fiftieth anniversary of the assassination of Mohandas Gandhi, the Father of the Nation, in 1998, he was being finally liquidated. Though the 'great man of history' theory holds out little appeal to sophisticated historians, we know that certain women and men require to be assassinated more than once or even twice. Ironically, Gandhi's very own friend, the great poet and writer Rabindranath Tagore, may have contributed towards Gandhi's eventual obliteration when he fatally transformed him from Mohandas into the Mahatma.[1] Students of history might recall also that Gandhi had emerged from his last fast, a final attempt by him to move India away from the degraded politics of the modern nation-state system and to pave the way for better relations between India and Pakistan, barely a few days before Nathuram Godse decided to dispense with his frail body, all ninety-five pounds of him.[2] A failed assassination attempt, some ten days before the fateful evening of 31 January 1948, left the nation-state scrambling to devise ways to offer Gandhi the 'security' for which he had, as described in the following chapter, little use. In those final days of his life, some of Gandhi's detractors relentlessly pounded away at him, holding him responsible for India's Partition, and they even taunted him with the word 'hijra'. Gandhi had not been man enough, so it was alleged by Godse at his trial, to protect the motherland from the rapacious ambitions and murderous instincts of the Muslim 'invader'; such a feminine figure who resorted to spinning, found solace in the inner voice, and employed the weapons of the weak (such as fasting), was scarcely equipped to provide guidance to India's beleaguered leaders.[3] India had been vivisected, and the Hindus no more wanted a divided nation than they wanted a castrated man. The Muslim was circumcised, 'cut up' as militant Hindus jeer;[4] so was Gandhi a castrated man, emaciated and emasculated.

First we kill in the flesh, then we must kill in the spirit: Gandhi had yet to be exorcized. In death, as in life, the old man refused to disappear into the dark of the night, and Gandhi would loom large in India's imagination, even as many people thought that his name existed only to be invoked at rituals and ceremonies, as a specimen of a pre-eminent Indian spirituality and moral probity. In 1974, less than three years after concluding a victorious war with Pakistan, India exploded what was called a 'peaceful nuclear device', as though even its nuclear explosions had to carry some of the burden of Gandhi's non-violence.[5] How else can one think of these three words existing in apposition rather than opposition to each other? For the subsequent twenty-four years, India exercised what was taken to be virtuous restraint, but then in May 1998 it broke the self-imposed moratorium with a series of five nuclear tests; two weeks later, Pakistan was to follow suit. Writing to Clinton and other political leaders, Prime Minister Atal Bihari Vajpayee pointed to the 'deteriorating security environment' in South Asia, and the purportedly aggressive designs of India's two principal neighbours, China and Pakistan: the geopolitical situation of India, Vajpayee suggested, furnished it with a sufficient warrant for seeking to acquire nuclear deterrence.[6] It is no accident that Vajpayee's Bharatiya Janata Party, whose predecessor was the Jana Sangh, numbers among its members some who have been active in political associations that were implicated in the assassination of Gandhi fifty years ago and which have ever been the ardent champions of Hindu ascendancy. What Godse could only gesture at, and what the Hindu Mahasabha and Rashtriya Swayam Sevak Sangh have willed for a long time, has finally been achieved: Vajpayee has removed the spectre of Gandhi which has been haunting India's modernizing elites. Even the land of the Buddha and Gandhi, as

India's modernizing hawks and political elites have long desired, must show its muscle, its willingness to move beyond the spiritual visions and agrarian bent of its greatest men and women, and demonstrate its capacity to survive and compete in the nuclear age. The Indian nation-state will no longer live in consummate fear of Gandhi's critiques of modernity, big science, instrumental rationality, development, war, and masculinity.

Consequently, while economists, foreign policy experts, and defence specialists will continue to debate the reasons that led India to assume nuclear testing at this particular juncture, the political and electoral calculations of the Bharatiya Janata Party, the cost to India and Pakistan of economic sanctions, the possible escalation of an arms race, the palpable failures of American foreign policy and intelligence gathering, the future of Indian relations with China, the wider geopolitical consequences of South Asia's nuclearization, and the probable effect of the nuclear explosions in triggering the conflict between India and Pakistan over Kargil the following summer, there are other, more interesting and poignant, considerations to which we should be attentive. No doubt the question, 'What Is To Be Done?', acquires an urgency which we ought not to resist, but it is imperative that we not allow our vision of what the future can promise to be shaped by those very policy planners, technoexperts, and masters of realpolitik who must be held accountable for turning South Asia nuclear. Too often have we turned over our futures to those very men from whom it needs to be protected, and too often have we made the state, which continues to be the most grotesque violator not only of human rights but also of India's cultural legacy, the custodian of our rights.

To reclaim our future, then, we should seek to understand the real significance of India's turn towards nuclearization. During the height of the Cold War, Nehru attempted to place India in a 'third camp', indeed at the helm of the leadership of the non-aligned movement. This was even, in some measure, a continuation of Gandhi's policy of repudiating realpolitik and the grossly functionalist politics of Cold War deterrence, and it was certainly an acknowledgment that neither the United States nor the Soviet Union, nor the political and economic systems of which they were the supreme representatives, had a monopoly on truth. As Nehru appeared to be indicating, there were yet other ways of imagining the world. It is in the forums of the United Nations, an organization itself purportedly founded to free humankind of the scourge of war and lead to increased cooperation and amity among nations, that India most made visible its presence, and likewise its disproportionately large contributions to the various United Nations-sponsored peacekeeping operations, to which it continues to commit more men than do the 'great powers', were an endeavour to persist with Gandhi's legacy of what might be termed militant non-violence. However, in the hostile environment of the Cold War, where the United States in particular adopted the view that any country purporting to advocate neutrality was clearly aligning itself with the enemies of 'freedom' and 'democracy', the non-aligned movement would over time become increasingly irrelevant, until the fall of the Soviet Union rendered it altogether obsolete. The United Nations, which had been treated with characteristic contempt by the United States through much of the Cold War, was now seen as a useful vehicle for advancing American interests, and the number of Security Council-mandated sanctions against regimes was to show an alarming increase in the early 1990s. Indeed, as more than one scholar has argued, there is no effective protection against human rights abuses perpetrated by the Security Council under American domination.[7] With the turn towards globalization, and the continuing American quest for markets, China took on an importance that, ever since its ascendancy to nuclear power status three decades ago, the other powers had always been willing to recognize. Once again, India seemed to be left out in the cold, and commentators have consequently interpreted the nuclear tests as India's cry for attention. Clinton appeared to have echoed this view when he noted that India, perhaps lacking in self-esteem, thought itself 'underappreciated' as a 'world power'.[8] The fireballs which reach out towards the sun are symbolic of India's efforts to find a place for itself under the sun.

There is perhaps, yet, a more complex history to India's nuclear tests, a history that extends back, in a manner of speaking, to the early days of India under colonial rule. The British were apt to describe Indians, I have elsewhere suggested in this book, as an 'effeminate' people, leading lives of indolence and womanly softness.[9] That India had been under the rule of 'foreigners' for centuries was for the British proof enough that, abandoning the work of fighting to men better endowed with military prowess and prepared to wield the sword, Indians were content to plough the land and lead the lives of agriculturists. The rebellion of 1857-58 was attributed not to a resurgence of military pride among Indians, but to ill-advised colonial policies calculated to wound the religious sentiments of Indians and increase racial hostility; and after its brutal suppression, the entire country was divided between 'martial' and 'non-martial' races.[10] Among the 'martial races' were the Rajputs, Pathans, various hill tribes, and what the British termed 'Muhammadans'; prominent among the non-martial races were the majority of the vast number of Hindus living in Bengal and the Gangetic plains. The contempt for the supposed effeminacy of Hindus continued to run deep among British officials, and in 1879 the Viceroy could state with barely concealed disgust, to quote once again a passage that never ceases to amaze, that 'the Baboodom of Lower Bengal, though disloyal is fortunately cowardly and its only revolver is its ink bottle; which though dirty, is not dangerous.'[11] Indian nationalists may have taken this as a perverse, backhanded compliment: certainly they would produce much seditious literature, and the large collection of Indian pamphlets and political tracts in the collection of the British Library is one testament to the power of the 'ink bottle' in the hands of fervently anti-colonial polemicists.[12] One other, unfortunately not less attractive, response among Indian nationalists was to embrace a certain kind of hyper-masculinity, which would enable Indians to be construed as a people just as 'manly' as the British. As numerous social and cultural historians have documented, the masculinization of Indian nationalism took on many manifestations: the cult of exercise and body-building was encouraged, martial figures from India's past were evoked, the rewriting of Indian history from the point of view of highlighting the resistance offered to invaders was attempted, and armed revolutionary activity gained many adherents.

Hindus have, nonetheless, never been able to live down the taunt of 'effeminacy', and those who know something of the cultural nuances of South Asian history are aware that many Indians imagine Pakistani Muslims as a meat-eating, virile, robust, and militaristic people. The Pakistanis themselves have largely adopted the colonial view of Indians: during the Kargil conflict, Indian newspapers drew attention to a recently completed study of the 'Indian personality', conducted by a senior Pakistani military officer at the Faculty of Research and Doctrinal Studies in the Command and Staff College, Quetta, which stresses that Indians are patient to the

point of absurdity, and unlikely 'to defend with the weapon' because of
their propensity towards 'intellectualism' and abstraction.[13] They are, in a
word, a decidedly 'non-martial' people, and can most likely be trod on
without the fear of repercussions or reprisals: this may doubtless have
been a consideration when the Line of Control was violated in 1999 and
peaks on the Indian side of the border were occupied by Pakistani troops
or by Mujahideen acting with the encouragement of Pakistan. All this
weighs heavily upon the minds of many Indians who are anxiety-ridden
that the Hindu should not appear too weak, and who are not averse to
engaging in their brand of representational politics. Where, for example,
in the traditional iconography of Rama he appeared as a smiling,
compassionate, and serene god, possessed even of a feminine softness and
androgynous appeal, in more recent years, under the inspiration of the
advocates of the Ramjanmabhoomi movement, he has been transformed
into an angry, militant, and punishing god, whose bow and arrow no longer
adorn him but carry the triumphant promise of annihilating defeat.[14] It is a
telling fact that the first comment of Balasaheb K. Thackeray, the chauvinist
leader of the militantly Hindu Shiv Sena party who is an open admirer of
Hitler, upon hearing of India's nuclear tests was, 'We have proven that we
are not eunuchs.'[15]

By signalling its departure from the body of world opinion, India has
sought to arrive on the world stage, though it may find that the place where
it seeks to arrive is one from which others seek to leave. No doubt the
present world order tolerates and encourages vast inequities in power, and
the spectacle of having the only world power that has ever deployed nuclear
weapons, and that too twice, moralizing to the rest of the world on the
virtues of non-proliferation is too nauseating for many other countries to
contemplate with equanimity. The emulation of those who have degraded
themselves, worshipping at the altar of naked power, can however never
be anything more than a Barmecidean feast, an empty thrill and a false
hope. The recent nuclear tests may represent the shallow triumph of India
as a nation-state, but they signify the saddening defeat of India as a civilization,
an irony made all the more bitter by the posturing in which Vajpayee's
Bharatiya Janata Party engages as the vanguard of 'Hindu civilization'. Only
a people who have abandoned their civilization, and their civility, for the
imagined munificence of 'great power' status would have had the effrontery

to test nuclear bombs on the auspicious occasion of Buddha Purnima. If in 1974 Mrs Gandhi was informed by her scientists and generals, after the apparently unsuccessful nuclear test at Pokhran, that the 'Lord Buddha is smiling', then the Buddha must now be roaring with laughter. This macabre display of enlightened hyper-masculinity is only as grotesque as the pretensions of a nation-state that, while it has been grossly negligent in feeding, clothing, and educating its people, aspires to be taken seriously as a great power. With what face can the present Indian government dare at all to evoke, even on purely ceremonial occasions, the name of Gandhi, who late in his life had this 'talisman' to offer: 'Whenever you are in doubt or when the self becomes too much with you, apply the following test: "Recall the face of the poorest and the weakest man whom you may have seen and ask yourself if the step you contemplate is going to be of any use to him. Will he gain anything by it? Will it restore him to a control over his own life and destiny? In other words, will it lead to Swaraj for the hungry and spiritually starving millions?" Then you will find your doubts and your self melting away.'[16]

It is not unnatural, given the modern nation-state system and the xenophobia that it promotes, that India should seek to be a great player in the world. Not every country will have this ambition, but India will be unable to avoid this temptation. Its detractors and admirers alike are cognizant of India's densely layered pasts, and though reverence for the past leads to no tangible good in the modern marketplace, its population of nearly a billion elevates it into the rank of nations that are stamped on our consciousness. There is much talk of India's emergence as an economic power, its stature as a giant exporter of software, and its reportedly 'vast reservoir of technical and scientific manpower'; and some people have begun to believe that even its numerous beauty queens have earned India the respectability that it craved. Who could ask for more than silicon breasts to complement silicon brains? As a nation-state, however, India does not seem poised to be much of a great player in the next few decades, not even with nuclear weapons, and the nuclearization of South Asia erodes the few advantages, such as its skilled scientific and computer personnel, of which India is presently possessed. Indeed, by having conducted its own nuclear tests, Pakistan has already considerably undermined the reputation of India's much-feted scientific establishment. But if it is the one resounding cruelty of our times that no nation-state which refuses to partake in realpolitik and the brutal zero-sum politics of our times can receive much of a hearing, then how might India be a great player? If Indians were not so consumed by the anxieties generated by colonial and neo-colonial modernity, and if they had the capacity to listen to the deep, still voices of their saints, savants, and littérateurs, they would surely understand that as a civilization, India has played, and will continue to play, an incalculable part in the continuing evolution of the human sensibility and spirit. For those less inspired by the vision of an Indian civilization, they have only to think of the world-wide proliferation of Indian art, music, and literature.

While everyone else speaks of the 'arms race' into which India and Pakistan have now entered, we may gain a deeper insight into the problem unfolding before us by thinking of it as a game. If there are, as James Carse so elegantly argued, finite and infinite games,[17] then the nuclearization of the Indian sub-continent represents a finite game which is played only for the purpose of winning. It is a different matter that, in this game, neither Pakistan nor India will be winners, both will be only losers; but this is not to say that, viewed against the backdrop of a larger canvas, there will be no winners, since in such situations the modern nation-state system, the armaments industry, the military and political elites, and the proponents of big science are always triumphant. There is still the other game, the infinite game, the purpose of which is to keep playing, and so continue too the conversation which can only remain inconclusive and in which we must always engage to ensure a communicative universe. This is a game in which the rules are not set, and where ambiguity is not only tolerated but prized. Advocates of Indian nuclearization have argued that, in exploding the nuclear devices, India removed the ambiguity in which its nuclear programme has been shrouded; moreover, by compelling Pakistan to demonstrate its prowess, it unmasked the naked reality of Pakistan's own nuclear programme. This is the characteristic aspect of finite games, and of the particularly modern sensibility of which they are supremely emblematic: ambiguity, uncertainty, and liminality are equally feared, and it is demanded of humans that they unequivocally declare whether they wish to be construed as Hindu or Muslim, secular or religious, modern or traditional.

Dissent in our times has become a difficult proposition, since the only forms in which we are allowed to express dissent are the ones which have been authenticated by those who set the rules of finite games, as rational, reasonable, legitimate, and conforming to the norms of what is construed as democratic. To do otherwise is to open oneself to the charge of being a lunatic, dictator, or religious fanatic, presiding over what the American leaders and commentators describe as 'rogue' nations. It would most emphatically be a mistake, however, to describe India as a non-player, since in emulating the power politics of the modern nation-state system, India has shown its willingness to be a player, albeit no longer (as it imagines) an insignificant one. Now that the ambiguity of South Asia's nuclear programmes has been dispelled, it remains to be seen whether anything noble can be salvaged from so ignominious a political decision. In true Gandhian fashion, one must allow the hermeneutic and moral possibilities to flower. True bravery and courage surely consist, not in an empty renunciation, but in forsaking the military force that one has at one's command. Thus might what Gandhi called 'non-violence of the weak', which is no non-violence at all, be transformed into 'non-violence of the strong', and from India's descent into nuclear madness might some good emerge.

Notes

1. It is Tagore who conferred the title of 'Mahatma', meaning 'great soul', upon Gandhi. The immensely engaging debate between Tagore and Gandhi can be followed in Jag Pravesh Chander, ed., *Tagore and Gandhi Argue* (Lahore: Indian Printing Works, 1945), and more recently in Sabyasachi Bhattacharya, ed., *The Mahatma and the Poet: Letters and Debates Between Gandhi and Tagore 1915-1941* (Delhi: National Book Trust, 1997). As Ananda K. Coomaraswamy explains, a Mahatma is one who is liberated in—not only from—this life; a Mahatma is one who is emancipated from himself, who is of developed stature, character, and prescience. See his essay 'Mahatma', in S. Radhakrishnan ed., *Mahatma Gandhi: Essays and Reflections on His Life and Work* (2nd enlarged ed., London: George Allen & Unwin, 1949), pp. 63-67.

2. For a more elaborate interpretation of the events preceding the assassination, and particularly Gandhi's recourse to fasting, see Vinay Lal, 'Gandhi's Last Fast', *Gandhi Marg* 11, no. 2 (July-September 1989), pp. 171-91.

3.   This was the substance of some of the allegations against Gandhi by his assassin, Nathuram Godse, who also charged Gandhi as guilty of having appeased the Muslims. See Godse, *May It Please Your Honour*; see also Ashis Nandy, 'Final Encounter: The Politics of the Assassination of Gandhi', in *At the Edge of Psychology: Essays in Politics and Culture* (Delhi: Oxford University Press, 1980), pp. 70-98.

4.   The speeches of Uma Bharati, Sadhvi Rithambara, and other militant leaders of Hindutva politics are liberally sprinkled with the observation that Muslims are circumcised. During communal riots, when the identity of a man cannot be ascertained with certainty, he may be asked to strip down: circumcision then becomes the passport to life or death. See, for instance, Sudhir Kakkar, *The Colours of Violence* (New Delhi: Viking, 1995), p. 161.

5.   For a pithy but enlightening discussion of India's 'peaceful nuclear explosion', see Itty Abraham, *The Making of the Indian Atomic Bomb: Science, Secrecy and the Postcolonial State* (London: Zed Books, 1998), pp. 137-47.

6.   The text of this letter appears as 'Indian's Letter to Clinton on the Nuclear Testing', *New York Times* (13 May 1998), p. A12.

7.   Hans Kochler, *The United Nations Sanctions Policy and International Law* (Penang, Malaysia: Just World Trust, 1995). I have advanced this argument in 'Sanctions and the Politics of Dominance, Multilateralism, and Legalism in the International Arena', *Social Scientist* 25, nos. 5-6 (May-June 1997), pp. 54-67.

8.   Steven Lee Myers, 'Clinton To Impose Penalties on India Over Atomic Tests', *New York Times* (13 May 1998), p. A1.

9.   The classic text, as already mentioned in the previous chapter, is that of Robert Orme, 'On the Effeminacy of the Inhabitants of Indostan', in *Historical Fragments of the Mogul Empire*; for a more recent study, see Mrinalini Sinha, *Colonial Masculinity: The 'Manly Englishman' and the 'Effeminate Bengali' in the Late Nineteenth Century* (Manchester: Manchester University Press, 1995).

10. Major G. F. MacMunn, *The Martial Races of India* (London: Sampson Row, Marston & Co., 1921).

11. Cited by Anil Seal, *The Emergence of Indian Nationalism*, pp. 140-41.

12. Graham Shaw and Mary Lloyd, eds., *Publications proscribed by the Government of India: A catalogue of the collections in the . . . British Library Reference Division* (London: The British Library, 1985). 1607 items are listed; many more than that were deemed to be seditious, contemptuous of British authority, or unacceptably patriotic.

13. Bimal Bhatia, 'The Enemy View of India', *The Hindustan Times* (17 June 1999).

14. Anuradha Kapur, 'Deity to Crusader: The Changing Iconography of Ram', in Gyanendra Pandey, ed., *Hindus and Others: The Question of Identity in India Today*

(Delhi: Viking, 1993), pp. 74-109.

15. Myers, 'Clinton To Impose Penalties on India Over Atomic Tests', p. A1, A12.

16. Raghavan Iyer, ed., *The Moral and Political Writings of Mahatma Gandhi*, Volume III: *Non-Violent Resistance and Social Transformation* (Oxford: Clarendon Press, 1987), p. 609.

17. James Carse, *Finite and Infinite Games: A Vision of Life as Play and Possibility* (New York: Ballantine Books, 1986).

Four

BLACK CAT COMMANDOS, GUNMEN, AND OTHER TERRORS:
THE INSECURITY OF INDIAN SECURITY

I

SECURITY FROM TERROR OR THE TERROR OF SECURITY?

In an article appearing in the New Delhi-based *Pioneer* in connection with India's Independence Day celebrations in 1993, it was noted that intelligence sources had unearthed the possibility of a 'missile attack' upon the then Prime Minister, Narasimha Rao, as he would speak to the nation from the precincts of Delhi's Red Fort to celebrate the achievement of Indian independence. The reporter, entitling his piece 'Unprecedented security for Aug 15', noted that the possibility of such an attack would necessitate the deployment of police forces not merely on the grounds of the Red Fort, but in various 'suspect spots', such as the Indira Gandhi Indoor Stadium, from where missiles could be launched. He had been informed that 'an unprecedented number of binoculars, 75 in number, will be provided to the staff on duty. These superior quality binoculars have been especially purchased by the Delhi Police to keep a watch of every human movement at the Independence Day show.'[1]

After the 'special' purchases and the 'unprecedented' security, one would have thought that something more than mere 'binoculars' were being furnished for the safety of the head of government. Indeed, the security arrangements provided for a great deal else, including 'mobile barricades' to separate Rao from the masses, and a 'special pink booklet' containing photographs and brief sketches of all 'known' terrorists with secessionist designs. (Perhaps only in India would have so 'feminine' a colour as pink been used in the makings of so masculinist an enterprise as employing specially trained commandos for the security of the head of the nation-state. The birthing of 'unprecedented' security measures seems to have been a curiously androgynous enterprise.[2]) 'The whole exercise', an official was said to have stated, 'has been scientifically and judiciously planned.'

Each year the security arrangements appear to have been even more elaborate, howsoever 'unprecedented' in previous years. Newspapers in 1994 spoke about 'top-grade protective measures' to make 'security foolproof' and the construction of a 'wide security net' to 'ensure that no untoward incident took place'.[3] One reporter described the 'impeccable security arrangements' as constituted of three tiers, with a large number of 'commandos' being posted in and around the Red Fort, on roof-tops adjoining the houses around the Red Fort, and along the entire route from the residence of the Prime Minister to the Red Fort. Where before police officers had been armed with binoculars to aid the human eye, now the 'sharp-shooters with latest automatic weapons were also posted at specially constructed platforms to keep a watch on miscreants.' All invitees were searched before they were allowed to enter the premises of the Fort, and cars likewise were examined to the point of having their under-carriages inspected with the aid of mirrors.[4]

If these concerns for the security of the Prime Minister and other VIPs appear to be comically excessive, we need only remember that two former Prime Ministers of India were assassinated in recent years, this also being the fate of the 'Father of the Nation'. A secessionist movement, which undoubtedly has received more than mere encouragement from Pakistan, is flourishing in Kashmir,[5] and has only subsided in the Punjab after the state applied brute force to eliminate 'terrorist' elements. Consequently, the security arrangements undertaken for very senior political leaders would appear to be not merely justifiable, but wholly necessary. The visible increase in political violence, the use of assassinations to create terror, and bomb outrages and scares in the capital city for extended periods of time, especially in the period from the mid-1980s to the mid-1990s, suggest that even the most absurd scenarios of the security threat to the Prime Minister may not be that farfetched. Indeed, to deny the Prime Minister and other persons of public pre-eminence the assurance of adequate safety, at however astronomical a cost to the nation, might appear to be not merely churlish, but a denial of the realities of the modern nation-state system, and particularly of the political realities which hold sway over the Indian nation today. Some might even argue that security arrangements devised for the Indian Prime Minister are comparatively mild, an impression that appeared to be bolstered by the visit of President William Clinton to India in March 2000. Clinton not only arrived in India, as one might expect, with a massive security entourage, but the (American) National Security Service, in an affront to the Indian security apparatus that the nation meekly overlooked, insisted that it would brook no intervention from the Indians.

However ungracious and unpatriotic it may be to question the supposed verities of Indian political life, and to suppose that the security and well-being of an entire people and its civilization have been seriously compromised by the fetish of security for a select few, it is incumbent upon us to question the realpolitik view by means of which India is sought to be governed today. Since it is the security of the 'nation' itself, through the persons of the Prime Minister, and other VIPs, that is at stake, we will take a long look at the security arrangements devised for Indian leaders since the time that India achieved independence. This trajectory takes us, by way of some detours, from the assassination of Gandhi less than six months after India became free to the massive arrangements devised in very recent years for the security of the Prime Minister and other VIPs, to the extraordinary cult of security which forms so ubiquitous a part of Indian political life today. As this 'history' suggests, an immense distance now demarcates the Indian political leader from his subjects; the body of the political leader has acquired immense significance, while the body politic itself suffers. The security paranoia that engulfs the Indian political leadership at all levels is easily seen as infected by the noxious nexus between criminality and politics. But that is, as I would argue, scarcely what is most objectionable and unacceptable about the cult of security. VIP security in India has become emblematic of despotic lifestyles; it betokens an incapacity to understand the nature of power in the modern world, and it fails to adhere to any notion of limits.

As I will further endeavour to demonstrate, solutions that seek to liberate us from certain supposed oppressions—the oppression of terrorism, the oppression of the 'foreign hand', 'miscreants', and 'anti-social' elements—may well unleash upon us a more terrible form of oppression. In the name of the security of the Prime Minister especially, the state infiltrates hitherto private spaces and arrogates to itself unprecedented powers, the exercise of which has the effect of eroding the rights of the citizen. The subjects vanish; there is only *the* subject, the newer incarnation of the Oriental despot. Thus, for example, on 2 December 1995, the crash of an Indian Airlines airplane carrying 108 people on board became a near reality: confused by a command from the control tower that the pilot conclude his landing movements within ten minutes, on account of the sudden intrusion of the jet of the Prime Minister in the near vicinity, the pilot lost his nerve and overshot the runaway by a large margin, only miraculously averting a crash.[6] Much more recently, a victim of the fanaticism of the security forces has written about how he was pounced upon by a large number of Indian policemen and brutally beaten with lathis, all because he did not recognize that the motorcade of the Prime Minister had not passed by at a Delhi traffic intersection before he himself ventured into the crossing.[7]

As in every other state governed by a constitution, a cloak of legality veils the actions of the Indian state, and extraordinary legislation becomes the normal law of the land, as the passage of the Special Protection Group Act—authorizing the constitution of a special force for the proximate protection of the Prime Minister and his immediate family—suggests. If we are to have state security, the more general rubric under which falls the security of leaders, self-styled or otherwise, what of people's security? To what extent can the cult of security claim a compatibility with both the norms of democracy and a civilizational ethos predicated on certain forms of cultural accommodation?

Finally, the entire political climate of India's modernizing elites is characterized by a selective emulation of the West, or more precisely by the endeavour to transform India from a 'soft' state to a 'hard' state. The cult of security is perhaps most indicative of this transformation. If the

Orientalist out-Hindus the Hindu, the political leadership of India and the modernizing elites are similarly enthused with the idea of showing that they can devise security arrangements more elaborate than any devised for the protection of the leadership of 'advanced' industrialized nations. It matters little that the security arrangements are so easily punctured so as to make a mockery of the Special Protection Group, or that attempts to picture India as a 'hard' state, endangered by bloodthirsty and ruthless terrorists aided and abetted by elements sworn to India's destruction, ultimately appear as parodic. To place protective, supposedly impenetrable, circles around political leaders is nothing short of placing a *cordon sanitaire* around Indian civilization, and thus to sacrifice Indian civilization to the Indian nation. If the vision of India's technocrats, defence experts, and modernizing elites were to triumph, India would become the exemplar of the professionally-managed state, exorcising—as did the nations of the West—all those elements which have conspired to render it 'soft'.

II

THE SECURITY OF MAHATMA GANDHI: THE BOMB VERSUS THE DARSHAN

On the evening of 20 January 1948, while Gandhi was leading a prayer meeting in the compound of Birla House, his occasional residence in Delhi during his visits to the capital over the past few years, a bomb exploded some twenty-five yards from where he was sitting. Gandhi escaped unscathed; no one else was injured. Upon interrogation, a young refugee from the West Punjab by the name of Madanlal Pahwa,[8] in whose possession a bomb was found, was revealed as bearing a grudge against the Mahatma. Like many other uprooted Hindus from the Punjab, Madanlal held the Mahatma responsible for the Partition of India. Though his statement to the police remains a matter of controversy, it is possible that Madanlal revealed the existence of a conspiracy among a number of young men, many of them associated with either the Hindu Mahasabha or with other associations advocating Hindu hegemony, to murder Gandhi.[9] Only a few days ago Gandhi had terminated what was to be his last fast, as a partial consequence of which the Government of India finally paid the sum of fifty-five crores of rupees to Pakistan, which it had held up in view of the belligerent action taken by Pakistan in Kashmir.[10]

No doubt the Mahatma's fast had antagonized Madanlal and his friends whose understanding of Hinduism was much too narrow to permit the more magnanimous interpretations that Gandhi was to provide, and the poorly conceived attempt on Gandhi's life on 20 January must be seen against that backdrop. Even before Gandhi's commencement of his fast, some apprehension existed of possible attempts on his life, and after Gandhi's return to Delhi from Calcutta in September 1947, Sardar Patel, Gandhi's close confidant and the Deputy Prime Minister to whom had also been entrusted the portfolio of the Home Ministry, had arranged to place a security guard of one Head Constable and four Foot Constables for Gandhi's protection at Birla House. 'Their main duty', noted Justice Kapur in his report on the assassination, was to prevent the 'mobs' from becoming a source of annoyance to Gandhi, and to 'deal with people who objected to the reciting of the Quran at Gandhiji's prayer meetings.'[11] The 'refugees were in an angry mood', Justice Kapur was told by a number of witnesses,[12] but the apprehension of danger to the Mahatma's life was perhaps fuelled less by that than by the fact that the Mahatma could easily be trampled upon by the hundreds of thousands who came to receive his darshan.[13] If at all a security guard was detailed 'to deal with people who objected' to Gandhi's recitation of the Quran at his prayer meetings, it certainly was not at Gandhi's instigation, for everything in Gandhi's teachings stood in opposition to even the contemplated use of force to compel compliance or to procure agreement with his views. Gandhi's method at prayer meetings was to forsake the reading of the Quran (or other scripture) to which objection had been found, to substitute in its place a discourse on tolerance and intolerance, and to wait until such time as the audience itself, feeling contrite, asked for the previously objectionable material to be read.[14]

After the bomb explosion on 20 January, security at Birla House was tightened. A small force was assigned for Gandhi's protection; additionally, one sub-inspector, four head constables, and two foot constables were posted in plain clothes and armed with revolvers. It was suggested to Gandhi that the police be allowed to exercise a strict supervision over the visitors at his prayer meetings, and be authorized to conduct searches of 'suspicious looking persons', but he most resolutely refused to allow the police these powers, although at least one witness thought Gandhi 'had no objection to the tightening of security measures in other respects.'[15] Manu, one of Gandhi's grandnieces, stated before Justice Kapur that when Gandhi was apprised of the danger to his life, 'he just laughed' and said that he would live as long as God wished him to live; moreover, his reaction to the proposed search of visitors 'was that he would have rather died than allowed it.'[16] In her testimony, Sushila Nayar, Gandhi's medical adviser and one of his closest confidantes, averred that Gandhi was unhappy, for reasons unknown to her, about the use of plainclothes policemen.[17] It is quite clear that Gandhi would have thought of the use of plainclothes policemen as a form of deception. In the Gandhian view, truth has no reason to hide itself, to feel mean and act cheap, and the triumph of truth is not to be achieved through dissimulation. The only form of security is to open oneself to every charge and tribulation, even to invite an attack upon oneself, for persuasion has not achieved its ends unless one's opponents have been able to act from a position of unmitigated strength.

If at the epistemological level Gandhi could not countenance the introduction of security measures designed to render him safe from the anger or fury of those who could not agree with him, on the ontological plane he could not brook the existence of measures that struck him as an effrontery to his idea of the real, and as a denial of his rootedness in God. Gandhi's followers recalled before Justice Kapur that, in his characteristic manner, Gandhi had said that 'his life was in the hands of God and if he had to die nothing would save him and that as long as God wills that he should serve the people, he will; and when God wills otherwise He will take him away.'[18] Manu agreed that Patel had sought Gandhi's permission to search people arriving at the prayer meeting, 'but the Mahatma refused saying that it would mean that he had no faith in God.'[19] Justice Kapur was inclined to believe that the Mahatma's faith in God prevented him from taking precautions for his own safety. The entire atmosphere of Birla House during Gandhi's visits, Justice Kapur was to maintain, rebelled against the provision of security measures equal to the preservation of a life as precious as that of Gandhi. The ashramites, trained by Gandhi himself, and inclined in any case to the belief that nothing could harm Gandhi, took the threats posed to him lightly. Wholly 'engrossed in their respective chores', and bound by a 'tight' schedule, 'they had no time to think about impending danger and were wholly heedless towards any danger to the Mahatma's life.'[20]

If Gandhi's own associates were unaware, and even unmindful, of the danger to his life, it scarcely helped that, on the fateful evening of 30 January 1948, a number of other circumstances had conspired to rob the Mahatma of that minimal safety to which he had agreed. The Superintendent of Police, New Delhi, had been given instructions to be present at Gandhi's prayer meetings; however, on 30 January, entrusted with another important task, he could not be present at Birla House. Justice Kapur found it 'difficult to imagine anything more important than the protection of the Mahatma's life, but evidently the Delhi Police thought differently.'[21] After the 'bomb' explosion of 20 January, Gandhi's associates had been led to believe that the safety of their leader was now securely in the hands of the police, and that 'nothing untoward would be allowed to happen'; as a consequence, their vigilance relaxed, and they did not henceforth enclose him on all sides as they were wont to do previously. Justice Kapur himself thought that 'four or five people flanking the Mahatma on all sides might have been a sufficient protection at prayer meetings.' On the evening of the 30th, coincidentally, Gandhi was late by a few minutes in arriving at his prayer meetings, a matter of considerable distress for someone as punctual as him, and was proceeding at more than his usual pace; 'it was not considered', Justice Kapur was told, 'to have people in front [of Gandhi] as well as at the back.'[22] It was at about thirteen minutes past five o'clock in the evening that Nathuram Godse elbowed his way through the crowd, 'joined his palms [before Gandhi] as if in a reverent obeisance', pushed aside Manu who was remonstrating with him, and fired three shots at point-blank range at the Mahatma.

What, then, was Justice Kapur inclined to think about the adequacy or otherwise of the security measures undertaken to preserve the life of the 'Father of the Nation'? He acknowledged that the police were confronted with no easy task, considering that Gandhi was himself quite oblivious of his own safety, and that Gandhi's unwillingness to allow the police to search persons entering Birla House 'put limitations on the efficacy and efficiency of the precautionary measures' taken by them. D. W. Mehra, the DIG of Police, had himself reached the conclusion that 'it was impossible for anyone to have stopped the tragedy considering Mahatmaji's aversion to placing any restraint on people coming to his prayer meetings.'[23]

Justice Kapur was nonetheless not prepared to concede that Gandhi's assassination was unavoidable. The 'bomb' explosion of the 20th had provided incontrovertible proof of the danger to Gandhi's life; interrogation of Madanlal had pointed to the presence of a conspiracy to murder Gandhi; and, in Delhi, the temper of feeling against Gandhi was such that during his fast, taunts like '*Marta hai to marne do*' ('If he wants to die, let him die'), were openly thrown at him. Under the circumstances, Justice Kapur thought that 'more attention should have been devoted to security and the crowds should have been kept at a little distance from the Mahatma.'[24] If Gandhi was not prepared to give his consent to having persons entering Birla House searched, could nothing else have been done? Justice Kapur noted that the police failed even to act on the intelligence they had gathered.[25] An inner and outer ring of policemen, dressed like Congress volunteers, could have been placed around Gandhi, but no thought had been given to this; and other 'spotters' or detectives, disguised as malis and domestic servants, could have been placed on the premises to detect Godse and his other accomplices. Justice Kapur recognized that with Marathi-speaking malis and domestic servants in Birla House, the operation might not have remained hidden from 'the Mahatma's observant eye'. Justice Kapur concluded that, despite the obvious difficulties in providing security for Gandhi, an 'unobtrusive method of giving protection to the Mahatma was worth trying and should have been given a trial.'[26] The police had certainly shown a singular lack of imagination in dealing with the most delicate task with which they were ever likely to be entrusted; and, much like Gandhi's associates, they had allowed themselves to be governed by 'pure fatalism' in supposing that Gandhi's life was in the hands of God.[27] Where Gods might be present, can mortals dare to intervene?

Thus far Justice Kapur appears as a man who, while mindful of the obligation of the state towards the Father of the Nation, and himself inclined to think of Gandhi with considerable reverence, could not take the 'hard' view that Gandhi's security was an open-and-shut matter, a relatively easy case of the interests of the state and the nation taking precedence over the foibles of an old man, and an even easier matter of ensuring that the protection of Gandhi proceeded with enough efficiency to obviate any danger to his life. Though it was suggested to him that Gandhi should have been overruled when he refused to authorize the search of persons, Justice Kapur did not think that Gandhi's wishes could have been ignored; as he was to put it more forcefully, 'it is unimaginable that anything could be done without his knowing it and against his wishes and in this matter it would have been a challenge to his faith in the protective hand of God if the police had persisted in searching or screening.'[28] What cordon of policemen, disguised or otherwise, could keep Gandhi from 'the milling crowds pushed forward to pay their homage to the unique leader that Mahatma Gandhi was, a combination of saintliness, of foresighted statesmanship and a very astute politician'?[29] Throughout India, Gandhi was known not only as a political leader, but as a saint. If people clamoured for a darshan of the Mahatma, how were they to be prevented from obtaining it? Finally, on the possibility of devising impenetrable security arrangements for Gandhi, Justice Kapur thought it sufficient to note that in other countries where elaborate precautions had been taken, 'mishaps have happened.'[30] No amount of efficiency could have provided a permanent assurance of the safety of Gandhi's life.

III

FROM NEHRU TO INDIRA GANDHI:

THE GRADUAL EROSION OF THE 'SOFT' STATE

There is, in Justice Kapur's remarks about the security arrangements devised for Gandhi, a notable ambiguity—an ambiguity perhaps enhanced by the passage of time between the assassination and the authorship of the report. Justice Kapur, pointing to Gandhi's visit to the shrine of Khwaja Qutub-ud-din at Mehrauli a few days before his death, adverted to the rather reckless manner in which Gandhi 'was prepared to go into any crowds where he thought he should go or was taken', and one almost senses that he might have been prepared to place restraints on Gandhi's movements. But the voice of the state is quickly contradicted; as Justice Kapur was ironically to add, Gandhi's visit perhaps showed that 'the Mahatma was safer in the shrine of a saint even though he was a Mohammedan saint than he was at his residence at Birla House under the protection of the Police whether in uniform or in plain clothes.'[31] From certain of his countrymen, Justice Kapur appeared to imply, Gandhi could not have been saved, and security was no more than an illusion under such circumstances.

The inquiry into Gandhi's murder was to suggest the possible existence of a plot to assassinate not only Gandhi but the top leadership of the newly formed Indian state. Nehru's security adviser, G. K. Handoo, was apparently told by Godse himself that Nehru would have been the next target of the assassins.[32] As Justice Kapur noted, in writing about the assassination more than twenty years after the fact, a mere sub-inspector had been placed in charge of security operations at Birla House, a palatial building where the poorest 'Father of the Nation' that any nation has known had been lodged, 'whereas in the case of VIPs, officers of a much higher rank are employed.' Justice Kapur did not doubt that, 'from the point of view of national security and [the] country's stability', Nehru and the members of his cabinet deserved the 'strictest police vigilance and protection', though there was at first a reluctance on the part of these ministers to avail themselves of such protection.[33] These leaders had been in the forefront of India's freedom struggle, and were not unreasonably inclined to the view that no one among the people could possibly wish them harm. Gandhi's assassination at once endowed the issue of security for the leader of the state and other VIPs with urgent importance.

Thus it is that rather more elaborate security arrangements were devised for Nehru's protection. Handoo stated before Justice Kapur that the principal objective was to ensure that the Prime Minister was *never* within twenty-five yards of the range of an assassin armed with a revolver; however, as physical searches of persons approaching the PM or some other VIP were not undertaken except when there was reason to be suspicious, a judgment that only the officer placed in charge was capable of exercising, it remains unclear how the safety of the PM or any other VIP could be assured.[34] Two rings were placed around the VIP: the inner ring at a distance of two-three yards from the VIP, and the outer one at a distance of no more than twenty-five yards.[35]

Certainly there was no special force, such as the Special Protection Group established during Rajiv Gandhi's time, for the protection of Nehru. The history of political assassination in independent India essentially commences at a much later date, and commensurably the history of security measures for VIPs also belongs to more recent times. The biographies of Nehru make no reference to the security arrangements devised for his protection, and the government 'Blue Book', a manual for the protection of the PM and VIPs, has long been unavailable for public use. It is only recently, with the publication of the memoirs of a few senior policemen, that some slight insights have been gained into the security arrangements for Nehru's protection. S. Venugopal Rao, who was Superintendent of Police at Guntur, now in Andhra Pradesh, has recalled how he was entrusted with providing for the security of Nehru when he was to come to Guntur in November 1955 to lay the foundation stone of the massive Nagarjuna Sagar dam project. He details the numerous obstacles he had to face in providing adequate security arrangements, and the measures taken to construct a special rostrum where Nehru and other political dignitaries would be seated. Satisfied that he had succeeded in placing a massive security net around Nehru, Rao sent a message 'to Police Headquarters that there were no grounds to apprehend any security risk to the Prime Minister.' The moment finally arrived: Nehru came to deliver his speech, and was finally introduced to the man in whose hands his security had been placed. As Rao recalled many years later, Nehru shook his hands, and then shouted in indignation, 'Why so many men? Why are you policemen standing between me and my people?' Nehru then rushed headlong into the crowd, while Rao 'was left with a heavy sense of rejection.'[36]

Nehru, like Gandhi before him, operated in a fundamentally democratic spirit. Unlike Gandhi, Nehru contested for office, and as a professional politician he was invariably at some remove from the masses. Nor did Nehru—or for that matter almost any other politician in the post-independence period—have the profound knowledge of, and insight into, village India that Gandhi could claim. By the late 1950s, if not earlier, the aura of the independence movement had largely vanished; and there is, by that time, a streak of populism in Nehru's ardent desire not to be separated from 'his people'. Nonetheless, one can be reasonably certain that Nehru had little use for security measures undertaken on his behalf, and that he was deeply concerned that these measures should neither inconvenience the people, nor prevent them from having ready access to him. One writer has recently claimed that 'Nehru would dash off a strong note to his security officer whenever he found security in excess of requirement.'[37] It is curiously the debate in the Lok Sabha over the introduction and passage of the Special Protection Group Bill, a measure designed to provide protection to the family and person of Rajiv Gandhi, the grandson of Nehru, that furnishes further evidence that Nehru certainly did not require much by the way of security protection. While acknowledging that '1988 is not 1958', Ataur Rahman, Member of Parliament from Barpeta, recalled that Nehru 'really enjoyed the confidence of the people.' Having travelled with Nehru after the earthquake in Jorhat in 1950, Rahman noted that Nehru rode on foot boards, or in open jeeps, while addressing crowds. Rahman admitted that now it would be difficult to do so, as 'dreadful things are happening'; as he was to inform the Lok Sabha, 'The Prime Minister's security is closely tied down with the trend of politics.'[38]

Evidently, in the years between Nehru's death in 1964 and Indira Gandhi's second stint as Prime Minister in 1977-80, a more extensive security system was gradually to come into place. In 1975, Indira Gandhi had imposed an internal Emergency on the spurious grounds that the stability and political integrity of the nation were threatened by enemies from within and without. There is nothing to suggest, however, that the political turmoil of the times, and the feelings of hatred that she undoubtedly engendered owing to the climate of repression that she had created, had necessitated any extensive overhauling of the system of security devised for her protection. Swept from power in 1977, Mrs Gandhi was nonetheless able to reclaim power with an overwhelming victory in 1980. It was in the aftermath of her electoral triumph that, over the next few years, a violent secessionist movement developed in the Punjab, which Mrs Gandhi sought to crush decisively with an attack upon Amritsar's Golden Temple, the sacred shrine of the Sikhs which, as the Government alleged, was being used to mount a terrorist movement aimed at the destruction of the Indian nation-state. Here militant advocates of a Sikh state designated as 'Khalistan' had sequestered themselves.

In the aftermath of the assault upon the Golden Temple by Indian armed forces, Mrs. Gandhi appears to have been informed that her security would have to be tightened, and she was urged to forgo the services of her Sikh bodyguards. It was conceivable that some Sikhs, angered by the desecration of their sacred shrine, would vent their fury upon the Prime Minister for having authorized the assault upon the Golden Temple. But Mrs Gandhi was not prepared to heed the counsel of her security advisers, and she chose to retain Sikh bodyguards in defiant demonstration of her devotion to secular and dynastic democracy. However considerable the element of authoritarianism in her political style and practices, she still belonged to a generation of political leaders for whom populism had both a rhetorical and charismatic appeal. She could not be separated entirely from 'her people', and as a consequence she insisted on maintaining, until the very last days of her life, the tradition initiated by Nehru of an 'open house', where commoners were welcome to her residence every morning to meet with her and air their grievances. Nor was she willing to allow that all the members of a certain community, in this case the Sikhs, were to be viewed with suspicion merely because some elements of that community had shown themselves to be hostile and disloyal to the state over which she presided. Much like the autocratic colonial rulers who governed the Punjab with an iron hand, Mrs Gandhi no doubt also believed that though some yeomen farmers might be led astray by the inflammatory rhetoric and gestures of a few evil-minded politicians, the greater part of the Sikhs would never abandon their loyalty to someone like her who, as she imagined, represented 'Mother India'. While her declaration of an emergency had revealed that Mrs Gandhi was unwilling to brook dissent, and her handling of Sikh insurgency was to mark her as an uncompromising proponent of India as a hard nation-state, her political style partook, nonetheless, of an earlier era of cultural pluralism and accommodation.

Thus it is that a number of Sikh security men remained within her personal retinue.[39] Her two bodyguards, Beant Singh and Satwant Singh, who would fire at her, had previously been removed from guard duties at her residence, but were brought back at her insistence. Mrs Gandhi, or certainly someone in the PM's office, is reported to have said that it would put the concept of secularism into question if they were removed solely on the grounds of being Sikhs.[40] From the point-of-view of professional police work, neither Mrs Gandhi nor her office ought to have been allowed to intervene in a matter where she was not in the position of being able to make an accurate judgment, and at least one senior police official has recalled that when Nehru similarly objected to the removal of two Muslim staff members from his house, his security adviser did not allow Nehru's view to prevail. Evidently, Mrs Gandhi, Nehru's daughter, was persuaded that it would be in the interest of her father's security to have those Muslims removed from the premises, and she used her influence to let the security officials have their way.[41] It is rather ironical that, though Mrs Gandhi counselled her father to privilege the principle of security over the principle of trust, she herself did not feel bound to follow that piece of advice. But Indira Gandhi was under much greater compulsion than her father to provide a demonstration of her capacity to live by the principles of secularism, and similarly she had less of a following among the people of India.

Mrs Gandhi's death at the hands of her own bodyguards was, in any case, to have the effect of putting into place a revised system of security operations for the PM and other VIPs. In its lead editorial, the *Times of India*, a leading newspaper friendly to the government, described her death as a 'security disaster', and provided a portent of the changes that were likely to be effected. It was noted that Mrs Gandhi's security had been furnished by the Delhi Armed Police, members of whom were by rotation attached to guard duty with Mrs Gandhi. Her security had thus been compromised, for Mrs Gandhi's guards should have been 'part of a small force permanently given this vital task [of protecting her], comprising men whose antecedents had been thoroughly investigated and whose loyalty had been firmly established.' As if this inept manner of providing Mrs Gandhi with security was not enough, the *Times of India* lamented, her security guards had acquired something of a reputation for 'drunkenness and loutishness' aboard the aircraft that took Mrs Gandhi on her tours abroad. Noting that the 'morale and efficiency' of the entire force had suffered as a consequence, the editorial condemned 'the scandalous failure of security arrangements for the most important public figure in the land.'[42]

What the *Times of India* did not comment on was the more obvious breaches of security apparently stipulated in the 'Blue Book' on the PM's security. Satwant Singh, as a mere constable, should not have been allowed within the inner ring placed around Mrs Gandhi, and that too within such extraordinary proximity so as to be virtually by her side. More astonishingly, how did Satwant Singh come to wield a sten-gun, when all the guards had been issued revolvers?[43] While these and other unresolved matters would eventually be turned over to a commission charged with investigating the circumstances under which Mrs Gandhi was assassinated, it had become imperative to provide Mrs Gandhi's successor with an impenetrable system of security. On the very day of her assassination, 31 October 1984, Mrs Gandhi's son, Rajiv Gandhi, was sworn in as the Prime Minister. What assurance was there that those security failings which had become manifest in the death of Indira Gandhi would not now claim her son's life?

IV

THE LANGUAGE AND APPARATUS OF SECURITY IN THE RAJIV ERA:
PARODIES OF PROFESSIONALISM, FANTASIES OF EFFICIENCY

Shortly after Rajiv Gandhi occupied his office, a special force, under the jurisdiction of the Cabinet Secretariat, was brought into existence in order to provide for the security of the Prime Minister. The Ministry for Home Affairs, in February 1985, appointed a committee headed by Birbal Nath to look into the issue of VVIP security at length, and in the following month the committee submitted a set of recommendations urging the government to create a Special Protection Unit. On 30 March, the President of India created 819 positions for the unit under the Cabinet Secretariat, and the Special Protection Group (SPG) was brought into existence. Described as 'a single specialized agency consisting of highly motivated professionals charged with the responsibility of ensuring [the] proximate security of the Prime Minister and members of his family',[44] the SPG was placed at the helm of all the agencies, such as the Delhi Police and the Intelligence Branch, involved with the Prime Minister's security. Over time the SPG appears to have grown into a force of 3,000 personnel, and though originating as a force concerned solely with the security of the Prime Minister and his immediate family, by amendment in May 1991 former Prime Ministers and their families were also brought under the SPG's jurisdiction.[45] Initially, at least, the ambition appears to have been that, acting on information furnished to them by the local police and the Intelligence Branch, Black Cat commandos of the SPG would be in the position of foiling any plan aimed at the life of the PM and members of his family. The public in India would henceforth be witness to the sight of Rajiv Gandhi travelling with a vast escort of commandos armed with sten-guns and automatic rifles.

Notwithstanding the creation of the SPG, and the restructuring of the entire security apparatus, the security system collapsed on 2 October 1986. Early in the morning of that day, Rajiv Gandhi, the President of India, and other dignitaries had proceeded to Rajghat, the national memorial to Mahatma Gandhi, to pay their respects to the Father of the Nation on the occasion of his 117th birth anniversary. Two shots were fired 'at' the Prime

Minister around 7:15 a.m. while the dignitaries were paying homage at the memorial, and a third shot was fired approximately *forty-five minutes later*, just as Rajiv and his wife Sonia were leaving Rajghat. The first two shots went wildly astray, while pellets from the third shot slightly wounded two officers of the SPG and a number of other men.[46] All the leaders of the nation, in the official jargon of piety, escaped entirely unhurt. Not unreasonably, the question on everyone's mind was why the would-be assassin was not apprehended after the first shot, and why so much time was allowed to elapse, during which he mustered courage to discharge his revolver again, before he was taken into custody. Apparently members of the SPG force mistook the sound of the first shot for the sound of a scooter backfiring, though how they could have been so foolish as to arrive at this interpretation, given the large distance between the memorial and the road, remains beyond comprehension. As relayed in one newspaper, the area from which the gun had seemingly been fired was immediately searched, and though a piece of the spent bullet was found, it was dismissed 'as something of no consequence.' Indeed, 'sniffer dogs, imported from Australia', were brought into service (no doubt poorly-fed, smaller, ill-trained canines from India being quite inadequate for this manly enterprise), and when one showed a degree of restlessness upon approaching the shrub where the incompetent assassin was hiding, and the matter was brought to the attention of the principal officer, the latter merely thought that the dog was needlessly excitable.[47]

None of the bullets came even remotely close to the PM, but his providential *escape* owed nothing to the efficiency of the system designed to ensure the protection of his life, or to the dedication and skill of the men constituting his personal bodyguard. If the would-be assassin, an unemployed Sikh youth by the name of Karamjit Singh, was not very competent with his gun, which he fired at a distance of only 30 metres from the PM, the officers of the Delhi Police and the Special Protection Group seem not to have acquitted themselves any better. Their shooting was so poor that *they* were 'disarmed' at the orders of Delhi's Lieutenant-Governor, H. L. Kapur![48] That their shots were fired *at* the gunman, when clearly the sensible thing to do would have been to have taken him alive, provides another commentary on the intelligence of the officers of an elite security force. Considering their poor shooting skills, Rajiv Gandhi must have had reason to be grateful that the men into whose custody he had delivered himself had not accidentally taken his own life.[49]

The failed attempt on the PM's life was bound to raise serious questions about the extraordinary lapses in security; and to aggravate matters, on the day following the incident at Rajghat, a number of terrorists breached the vast security net surrounding J. F. Ribeiro, the chief of police in the Punjab, a man himself chosen to wipe out Sikh terrorism, and launched a daring if unsuccessful attack on Ribeiro's life.[50] 'Security shambles', noted one editorialist, while another writer entitled his column, 'Glaring loopholes in security.'[51] Both incidents boded ill for the country: in one instance, a special force then constituting of 2,000 members had proven to be entirely derelict in providing security for the head of government, while in the other instance terrorists, donning the uniforms of police, had managed to infiltrate the headquarters of the police chief into whose hands had been placed the task of bringing them into submission, and had then made good their escape from the lion's den.[52] The 'common man', noted the *Hindustan Times* editorial, was entitled to ask questions about the safety of the nation's political leadership when he himself had been subjected to 'harassment and delay in the name of security', but the editorial did not dare any further. What of the security of the common woman and man, of the fear that the public entertains both of terrorists and of the state agencies armed with the task of eliminating them?[53]

As reports on the failed attempt on Rajiv Gandhi's life were to reveal, both the Delhi Police and the SPG had claimed to have conducted a thorough search of the premises at Rajghat for a number of days before the arrival of the PM, and indeed on the very morning of the incident. Specially trained dogs had been employed; entry of people and vehicles had been strictly regulated; commandos had been posted 'on top of all vantage points around the venue' of the site 'to spot any suspicious movement'; and two DIGs of the SPG had personally inspected Raj Ghat on October 1st and 2nd 'as an added precaution because of the alert given by the Intelligence agencies of a possible assassination attempt' and had 'declared it clear' of any terrorist and antisocial elements. Nonetheless, the would-be assassin, Karamjit Singh, had managed to conceal himself in a structure overlooking the memorial and the 'VIP path,' and what is more wondrous, he had spent the entire night and the previous day at his hideout.[54] When he was apprehended and his hideout searched, a bottle of water, biscuits, and a tube of toothpaste were found on him.[55] Apparently Karamjit Singh must have restrained the impulse to clear his throat in the loud manner commonly associated with Indians, but we do not know whether the police officers found commendable his devotion to dental hygiene. The man was clearly not foolish, nor was he without 'some guile': in an attempt to turn him into a possible master plotter, the *Times of India* noted that he had disguised himself in 'olive green clothes and had wrapped himself in a green blanket so that he could get lost in the bushes.'[56] Karamjit Singh, if the newspapers were to be believed, was clearly an old hand in the game of political assassinations: not only had he attempted to deceive the police by providing them with 'different names', he also changed his statements several times, and was even an 'expert in several dialects, especially those spoken in Mathura district.'[57]

However, it was not enough merely to characterize Karamjit Singh as a clever assassin, from whose clutches the PM and the political leadership of the nation providentially made good their escape, for a lone assassin can, if he is permitted to be heard, command sympathy. The lone assassin seldom makes for a good story, particularly if he is motivated by none other than a personal grudge, or if he is an alienated young man, searching for livelihood and meaning in life. Though they were no grounds to substantiate a theory that Karamjit Singh was merely a pawn in a conspiracy, or perhaps even the linchpin of a larger and diabolical plot, a conspiracy theory had perforce to be invented. To begin with, as there were doubts that the PM was even the target of any attack, considering that his purported assassin missed him by several feet when he himself was not at any great distance from his victim, witnesses had to be brought forth to testify that the shots had been aimed 'at' the PM. Yet, curiously, the very man who claimed that he had been hit, when the bullet was intended for the PM, had to admit that he had been struck only by a pellet, for the range at which the bullet had been fired had led to its disintegration upon impact.[58] Karamjit Singh himself was reported as having confessed that 'Mr Gandhi was his target', not the other VIPs', and this disclosure was stated to have been signed by 'the seemingly well-educated man' in 'English, Hindi and Gurmukhi.'[59] Secondly, it had to be suggested that Karamjit Singh had been acting in consort with others, and his 'associates' were thus taken in for questioning.[60] A few days after the incident, numerous arrests were effected, and when asked if Karamjit Singh was part of a conspiracy, police officers placed in charge of the investigation replied, 'why should we be arresting people if there was no conspiracy?'[61] Journalists such as A. R. Wig, who pride themselves on their tough realism, were at once willing to support the conspiracy hypothesis, though at this time little more was known than the name of the culprit; in reprimanding the SPG for firing at the gunman, and risking his death, Wig noted: 'The investigating agencies would not have known the people behind the whole conspiracy.'[62] And what might this conspiracy be, if not the 'foreign hand'? And if the 'foreign hand', who else could want to destabilize India but Pakistan, whose attempts at fomenting insurrection in Punjab had so decisively been crushed by Ribeiro?[63] And, finally, if the supposed attempt upon the PM's life had not already been magnified enough into a sinister plot to render chaotic and fractious the world's largest democracy, when the would-be assassin was nothing more than a country bumpkin armed with a rough pistol that he scarcely knew how to fire, the Indian public had to be assured that the world's leaders had expressed their most profound shock at the attempt upon the life of Rajiv Gandhi, a man whose mother had cruelly been snatched away from him, and who had so graciously assumed the burden of leading India to the height of its power and glory. 'Widespread condemnation', noted one headline in the *Times of India*, while another stated: 'World community shocked'.[64]

In the midst of this incident, the Father of the Nation, whose memory was to be honoured on the day of the supposed assassination, was entirely forgotten. In India, he has been largely overlooked, especially by the ruling elements (where hooligan and criminal elements now predominate), though the observance of his birthday and death anniversaries each year allows the principal functionaries of the Indian state to declare their readiness to live by his principles. It is this mask that Karamjit Singh was able to lift, revealing the ordinariness of an otherwise extraordinary day, and it is this merciless (if inadvertent) unmasking that could not be forgiven. 2 October was really, as Karamjit Singh appeared to be suggesting, any other mundane day, though the nation-state might pretend otherwise. Secondly, as a formidable solemnity had been ascribed to the incident, no suggestion was allowed to be entertained of the sheer incongruity of supposing that the would-be assassin was enacting a parody of the security fantasies that afflict the Indian nation-state. The infiltration of India's most heavily guarded buildings, emblematic of the power of the state, has become notoriously easy, though security has now been placed in the hands of several so-called 'elite' or 'crack' units of securitymen: in one incident, a visitor to the residence of the then Prime Minister Narasimha Rao, who had been searched by members of the SPG and cleared, calmly took out a concealed camera with which he proceeded to take photographs of the PM. The visitor stated that he had placed it in his armpit, and officials conceded he could just as easily have concealed a small pistol.[65] In another incident around the same time, a 'rum-drinking' Swami, posing as a Member of Parliament and friend of numerous political leaders, was not only able to 'breach the security cordon' in sensitive areas of Kashmir, he was also able to obtain the services of security agencies keen to oblige a holy man.[66]

As the purported assassination attempt had been turned into a sinister attack upon the nation, so proportionately severe remedies had to be initiated in order to atone for the lapses of security and minimize the ridicule that had been unleashed upon India's security regime. Both the BBC and ITV in London had reportedly referred to the 'so-called elite security force' set up to guard the PM, and the knowledge that the 'gunman' had been allowed 'to fire shots at intervals over a long period' before the PM's elite guards even attempted to apprehend him had led television observers in the US to ask, 'what kind of security do the Indians have? In which century are they living?'[67] While Rajiv Gandhi presented himself as a total modernizer, a dashing young man who had been so unfazed by the attempt upon his life that he was able to direct his security guards to fire at the gunman,[68] the men entrusted with his life seemed to evoke the timeless image of an India that is inefficient, chaotic, and quite incapable of dealing with the demands of the present. This damage had perforce to be repaired; and in the days following the purported attempt, there was widespread reportage of actions taken to restore the credibility of India's security regime. Various officials from the Delhi Police, Intelligence Bureau, and the NSG were relieved of their duties; the leave of all Delhi policemen was cancelled; a 'red alert' was sounded throughout the capital; and the idea was mooted of curtailing the PM's exposure to crowds over long periods.[69]

Most significantly, numerous high-level meetings attended by police officers, members of the SPG, and officials of the Home Ministry and the Prime Minister's Secretariat established that security arrangements had been compromised by leaving security in the hands of diverse agencies which had not merely been unable to coordinate their activities, but which were often hostile to each other. The Intelligence Bureau had intimated the possibility of an attack upon the PM four days prior to the incident, but apparently neither the Delhi Police nor the SPG had been similarly informed.[70] Though the SPG, a 2,000-strong force 'constituted by men specially picked from the Delhi police and the paramilitary forces and given specialized training', enjoyed overriding powers in the matter of the PM's security, it apparently did not get the benefit of the information gathered by the various intelligence agencies operating under the auspices of the Home Ministry.[71] That the SPG itself had been grossly derelict was not to be doubted: under its own guidelines, the PM should have been taken away by the SPG as soon as the first shot had been fired, but instead the PM was left in the same spot for another 45 minutes. After the incident at Rajghat, one journalist opined, the 'only thing that the different agencies [could] do is to blame one another' as it was 'now happening'.[72] The PM's security had been placed in his own hands, as the SPG was under the care of his Secretariat, but perhaps the fundamental stipulation that the PM's security was one matter in which he should have been allowed no say had been violated, for this interfered with the effort to 'evolve a system that [would] be completely professional, insulated from any other influence.'[73]

Less than two years after the purported assassination attempt on the life of Rajiv Gandhi, and after the resolve to place the security of the PM in the care of one central agency, the Lok Sabha passed the Special Protection Group Bill, 1988, which then sought to provide 'proximate security' to the PM and members of his immediate family, whether in India or abroad. If the necessity for such legislation appeared to be obviated by the fact that the Special Protection Group, 'a specialized force consisting of well-trained motivated professionals', had already been raised on 1 April 1985, the Minister of State for Home Affairs, P. Chidambaram, sought to argue that the bill provided for the SPG as a permanent and statutory force, and so sought to place the SPG on a more secure footing than was furnished by the Executive Order that had kept it in existence for three years.[74] Though Chidambaram did not state so, in endowing the SPG with statutory backing, the Government of India was seeking to give members of the SPG immunity from prosecution. In justifying the bill, Chidambaram noted only the increased incidence of 'terrorist violence' in India during the last few years, 'the aim of the terrorists being to destabilize the democratically elected government by resorting to selective killing of prominent members of the public including those in the Government.'[75]

Notwithstanding the overwhelming majority of the Congress party in the Lok Sabha, the opposition parties did not allow the bill to remain uncontested. Sobhanadreeswara Rao, MP from Vijaywada, bemoaned the necessity of bringing the bill before the House of the 'largest democratic country in the entire world', and asked if it was not 'pathetic' that the PM had to address the country from the ramparts of the Red Fort on Independence Day from behind a bullet-proof enclosure. Rao noted that Rajiv Gandhi's predecessors had not required such security as was now being proposed for the PM. Keeping in mind the changing political circumstances, and the ascendancy of violent insurrectionist movements, Rao nonetheless sought to impress upon the House that Nehru never ceased to mingle with the crowds, though there were security arrangements in his days as well. If Nehru was in no need of exceptional security, was it not because 'the people were the real guards to him'? As Rao pointed out, Mrs Gandhi's assassination had a singularity all its own by virtue of the fact that her assassins, unlike those of Kennedy or Mahatma Gandhi, were her own security guards. Did this not demonstrate that a force of 1,500 to 2,000 men, howsoever well-trained, cannot provide 'foolproof protection'? In articulating his reservations about the bill, Rao suggested that the only solution to the security of the PM and other leaders is a political solution.[76]

In resuming the debate the following day, Rao went on to articulate other reservations about the bill. As he was to note, if the SPG was to be rendered into a permanent and statutory force, the day when other VIPs, such as Union Ministers and Chief Ministers, would demand similar privileges was not too far removed. The effect of all such legislation would be to increase the distance between the rulers and the ruled, between the functionaries of the state and the people they were empowered to serve.

Not to mention the extraordinary expenses entailed in raising special forces for the protection of political leaders. Rao thought that the advent of such forces would have the effect of pushing India towards a 'police raj', and undermining the country's democratic institutions. 'My point', Rao further stated, 'is that the Government should be in a position to give protection even to a common citizen of this country.'[77]

Several of Rao's arguments were to be extended further by opposition MPs in the Lok Sabha. Though the bill appeared to be innocuous, Jaipal Reddy submitted that it had 'some outrageous, obnoxious and atrocious features.' First, in the warrant of precedence, the offices of the President and Vice-President commanded superiority, whatever *de facto* precedence the office of the PM might have had. Far from acknowledging this order of precedence, the bill effectively contradicted it by offering 'proximate security' to the PM and his family alone. Secondly, could the Government of India, and the ruling Congress party, point to a 'parallel in any part of the world' for the existence and statutory justification of an organization created to provide 'for the protection of a person holding a particular office'? Reddy did not think that a special extra-constitutional paramilitary force for the protection of a 'single individual' existed anywhere except perhaps in a 'Banana Republic', certainly not 'in any major democratic nation.' Thirdly, as the SPG was to be under the control of the PM himself, was there any such force elsewhere in the world that was 'directly under the control of the Office of the Chief Executive of the nation'? Fourthly, as the bill provided no upper limit for the number of men that could be admitted into this special force, what would prevent the PM from raising the strength of the force to a formidable number, and then using this paramilitary force to enhance his standing, or to remain in power when he could no longer command a majority in Parliament? As Reddy was at pains to note, the 'implications' in such circumstances 'for the democratic polity can be, theoretically and hypothetically, hazardous.' Finally, Reddy did not think it advisable to offer members of the force immunity from prosecution or other legal proceedings.[78]

Rao and Reddy had not exhausted all the objections to the bill, and in the ensuing debate, other considerations were brought to the fore. The bill provided no guidelines for admittance to the SPG, this being no small matter, considering that anyone so admitted was immune from prosecution or legal proceedings. Moreover, under clause 18, such immunity was to be seen as being conferred with retrospective effect, that is to say from the moment of the SPG's inception in 1985, when the SPG had been raised without approval of either the Cabinet or Parliament. If all this was not objectionable enough, what had the government to say in defense of clause 14, which required it as the 'duty of every Ministry, and Department of the Central Government or the State Government or the Union Territory Administration, every Indian Mission [Embassy], every local or other authority or civil authority or military authority to act in aid of the Director or any member of the Group whenever called upon to do so'? By what right could *any* member of the SPG demand services of higher military, civil, or political authorities? Did not the bill concentrate arbitrary power in the person not only of the PM, but also of his chosen henchmen? Did not the refusal to accede to the wishes of the SPG subject various legitimate authorities to sanctions?

In his reply, the Minister of State for Home Affairs, P. Chidambaram, was constrained to admit that no comparable force raised under the law to protect one person existed anywhere else in the world, certainly not in any democracy. But Chidambaram did not think it fit to address the other pressing questions raised in the House, and with scarcely any more debate, the bill was passed in the Lok Sabha by an overwhelming majority. Similar objections to the bill in the Rajya Sabha were brushed aside, and when Ram Jethmalani charged the government with creating a praetorian guard for the PM and subverting the constitution, Chidambaram replied: 'We do not want to make a laughing stock of ourselves knowing full well the security risks were there for the Prime Minister and members of his family who could be kidnapped, blackmailed and even killed.'[79]

In his haste to occlude the possibility that he, or other members of the government, might become the 'laughing stock' of the world, the Minister had ceased to reflect on the political shortsightedness of his position, and on the absurdity of tolerating a frightful regimen of security in the name of providing freedom from terror. As the events in the aftermath of the passing of the bill were to show with utter clarity, security is but an illusion, and the anxieties of a nation-state confronted with modernity, and pressed to demonstrate its resilience and toughness, are not so easily resolved. The only security we may have resides in the understanding that though the nation-state does not show ways of accommodation, an old civilization might yet point to a more complex comprehension of the relationship between the rulers and the ruled, between practitioners of varying faiths, and between 'patrons' and 'clients'.

V

FROM SECURITY OF VIPs TO SECURITY OF CITIZENS

Three years after the passage of the Security Protection Group Bill, Rajiv Gandhi and twenty others, including his own Personal Security Officer, were killed in a bomb blast. Having sent Indian troops at the 'request' of the Sri Lankan government to aid in the suppression of Tamil militancy, Rajiv himself became the target of secessionist politics, the complexity of which he was scarcely equipped to understand. A woman, believed to be a member of the LTTE [Liberation Tigers of Tamil Eelam], strapped a bomb to her body, and as she bent down in an apparent gesture of greeting Rajiv, the bomb exploded, scattering him into pieces.[80] In the wake of the assassination, a 'red alert' was sounded, and 'security of VVIPs strengthened.' It was noted that the numbers of 'National Security Guards and the Special Protection Group' had been increased and put on 'an extraordinary alert', and 'Black Cat commandos' had been 'deployed to protect Mrs Sonia Gandhi and her children.'[81] As 'mobs' desirous to catch a darshan of the body of their dear and departed leader had attempted to lay siege to Teen Murti House, where Rajiv Gandhi's body lay in state, BSF men had thrown a cordon around the building, and a '50,000 strong force', consisting of troops from the NSG, CRPF, and BSF, was mobilized to patrol the streets of the capital, though ordinary citizens themselves had been requested to cooperate with law enforcers in preventing antisocial activities. All this preparation was, no doubt, by way of a prelude to the security arrangements for Rajiv Gandhi's funeral, which was expected to be attended by leaders from around the world. With great solemnity, and no less predictability, the national newspapers were to report that Mr Gandhi's funeral site, which was 'declared out of bounds', was being combed at regular intervals by 'sophisticated mine detectors', and that the entire route of the funeral procession was being manned by police and sharpshooters.[82] Though the former Prime Minister's life could not be preserved, and though his much-vaunted security was reduced to shambles, the Government of India would continue to insist on maintaining the charade of being possessed of an elite, professional, and impregnable security network.

The former Prime Minister, who had to surrender his office when his party lost at the polls, was engaged in some last-minute campaigning in Tamil Nadu for the tenth general elections to the Lok Sabha when he was killed. Following the defeat of the Congress party in the 1989 elections, the V. P. Singh Government took a decision to withdraw SPG cover from Rajiv Gandhi, as it was contended, quite rightly, that the legislation authorizing the SPG did not sanction SPG protection for former prime ministers.[83] At a meeting of the cabinet on 30 January 1990, it was decided that the SPG Act would not be amended, and any arrangements for Rajiv Gandhi's security would have to be provided by other agencies.[84] A parliamentary committee, however, is said to have decided on 4 December 1989 that the SPG cover for Rajiv Gandhi ought to be maintained, unless fresh circumstances suggested that Rajiv Gandhi had no reason to fear for his life. Justice Jagdish Sharan Verma, who was appointed to inquire into the circumstances surrounding Rajiv's assassination, was later to note that the findings of this committee were effectively ignored by the Intelligence Bureau (IB) and Home Ministry. Apparently, both on 21 March 1991, and again on 20 May, one day before Rajiv's assassination, the IB had sent out memos suggesting that an attempt might be made on Rajiv's life. On the strength of observations made by Directors General of Police throughout the country, the IB had recommended that three Personal Security Officers be attached to Rajiv Gandhi; on the latter occasion, the IB recommended that an escort of National Security Guards be provided to him 'immediately': neither recommendation was implemented. Verma found that no attention had been paid to the warnings; more significantly, the most elementary rules of security had been flouted: for example, women were barely searched before being allowed to approach Rajiv. Thus his assassin had been able to approach him unhindered, and though police officers had previously been informed that 'garlands and bouquets were to be checked' before being presented to Rajiv, no such measures were taken when Rajiv's assassin went up to him.[85]

Notwithstanding the withdrawal of SPG cover for Rajiv Gandhi, he continued to have a very large security force attached to him, and various reports indicate quite clearly that the negligence of his own security forces, his party men, and the security forces of the state and the central government made it possible for his assassin to so easily infiltrate the security net purportedly placed around him. Yet, on the day before his assassination, national newspapers reported that there was 'unprecedented security' in preparation for the elections.[86] The supposition that Rajiv might have been saved by more professional security experts, which the Verma and Jain Commissions viewed as axiomatically true, ignores the debacle at Rajghat in 1986 and the almost comical bungling by securitymen on numerous other occasions; it also feeds the illusion that the security of senior political leaders is mainly a matter of resolving certain problems of bureaucracy, coordination, and technology, and raising the standards of the security forces to those which are believed to obtain among 'hard', no-nonsense states such as Israel and the United States.[87] Moreover, to enter into the 'debate' of whether such security as was provided to him was adequate, or whether the V. P. Singh-led National Front Government was niggardly in withdrawing the SPG cover for Rajiv, is to concede that the security fantasies of the state are justified, and that the state and its supporters, along with India's modernizing elites who would like to turn India into a 'hard' and masculinist state, should be allowed to determine the contours of this debate.

The question of whether it is possible to design an unbreachable security mechanism, which can be rendered immune from infiltration by terrorists, and which is (just as importantly) resistant to the interventions of 'soft' and wily intellectuals, activists, and democrats, who allegedly fail to recognize the real nature of the threat, has occluded rather more important considerations. Can there be any security for political leaders when the citizens of the country no longer feel safe? Is it tolerable that nearly one-third of the nearly 60,000-strong Delhi Police Force should be employed for the security of 500 protected persons living in the capital, of whom a dozen are placed in what is described as the Z-plus category?[88] And what are these categories of classification—Z-plus, Z, X-plus, X, Y-plus, and Y[89]—if not forms of mystification and obfuscation? What else do these categories do if not oppress, and how effectively do these categories silence nagging questions about political responsibility and accountability, about the advent of managerial 'knowledge', and about the fictions of terrorism generated by the state's own information industry? Must security be turned over to the technocrats, bureaucrats, and other experts? Does the only assurance of providing foolproof security reside in enhancing the distance between the ruled and the rulers, between the state and the subjects? Must security come at the price of creating an altogether asymmetrical relationship, so that the notion of the private collapses in respect of the lives of ordinary Indians, and conversely is deified when there is only *the* subject? How far have we travelled from the days of Mahatma Gandhi to the development mandates of Narasimha Rao and the nuclear fantasies of the Hindutvavadis, and what does this distance, and the mode of traversing it, portend for the future of India, both as a nation-state and as a civilization?

First, it can scarcely be doubted that in the name of security, the citizenry of India has been reduced to mere rubble. Consider these two reports from an Indian newspaper:

> T. N. Seshan [the Chief Election Commissioner] orders his National Security Guard (NSG) commandos to fire at a car which has overtaken his motorcade.
> Former Prime Minister Chandrasekhar becomes so incensed by a Ramjas College boy overtaking his convoy that security-men come knocking at the boy's door next morning at 4 a.m. and drag his family to the police station.[90]

Occasionally, when Indian elites themselves must suffer on account of the security paranoia of the state, and the grossly cavalier attitude of security personnel, the discomfort of citizens becomes a news item. Such was the case when Rajiv Gandhi's securitymen repeatedly invaded the precincts of the exclusive Gymkhana Club, whose members number 'senior civil servants, powerful politicians and affluent businessmen', and behaved in such a brutish manner as to occasion complaints from a 'number of ladies'. Since these policemen were acting in the name of the PM's security, members were 'reluctant to lodge a formal protest.'[91] In point of fact, while less privileged citizens may not have to contend with similar violations of 'privacy', they have to make do, all in the name of security, with daily inconveniences and nuisances such as needless roadblocks, the diversion of traffic,[92] the prohibition on carrying personal belongings into public buildings, the interruption of music concerts and other cultural events, the unannounced closure of public buildings, and laborious personal searches. This modus operandi, a deplorable demonstration of the lack of respect for the lives of ordinary citizens, if not contempt for them, has also been followed by the Delhi Police. In one notable instance, that would have been comical but for the evident inconvenience caused to a large part of Delhi's population, an order to the Delhi Police by the Supreme Court to produce before it, by a certain time, an inter-caste couple that were suspected to have been kidnapped at the behest of the bride's father, occasioned a massive search in which vehicles on roads were searched and roadblocks placed everywhere; as though any criminal would be so astoundingly stupid as to transport his victims in broad daylight. One newspaper commented: 'The task was gigantic and the result, a chaos', and road journeys that ordinarily took 15 minutes were taking as long as two and a half hours.[93] It is these kinds of hardships that the opposition sought to call to attention during the parliamentary debate on the Special Protection Group Bill. Recalling Rajiv Gandhi's visit to Ooty, the member from Madras informed the House that 'shops have totally been removed even though they paid municipal taxes and lot of harassment is caused to the general public.'[94]

Though such inconveniences are deplorable enough, the more serious problem is that no checks exist to protect citizens from the depredations of securitymen themselves, who then seek immunity by virtue of their close association with politicians. There have been reports of Black Cats thrashing people in full public view, and firing at them, for the no greater offence than that of having blocked their view on the road, or for failing to stop at a security cordon.[95] The case in the mid-1990s of the abduction and possible rape of a French woman, in which the grandson of the Punjab Chief Minister and his two personal security guards were found to be chief villains, provided a macabre demonstration of the danger to the security of citizens posed by securitymen and their political patrons.[96] Indeed, in the hierarchy of police and security forces, ordinary policemen themselves have no assurance of security from the depredations of the more elite security forces, and there have often been reports of Delhi policemen themselves being beaten up by NSG and SPG commandos, who act with the utter impunity of those assured of immunity, subject to the usual and worthless caveats of having acted in good faith, from prosecution.[97] When policemen can be subjected to such treatment, the ordinary citizen must learn to live with fear.

Third, as is now widely known, it is not only the top political leaders of the country that have security guards attached to them, for even the meanest of the small fry can boast of a security retinue. In Uttar Pradesh, where over the years at least a quarter of the state legislators have proven criminal records, politicians have at various times been ardently vying to have securitymen or 'gunmen', as they are accurately termed by the media, attached to them: the larger the security retinue, the greater the prestige. The former Chief Minister, Mulayam Singh Yadav, was in the enviable position of being placed in the 'Z' category, which meant that he was entitled to seven Black Cat commandos, guarding him day and night. The Bharatiya Janata Party had, a study conducted in 1993 showed, seventy-three politicians with criminal records who had also been sanctioned personal security guards. Among these men were Brij Bhusan Sharan Singh and T. P. Shukla, each of whom had two dozen or more cases registered against him for murder, dacoity, and other offences. Each man had at least one 'gunner', wielding a stengun or .38 carbine, attached to him; Sharan Singh also had a 'shadow', an officer of the rank of a sub-inspector, armed with a revolver, following him.

The Congress (I), no great bastion of virtue, had forty-eight politicians provided with security when they had also been charged with heinous crimes. As the former Governor, Motilal Vora, was to concede, 'Official security cover is in great demand amongst politicians these days.' In an analysis carried out by his predecessor in 1993, it was found that 958 politicians in Uttar Pradesh were being provided with security, at an expenditure of over Rs 20,000,000, when most of these politicians were not entitled to this privilege.[98] It is a grotesque irony that the very politicians from whom the public must demand security, so ruthless are their records, are themselves furnished with security at public expense; and it is no less ironical that while the state has given security to these criminals, it is also attempting, through the courts, to put them behind bars. But this scenario is scarcely confined to Uttar Pradesh, for everywhere politicians, many of them implicated in murder, arson, dacoity, kidnapping, and incitement to hatred of minorities, have been insisting upon being provided with official security. As late as February 2000, when the Indian government announced a new VIP security policy designed to reduce the immense cost of VIP security and allay concerns about the public display of gun-toting securitymen, one of the nineteen individuals throughout India entitled to NSG security cover, which is reserved for VIPs other than the Prime Minister, was H. K. L. Bhagat, who is widely believed to have been a major force in orchestrating the pogrom against Sikhs following the assassination of Indira Gandhi in 1984.[99] Indeed, in the early 1990s, foreign governments had been so harassed by the Government of India, who had been requesting them to provide security for various Indian VVIPs travelling abroad, that the Government of India was curtly told that it would have to provide such security through its own devices.[100]

Fourth, securitymen have, more often than not, only succeeded in making a foolish and parodic display of themselves. The purported assassination attempt on the life of Rajiv Gandhi presented one instance of that, as did the attempt on the life of Ribeiro, and as has the repeated infiltration of high-security buildings, including the Prime Minister's own office, by members of the public.[101] In a not altogether rare incident in 1991, the hijacker who commandeered an Indian Airlines jet to Srinagar, and was subsequently killed by Black Cat commandos who stormed the aircraft, was discovered to have passed by securitymen disguised as a cripple. The newspaper called it a case of 'misplaced sympathy', and further noted that none of the securitymen appeared to have found anything odd about the fact that the hijacker was moving about in hot and humid weather dressed in a jacket; nor did they consider anything amiss when the metal detector started beeping, as they assumed that the cripple's metal or aluminum crutches had detonated the alarm.[102] Every instance of such bungling is seen, by the security experts, as just that—an instance of amateurism, lack of professionalism, improper training, failure to abide by standards, and the negligence of human beings. No other reading is ever allowed to disturb the placid banality of the dominant view. Try as hard as it might, the Indian nation-state finds that it cannot keep out human emotions from its operations; always poised to take on the efficiency, professionalism, and ruthlessness of the states it emulates, it falters at the last moment. Perhaps, as the purported assassination attempt of Rajiv

Gandhi at Rajghat in 1986 was to show, Indians have within their arsenal such actions, gestures, and antics of dissent as are not recognized by the FBI, CIA, M5, ISI, RAW, and other agencies that have decoded and categorized insurgency and authored manuals on counter-insurgency operations. Perhaps, too, the dedication to their work and to realpolitik among the superior officers takes no cognizance of the lifestyles of the subalterns within the ranks, and of their closer contact with the denser ranks of humanity.

Every incident in which the security is shown to have been circumvented, indeed ridiculed, as in the attempt on the life of Youth Congress President Maninderjit Singh Bitta, where eight others died though the main target escaped unhurt, is followed by frenzied and loud meetings on security, and with a sworn resolve to tighten the loopholes, increase efficiency, and remove corrupt policemen.[103] Each year the security at state gatherings and national celebrations is declared to be 'unprecedented', unusually tight: witness the following newspaper headlines, on the occasion of either Republic Day or Independence Day: 'Tight security for parade' (1985); 'Tightest security this year' (1988); 'Tightest-ever security for PM' (1989); and 10 years later, 'Tightest-ever security arrangements' (1999). After every disaster or near-disaster, the counter-terrorist experts, technocrats, defence-policy experts, and security specialists take to the pen, and the public is reminded that the security apparatus is in a shambles and requires refurbishing;[104] and additionally it is stressed that India must avoid the ignominy of being laughed at by the rest of the world, and cannot hope to be considered a respectable nation-state unless it becomes hard-nosed and tough-minded, handed over to the charge of men who can turn it into a real nation-state. More pointedly, the experts are keen to remind us, Indian intellectuals have been 'soft' on terrorism,[105] and they must understand that 'a "soft" state cannot endure'.[106] 'No other "soft" state in history', writes K. C. Khanna, 'has had so many hardened killers as India has in so few years in its heartland', and thus 'softness' is a luxury that the Indian state can ill-afford: 'It must harden its heart and meet the threat head-on to survive.' The suggestion that the PM or the President, and indeed all other VIPs and elected politicians, must not be isolated from the public, an invariable consequence of the security regime that has come into place, appears as sheer 'woolliness' on the part of the intelligentsia.

No matter, then, that the public must now always be addressed by the PM or the President from behind bulletproof glass enclosures,[107] that the PM is no longer available to the public, and that the President of India, who used to arrive for the Republic Day parade in a ceremonial horse-drawn carriage, is now driven in a bulletproof car.[108] For the modernizers, eager to usher a strong India into the twenty-first century, horse-drawn carriages are in any case relics of the past, and horse-dung an acute embarrassment, an effrontery to man's visual and olfactory senses, and even the slightest mention of such contraptions as horse-driven carriages evokes accusations of endorsing nostalgia and sentimentality.

Though India is now signatory to various agreements for the suppression of terrorism, and cooperation with international agencies such as Interpol for the apprehension of terrorists has been significantly increased, and though aircraft ('to shoot down unauthorized flying objects'),[109] security gadgets,[110] sniffer dogs,[111] and sophisticated computers[112] have been brought into service to combat terrorism, insurrectionist movements, and risks to the lives of political leaders, the brute fact remains that a 'foolproof security system' for the Prime Minister and other VVIPs remains a complete chimera.[113] Even as the state struggles to be more scientific in its management of security problems, the ineffectiveness of its measures appears all the more glaring. The mode of addressing this situation is not to seek more complex technology, more repressive legislation, a larger, better-equipped and better-trained force, the isolation of VIPs, or some other solution dictated by unthinking bureaucrats and masters of realpolitik, but to begin with the recognition that there is something quite lamentable about the Indian state's attempt to take on the appearance of being 'hard' when there is too much within it that is still amenable to the lived practices, processes of accommodation, and styles of thought of an ancient and pluralistic civilization. Not every important site can be manned by security personnel, much less around the clock, and it is a pleasing thought that, amidst the current paranoia of security, the committee placed in charge of Mahatma Gandhi's samadhi at Rajghat opposed some years ago the permanent deployment of armed securitymen at the samadhi.[114] (Against this, one can set the fact that for an entire three days before Clinton's visit to India in early 2000, Rajghat was closed to the public: this represents a different form of desecration of the memory of the Father of the Nation, who, one can be reasonably certain, would have rebelled against this inexcusable privileging of foreign elites and the forcible separation of the public from those who have entered the life of 'public service'.) The question is not whether 'foolproof security' is possible, and even less how it might be achieved, but how it came to be considered desirable, and what might be the hazardous consequences of labouring for such a system of security.

The need, even craving, for security is one without which few individuals can do,[115] and the state must surely do all within its means to fulfill this need. The more expansive the notion of security, such that it would not only include freedom from the fear of political repression, but also the assurance of food, clothing, shelter, education, clean air, employment, medical facilities, and equal opportunities, the more the state is found wanting. Though it is not the Indian state alone that has been remiss in the matter of providing this more expansive notion of security to its citizens, what is indubitably certain is that a security regime, with a sensibility that thinks the lives of ordinary Indians unworthy of protection, and whose functionaries in the security business have contempt for ordinary humanity, has taken possession of this country. The 'Delhi security man', the columnist V. N. Narayanan observed, 'stands there as a symbol of the unbridgeable chasm between you and the great Indian state', and he went on to recommend that politicians rediscover the India that exists outside Delhi, and—one might add—other state capitals.[116] The delusions of grandeur from which rulers have habitually suffered are too well known to require enumeration, and we have the stellar example of Muhammad Tughlaq, who, mindful of the disobedience of his subjects in Delhi, had the entire city evacuated.[117] This option is fortunately no longer available to the political elite of Delhi, who are otherwise disposed to isolate themselves from the subjects whom they govern, and have gone as far as they can to surround themselves with the trappings of power on display. The barricades that are to be found all over Delhi *after* the assassination of a political figure, in yet another parodic display of bumbling state power, succeed only in barricading rulers from their subjects. The inaccessibility of the ruler, Elias Canetti has reminded us in *Crowds and Power*, is a mark of the power that the despot exercises; the visibility and exercise of power was, until modern times, the irrefutable manifestation of its possession by the ruler. Though the hallmark of an efficient and less oppressive system of security must remain its invisibility,[118] to Indian rulers and potentates the primary consideration is the display of sovereignty through an ostentatious demonstration of its privileges. How else are we to explain the convoy of white Ambassadors that hold up the traffic, the lecherously swerving lead cars, the screeching sirens, the gun-toting commandos, and the unwieldy barricades that have sent many an innocent man to the hospital with grave injuries? The ruling elite in India is yet to understand that power is never as effectively wielded as when it is invisible.

Never hesitant to walk alone, Gandhi nonetheless mingled with ease among large crowds of people; the politicians of today, by contrast, though they claim to be public servants, are all too eager to set themselves apart from crowds and so mark the singularity of their importance. The ironies of this contrast are all too evident, and we can easily set apart Gandhi, with his truly democratic sensibility, from the common herd of Indian politicians. It will always be claimed that, in the matter of security, this distinction cannot carry us very far, for the political realities of the present moment would have been all but inconceivable in Gandhi's time. Notwithstanding the terrors of the Partition, that was a 'softer' time; the madness—what in Hindi would be called *pagalpan*—of those killings had yet little of the professional, calculated, orchestrated, cost-effective characteristics of the pogroms of the last two decades. The political realist and anti-terrorism expert, who takes it upon himself to be the true custodian of India's future, can always point to the insurgencies in Kashmir, Punjab, and the North East, and to the insidious hand of Pakistan's Interservices Intelligence in fomenting violence, hatred, and revolution in India.[119]

Nonetheless, in the name of providing security to the political leadership, some serious and irreversible transgressions have taken place, and continue to take place with impunity. Those who speak the language of realpolitik should perhaps be reminded that each profession carries its own risks, and that men and women in public service must perforce habituate themselves to the idea that protection, particularly when it is an enormous drain on the resources of the state, is not an inalienable privilege of the life of a politician. If there is equality before the law, as Article 14 of the Indian Constitution promises, then that legislation cannot be usurped to render some people superior to others and indeed to the law, which is precisely what the entire regimen of VIP security is designed to accomplish. When Gandhi scarcely saw himself as indispensable, far much less can anyone else make that claim for himself or herself. What has been offended by the publicly enacted security fantasies of the nation-state and many of its political representatives are not only the sensibilities of a people, but the sensibilities of a civilization that has generally lived within a sense of limits, recognizing that the transgression of these limits must always lead to a reign of oppression. One form of terror cannot save us from another form of terror.

Notes

1.   See *The Pioneer* (Delhi edition), 13 August 1993, p. 1. All quotations from this paragraph and the following are drawn from the same source. Henceforth citations to Indian newspapers will always be to the Delhi edition of the newspaper, unless otherwise noted. The following abbreviations have been used in this chapter:

BSF	Border Security Force
CBI	Central Bureau of Investigation
CP	Commissioner of Police
CRPF	Central Reserve Police Force
DIG	Deputy Inspector-General (of Police)
IP	Inspector of Police
MP	Member of Parliament
NSG	National Security Guards
PM	Prime Minister
SP	Superintendent of Police
SPG	Special Protection Group
VIP	Very Important Person
VVIP	Very Very Important Person

2.   Just how resolutely pink is associated with girls and blue with boys can be gauged by the fact that in most Western countries, particularly the United States, a pink ribbon is placed at birth upon the head of a girl, just as a blue ribbon marks a new-born boy.

3.   'Tight Security at Red Fort', *Hindustan Times* (16 August 1994), p. 5, and 'I-Day fete held amid tight security', *Pioneer* (16 August 1994), p. 3.

4.   'Tight Security at Red Fort', *Hindustan Times* (16 August 1994), p. 5.

5.   In so designating it, I by no means wish to imply that the people of Kashmir do not genuinely aspire to be free, or that grave human rights violations by the Indian state have not played a critical role in further alienating the Kashmiris and encouraging secessionist tendencies.

6.   See daily newspapers, such as *Times of India*, *Hindustan Times*, and *Statesman*, for 3 December 1995.

7.   See the account by Martin Massey at <http://www.redif.com/news/may/15mass1.htm> as well as Sangeeta Mall, 'Citizens' Rights and Security of VVIPs', *Mainstream* (24 May 1997), pp. 33-34.

8.   He is also referred to in the records as Madan Lal; as is common with many Indian names, he is known by his first name, and throughout I shall refer to him as Madanlal.

9.   Justice J. L. Kapur, *Report of [the] Commission of Inquiry into [the] Conspiracy to Murder Mahatma Gandhi*, 6 volumes published in two parts (New Delhi: Government of India, 1970), Part I, p. 13.

10.   For a detailed study of the circumstances under which Gandhi commenced his last fast, and the politics of fasting, see Vinay Lal, 'Gandhi's Last Fast', *Gandhi Marg* 11, 2 (July-September 1989), pp. 171-191.

11.   Kapur, *Report of Commission of Inquiry*, Part I, p. 207; Part II, p. 15.

12.   Ibid., Part I, p. 190. This becomes apparent upon reading Gandhi's *Delhi Diary* (Ahmedabad: Navajivan, 1948), and virtually any other work on the Partition of India.

13.   Ibid., Part I, p. 193. With respect to the darshan of the Mahatma, no better interpretive study exists than Shahid Amin, 'Gandhi as Mahatma: Gorakhpur District, Eastern UP, 1921-22', Ranajit Guha ed., *Subaltern Studies III* (Delhi: Oxford University Press, 1984).

14.   Cf. Dennis Dalton, *Mahatma Gandhi: Nonviolent Power in Action* (New York: Columbia University Press, 1993), p. 163.

15.   Kapur, *Report of Commission of Inquiry*, Part I, pp. 208-213.

16.   Ibid., p. 192.

17.   Ibid., p. 198.

18.   Ibid., pp. 208-213.

19.   Ibid., p. 204.

20.   Ibid., p. 207.

21.   Ibid., p. 208.

22.   Ibid., pp. 193-96. See also p. 197. Manu relates that, just before his assassination, Gandhi scolded Abba and her for not having reminded him that he was running late for his prayer meeting. Gandhi told Manu, 'I do not like being late for the prayer meeting. Today's delay is due to your negligence . . . .

Even a minute's delay for the prayer causes me great discomfort.' See Manubehn Gandhi, *The End of an Epoch*, Gopalkrishna Gandhi tr. (Ahmedabad: Navajivan Publishing House, 1962), p. 41. Gandhi's notion of time, and his mode of dealing with it, is a subject for another paper. But as the matter of security has a great deal to do with the manner in which Gandhi associated with the masses, it is well to remember that unlike modern politicians, who are likely to keep crowds waiting as a measure of their importance, Gandhi was most particular in being as observant of time with the masses as he would have been with dignitaries and leaders. In more than one way, Gandhi kept time with the masses; similarly, I would suggest, he relinquished space to them, whereas the characteristic move of the colonialist has been the conquest of space. The standardization of time over the last 150 years points to attempts not merely to regulate and synchronize time, but also to ensure the predominance of one conception of time over competing notions of time. For an extended discussion, see Vinay Lal, 'Relocating Time: The Politics of Time at the Cusp of the "Millennium"', *Humanscape* 6, no. 12 (December 1999), pp. 6 -13.

23.   Kapur, *Report of Commission of Inquiry*, Part I, pp. 217, 211, 209.

24.   Ibid., pp. 217-18.

25.   Ibid., pp. 222-23.

26.   Ibid., pp. 225-26.

27.   Ibid., p. 226.

28.   Ibid., p. 219; cf. also p. 223, where Justice Kapur says that 'obtrusive interference' with his way of life would have been 'promptly resented' by Gandhi.

29.   Ibid., pp. 224-25.

30.   Ibid., p. 226.

31.   Ibid., p. 217.

32.   According to Justice Kapur, 'Fortunately after the murder high ranking police officers who knew something about security and were themselves active and alert were called in and the danger to the Cabinet Ministers was thus averted.' Ibid., p. 221. Writing to the premiers of the various provinces, Nehru averted to a 'deliberate *coup d'état* . . . involving the killing of several persons and the promotion of general disorder to enable the particular group concerned to seize power. The conspiracy appears to have been a fairly widespread one, spreading to some of the states.' See in G. Parthasarathi ed., *Jawaharlal Nehru, Letters to Chief Ministers 1947-64* (Delhi: Oxford University Press, 1985), vol. I: 1947-1949, p. 57. But it is surely pertinent to add that the same ideological reasons which led to Gandhi's assassination cannot be said to have existed with reference to other political leaders; quite to the contrary, the greater

majority of them would have found Godse's defense of the strong nation-state and the projects of modernization and industrialization eminently reasonable. Consequently, the entire narrative of a plot to eliminate other political leaders should be dismissed as largely a fiction. I cannot, however, here discuss whether the alleged conspiracy did exist, but suffice to note that the 'conspiracy motif' has always furnished the strongest grounds in official discourse for state repression, curtailment of civil liberties, and the paranoia of security. On the pretext of dealing with terrorism and political conspiracies, the state can arrogate to itself powers that constitute a terror greater than any terror they are designed to alleviate. For a greater elaboration of this point, see Vinay Lal, 'Anti-Terrorist Legislation: A Comparative Study of India, U.K. and Sri Lanka', *Lokayan Bulletin* 11, 1 (July-August 1994), pp. 5-24.

33.   Kapur, *Report of Commission of Inquiry*, Part I, p. 226.

34.   The category of VIP appears to have been reserved for Central Ministers and perhaps a few other persons (such as the Chief Justice) in Nehru's time. That is the usage intended in this paragraph. Now the designation VVIP plays the same part, given that even members of the cabinet in state governments, many of them with proven criminal records, have arrogated to themselves, or have obsequiously been conferred with, the designation of VIP. There is clearly no dearth of VIPs in India today!

35.   Ibid., p. 221.

36.   S. Venugopal Rao, 'Nehru and I', in S. K. Ghosh ed., *Police Administrators: Reminiscences* (New Delhi: Ashish Publishing House, 1989), pp. 160-176.

37.   Gurmukh Singh, 'Our VIPs are very important parasites', *Sunday Times of India* (10 December 1995), p. 17. His formulation is not particularly helpful, as it leaves the question of what is a proper 'requirement' open to the attack that as the threats have become more pronounced, the PM and VIPs are deserving of greater security today.

38.   *Lok Sabha Debates* 39, no. 51 (11 May 1988), col. 273.

39.   Mrs Gandhi had Sikh bodyguards for a number of years preceding the assault upon the Golden Temple in 1984. At least Bruce Chatwin found this to be the case when he visited her shortly before the election of 1980. See Bruce Chatwin, 'On the Road with Mrs. Gandhi', *Granta*, no. 26 (Spring 1989), p. 125.

40.   'Killers brought back by P.M.', *Times of India* (1 Nov. 1984), p. 7; G. C. Dutt, 'My Experiences of Police Work', in Ghosh ed., *Police Administrators*, p. 69.

41.   G. C. Dutt, 'My Experiences of Police Work', in Ghosh, ed., *Police Administrators*, p. 70.

42.   'A Security Disaster', *Times of India* (2 November 1984), p. 6.

43.   These points are made by Dutt, 'My Experiences of Police Work', pp. 70-71.

44. 'Bill on PM's security moved in L[ok] S[abha]', *Times of India* (5 May 1988), p. 5.

45. The protection of the President is generally entrusted to the 'President's Bodyguard', though SPG personnel have been assigned to that duty as well. A capsule history of SPG is furnished at <http:www.bharat-rakshak.com/LAND-FORCES/Special-Forces/SPG.html>

46. 'PM, VIPs escape attempt on life', *Times of India* (3 October 1986), p. 1.

47. K. C. Khanna, 'Protecting Precious Lives: A "Soft" State Cannot Endure', *Times of India* (7 October 1986); 'The Shots at Rajghat', editorial in *Times of India* (3 October 1986); A. R. Wig, 'Glaring loopholes in security', *Hindustan Times* (5 October 1986), p. 5.

48. 'Securitymen not firing fit', *Times of India* (10 October 1986), p. 1.

49. Apparently, on a number of separate occasions in the months prior to the attempt on the PM's life, securitymen attached to VIPs had succeeded in shooting themselves accidentally, suggesting that 'the Delhi police securitymen are not very comfortable with the weapons with which they are supposed to train regularly.' Ibid.

50. For details of the Ribeiro assassination attempt, see 'Ribeiro escapes bid on life; two cops killed', *Times of India* (4 October 1986), p. 1.

51. See *Hindustan Times*, 4 October and 5 October 1986, p. 9 and p. 5, respectively.

52. 'Ribeiro escapes bid on life; two cops killed', *Times of India* (4 October 1986), p. 1.

53. 'Security Shambles', *Hindustan Times* (4 October 1986), p. 9.

54. 'SPG officers inspected Raj Ghat', *Times of India* (7 October 1986), p. 3; 'Karamjit's associates held for questioning', *Times of India* (5 October 1986), p. 3.

55. 'Serious security lapse', *Times of India* (3 October 1986), p. 1.

56. 'The Shots at Rajghat', editorial in *Times of India* (3 October 1986), p. 8.

57. 'PM assailant from Sangrur', and 'Gunman confuses interrogators', both in *Times of India* (4 and 3 October 1986), p. 1 and p. 3, respectively.

58. 'Shots aimed at PM, says eyewitnesses', *Times of India* (3 October 1986), p. 3.

59. 'I wanted to kill PM: Karamjit', *Times of India* (4 October 1986), p.9

60. 'Karamjit's associates held for questioning', *Times of India* (5 October 1986), p. 3.

61. '5 held for bid on PM's life', *Times of India* (8 October 1986), p. 1.

62. Wig, 'Glaring loopholes in security', *Hindustan Times* (5 October 1986), p. 5.

63. 'Foreign hand in plot suspected', *Times of India* (4 October 1986), p.1.

64. *Times of India* (3 October 1986), p. 9.

65. Rahul Datta, 'Breaches PM security with a camera', *Hindustan Times* (2 Sept. 1994), p. 1.

66.   Girja Shankar Kaura, 'Journalists expose rum-drinking MP', *Hindustan Times* (25 Aug. 1994), p. 10.

67.   K. N. Malik, 'Foreign hand in plot suspected', *Times of India* (4 October 1986), p. 1; 'World community shocked', *Times of India* (3 October 1986), p. 9. The five-column headline in *The Guardian* (London) described the view of the British press: 'Gunman misses Gandhi after security guards blunder.' *The Times* [of London] opined that the 'worldwide concern that even so unprofessional an assassination attempt has aroused illustrates the speed with which Rajiv Gandhi has established himself as a world leader.' What is most arresting in the reaction of the English press is the depiction of India as a dynastic democracy, a country unable to prevent itself from being unstitched without the Congress, and in particular without the leadership of the Nehru family. This made the assassination attempt especially troublesome, as India stood on the verge of losing not only its political leader, but a man on whom hinged, in the words of *The Guardian*, 'the survival of coherent national politics across the subcontinent.' See 'British Press critical of security lapses', *Hindustan Times* (4 October 1986), p. 6. It is India's fate, on this view, that it requires a despot.

68.   'British TV shows incident', *Times of India* (3 October 1986), p. 9.

69.   'Gautam Kaul, others suspended', *Times of India* (3 October 1986), p. 1; 'Panel to probe security lapse at Rajghat', *Times of India* (8 October 1986), p. 1; 'Major reshuffle in Delhi police soon', *Times of India* (4 October 1986), p. 1; 'Delhi policemen's leave canceled', *Times of India* (5 October 1986), p. 3. It was imperative for the police and intelligence agencies, at this juncture, to look *busy*: thus, as the *Times of India* reported, CBI and IB officers visited Raj Ghat 'and took measurements of the structure from where the suspect had fired and the spot where some of the pellets had landed', though what was to be gained by these measurements was scarcely conveyed.

70.   'Security set up to be overhauled', *Times of India* (5 October 1986), p. 9. See G. C. Dutt, 'My Experiences of Police Work', in Ghosh, ed., *Police Administrators*, p. 68.

71.   'Security plan being reviewed', *Times of India* (3 October 1986), p. 7.

72.   'Security set up to be overhauled', *Times of India* (5 October 1986), p. 9; 'Unified security outfit soon', *Times of India* (7 October 1986), p. 1.

73.   'Unified security outfit soon', *Times of India* (7 October 1986), p. 1; see also 'Security plan being reviewed', *Times of India* (3 October 1986), p. 7.

74.   As Chidambaram was to explain subsequently, the bill sought to constitute the SPG as an 'Armed Force of the Union within the meaning of article 33 of [the Indian] constitution.' *Lok Sabha Debates* 39, no. 51 (11 May 1988), col. 285.

75. *Lok Sabha Debates* 39, no. 50 (10 May 1988), col. 450; 'PM security Bill introduced', *Hindustan Times* (5 May 1988), p. 9.

76. *Lok Sabha Debates* 39, no. 50 (10 May 1988), cols. 451-54.

77. Ibid., no. 51 (11 May 1988), cols. 242-43.

78. Ibid., cols. 245-46, 249-58. Reddy noted that the American Secret Service did not exist exclusively to protect the President of the US; similarly, the SDECE, Scotland Yard, and KGB, which provided protection to the head of state in France, Britain, and the (then) Soviet Union, respectively, offered security to other political leaders as well, besides fulfilling numerous other functions.

79. Ibid., col. 295; see also 'Security Bill passed', *Hindustan Times* (13 May 1988), p. 20.

80. For details, see Chand Joshi, 'Rajiv Assassinated', *Hindustan Times* (22 May 1991), p. 1, and 'Bomb was strapped on woman's body', *Hindustan Times* (24 May 1991), p. 18. The lengthiest accounts of the assassination are furnished in the reports of the two commissions of inquiry, headed by Justice J. S. Verma of the Supreme Court and the retired Chief Justice of the Delhi High Court, M. C. Jain, appointed by the Government of India. For the circumstances under which two commissions came to be appointed, see the Interim Report of the Jain Commission (August 1997), Chapter I, sec. 1, 'Genesis of Commission of Inquiry.'

81. 'Red alert declared', and 'Security of VVIPs tightened', both in *Hindustan Times* (22 and 23 May 1991), p. 1 and p. 5, respectively. Sonia Gandhi and her two children continue to receive SPG cover by Black Cat commandos; though she is statutorily entitled to such security arrangements, by the previously referred to amendment of the SPG in 1991, which extended SPG protection to former PMs and their families, there is no demonstrable threat to her life, or to the lives of her two children. The SPG, reserved for the PM, former PMs, and their families, costs the exchequer rupees 340 million annually as of 1995; in 1997-98 budget, the amount had been raised to Rs 751 million. See the 'Special Report' on Security in *Sunday Times of India* (10 December 1995), p. 17.

82. From the *Hindustan Times*: 'Capital tense but peaceful' (23 May 1991), p. 5; 'Massive security cover to funeral procession today' (23 May 1991), p. 3.

83. The Jain Commission passed unusually strong strictures on V. P. Singh and barely stopped short of laying the blame for Rajiv's murder on him. Justice Jain took it upon himself to inquire 'whether Shri V. P. Singh was actuated by malice, bias or animus in not providing security of such nature and level as would have protected Shri Rajiv Gandhi', and declared himself as not persuaded that the SPG act could not have been amended [as it would be after Rajiv's death] to provide for the security of Rajiv [a former Prime Minister] and his

family, or that some other security arrangement at the Central government level could not have been devised for him. Justice Jain thought that the 'threat scenario of Shri Rajiv Gandhi' was not taken seriously, and that the 'concerned bureaucrats', in the changed political climate of the day, decided to serve their present 'political masters', that is V. P. Singh and others in the Janata government. Justice Jain found the 'required seriousness, anxiety and concern' among members of V. P. Singh's government 'lacking', and characterized the relations between V. P. Singh and Rajiv Gandhi as 'strained', 'far from normal and satisfactory.' In conclusion, 'the consequence (assassination) may not have been intended [by V. P. Singh] but the devising of such an inadequate alternative security scheme resulted into such an unintended consequence.' See *Jain Commission Interim Report*, Chapter II, Sec. 34, accessible on the internet at <http://www.tamilnation.org/intframe/india/jaincommission/vol14>. The politics of the Jain Commission, and the immense controversy raised by the report, are complex matters around which an entire volume could be written.

84. 'File submitted to Jain panel fabricated: Vinod Pande', *Statesman* (22 September 1995), p. 9.

85. Rahul Pathak, 'Everybody's to blame: The Verma report carries disturbing implications', *India Today* (15 January 1993), p. 53. Women were not searched, largely because the idea of a *female terrorist* appears to be something of an impossibility, one might even say an oxymoron, particularly in a country like India where the principal associations of the word 'female' are with notions of fertility, fecundity, maternity, nurturance, and so forth. The trope of a female terrorist is, however, quite old in the Indian context: she makes her appearance in Tagore's story *Char Adhyay*, 'Four Chapters', and the revolutionary armed struggle in India against colonial rule, the participants of which were characterized as 'terrorists' and 'extremists' by the British, had within its ranks a not inconsiderable number of women. Suicide bombers among the ranks of the LTTE have been largely women: this suggests not so much the exceptional bravery of women, though this should not be discounted, as much as the extreme cynicism and opportunism of the LTTE leadership, which has understood not only that women can permeate security cordons more easily, but that women might perhaps with greater disregard for human life be manipulated in the name of the nation.

86. 'Massive security for first phase of polling', *Hindustan Times* (20 May 1991), p. 1.

87. The assassination of Rabin, one then hoped, would have the effect of diminishing Israel's reputation as a 'hard' state, and one expected that the ambitions of India's security cops to outdo Israel's allegedly impregnable

security apparatus would be suitably curtailed. However, judging from the vastly increased collaboration between India and Israel since the BJP's two recent electoral triumphs, India is evidently still inclined to consider Israel as a tough state that brooks no nonsense from terrorists. Israel has been delighted by the attention bestowed on its retired security personnel by the BJP government and by recent pacts for enhanced security and intelligence-sharing signed between the two countries. For all of the BJP's advocacy of swadeshi, it tends to go outside India for 'consultants' and 'experts'. Meanwhile, with respect to the US, it is worthwhile noting that it has required an ultra-nationalist government in India to allow the FBI to commence operations in India. Following Clinton's visit in March 2000, the Indian government reported that the FBI would be opening an office in Delhi.

88. Various figures have been furnished about the percentage of the Delhi police force deployed for VIP security. Home Minister L. K. Advani, speaking in the Lok Sabha on 8 December 1999, stated that 7,000 policemen were entrusted with the responsibility for VIP security out of a police force of 57,000 in Delhi; however, a newspaper article later that month described 10,000 policemen from the Delhi police as engaged in VIP security duties. Neither figure appears to include the 3,000 members of the SPG, who are largely stationed in Delhi. See *Lok Sabha Debates*, Session II (Winter), 8 December 1999, accessible on the internet at <http://alfa.nic.in/lsdeb/ls13/ses2/3608129901.htm> and Inder Sawhney, 'Scale down VIP security', *Times of India* (23 December 1999).

89. See 'Special Report' on security, *Sunday Times of India* (10 December 1995), p. 17, and Sawhney, 'Scale down VIP security', *Times of India* (23 December 1999).

90. 'Special Report' on security, *Sunday Times of India* (10 December 1995), p. 17. It is rather ironic that Seshan should now have become a resounding critic of the terror generated by VIP security: see T. N. Seshan, 'Internal security: a picture of anarchy'. The National Security Guards (NSG) was created by the National Security Guard Act of 1985 as a special anti-hijacking and counter-terrorist force; its use for the protection of VIPs is not within the letter of the law. That is not the NSG's only problem: there are no Sikhs or Muslims among its 7,500 members, who are all Hindus. The 'communalization' of the various security forces is a subject on which little or no work has been done, and figures are not easily available; I have, as a consequence, desisted at this moment from drawing out the troubling implications of such 'communalization' of the forces. See Patwant Singh, 'A contempt for law', *Hindustan Times* (3 October 1995), p. 13. For a hagiographic view of the NSG, see <http://

www.bharat-rakshak.com/LAND-FORCES/Special-Forces/NSG.html>
Strictly speaking, it is NSG personnel who are referred to as 'Black Cats',
though sometimes the designation is used to include SPG forces.

91. Ravi Bhatia, 'PM security invades Gymkhana privacy', *Times of India* (5 October
     1988), p. 1.

92. The diversion of traffic on special occasions, such as Republic Day, is scarcely
     an unusual step, but what has not been so common is the measures adopted
     to check vehicles. See, for example, 'Traffic restrictions for I-Day', *Times of India*
     (15 August 1988), p. 3; 'Traffic curbs for Independence Day', *Times of India* (14
     August 1989), p. 3; 'Tight security for I-Day function', *Times of India* (15
     August 1990), p. 10.

93. 'Cops given time to produce missing couple', and 'Search throws life out of
     gear', both in *The Pioneer* (23 Sept. 1993), p. 1.

94. *Lok Sabha Debates* (11 May 1988), col. 282.

95. See 'Special Report' on security, *Sunday Times of India* (10 December 1995), p.
     17.

96. 'Cops mum on rape case', and 'Grandson of Beant Singh, 2 cops held',
     Hindustan Times (5 and 9 Sept. 1994), p. 1 and p. 1, respectively. The immunity
     from prosecution for heinous wrongdoing sought, or rather assumed, by sons
     of ministers is a common motif of the popular Hindi film.

97. See, for example, 'Black Cats maul two Delhi cops', *Hindustan Times* (7 May
     1988), p. 20.

98. This paragraph relies largely upon Dilip Awasthi, 'Gunning for Cover', *India
     Today* (15 August 1993), pp. 58-63; see also Bishwadeep Ghosh, 'Armed
     securitymen a status symbol', *Pioneer* (17 August 1994), p. 5.

99. 'A "total relook" of VIP security', *The Hindu* (8 February 2000); 'New VIP
     security policy', *The Tribune* (Chandigarh), 8 February 2000; and, for a more
     detailed consideration of security considerations in a modern democracy, see
     P. L. Prasada Rao, 'VIP security in a democratic polity', *The Hindu* (6 June
     2000).

     The Ministry of Home Affairs' web site makes available the 'New Policy
     on Security of Individuals', 7 February 2000: <http://mha.nic.in/vip.htm>
     Too much should not be made of this 'new' policy, though the document
     suggests a new awareness on the part of the state that security should neither
     be obtrusive nor an extraordinary drain on the financial resources of the state.
     Para (1) notes that 'in public perception the term VIP security has termed to
     connote a picture of more VIP than security', and in an effort to suggest that
     such security will no longer be manipulated by politicians as a sign of 'social
     status', it states that the nomenclature of 'VIP security' is being abandoned

for 'personal security'. With respect to practical measures, about whose implementation—if at all that has occurred—little is known, the new policy proposes cutting down the number of individuals entitled to NSG security protection from nineteen to eleven, the number of VIP protectees in Delhi from 472 to 355, the elimination of perks to such protectees and their guards, a semi-annual review of the list of protectees, and so on. This is the sort of mechanical tinkering that one has come to expect of democracies that purport to be sensitive to public concerns, and it is striking, of course, that the more far-reaching questions of security for ordinary citizens in all realms of life are never entertained in such policy documents—not to speak of various other political, socio-cultural, and epistemological problems of the sort that I have attempted to raise.

100. 'No gunmen for VVIPs on foreign jaunts', *Indian Express* (10 September 1993), p. 10.

101. Amita Malik, the film critic, has pointed to an extraordinary lapse of security to which she was witness. At the function for the National Film Awards at Delhi's Siri Fort Auditorium in 1991, at which the President of India presided, the power supply failed while the President was delivering his address, and the auditorium was suddenly plunged into darkness. The generators did not come on for several minutes. More horrifyingly, Malik noticed that the President's security staff failed to surround him: 'The security kept on standing', she noted with evident consternation, 'where they were presumably still star-gazing. There did not seem to be any state of alert on their part, certainly not visibly.' See 'What price security?', *Hindustan Times* (Magazine Supplement), 25 May 1991, p. 2.

102. 'IA plane hijacker shot', and 'A case of misplaced sympathy', both in *The Hindu* (Madras), International Edition (1 May 1993), p. 1.

103. On the unsuccessful attempt on Bitta's life, see newspaper reports for 12-13 September 1993, and in particular 'Frenzied meetings on nationwide security', *Pioneer* (13 Sept. 1993), p. 1.

104. 'VIP security has become a sham, says expert', *Pioneer* (14 September 1993), p. 4.

105. See, for example, Chandan Mitra, 'Why is the intelligentsia soft on terrorism?', *Times of India* (5 May 1988), p. 3.

106. K. C. Khanna, 'Protecting Precious Lives: A "Soft" State Cannot Endure', *Times of India* (7 October 1986), p. 8.

107. It was only on a rare occasion, such as on 15 August 1989, that Rajiv Gandhi addressed the nation without being sheltered by a bulletproof shield. See 'Despite the threat, there was no shield', *Times of India* (16 August 1989), p. 3.

'At the end of the speech,' added the journalist, 'the Prime Minister said 'Jai Hind' ['Long Live India'] but the crowd failed to respond loudly. He exhorted them to say it again remarking '*Maja nahin aya*'. Even the second 'Jai Hind' was quite feeble and consisted of mostly children's and women's voices.'

108. 'Strict security during parade', *Times of India* (27 January 1987), p. 3; 'Parade reflects new mood of the nation', *Times of India* (27 January 1985), p. 1.

109. 'Special air security steps for I-Day', *Times of India* (15 August 1989), p. 1; see also 'Flying VIPs through thick and thin', *Times of India* (15 August 1989), p. 18, and 'Special security force for airports', *The Hindu* International Edition (8 May 1993), p. 5.

110. 'Security gadgets on display', *Times of India* (4 October 1989).

111. 'Even dogs are used for VIP security in Kerala', originally published in *Times of India* (1997), accessed on the internet: <http://www.kerala.org/news/online/1997/march/news/news11.html>

112. Ajit S. Gopal, 'Computers to Fight Terrorism', *Times of India* (28 June 1988), p. 4.

113. Such is the demand made by, among others, A. R. Wig, 'Glaring loopholes in security', *Hindustan Times* (5 October 1986), p. 5.

114. 'No security set-up at Rajghat', *Hindustan Times* (4 October 1986), p. 3.

115. For some considerations on this, see R. N. Berki, *Security and Society: Reflections on Law, Order and Politics* (London: J. M. Dent & Sons Ltd, 1986).

116. V. N. Narayanan, 'Rediscovering India', *Hindustan Times* (11 September 1994), p. 13.

117. Hermann Kulke and Dietmar Rothermund, *A History of India* (3rd ed., London: Routledge, 1998); more enlightening is Elias Canetti, *Crowds and Power* (New York: Seabury Press, 1978), pp. 424-34.

118. In India this is all the more difficult, as most security guards, not excepting those who are attached to VIPs, come from lower-class working families, and the exercise of power is to them a novelty. By this I mean also to suggest that the business of security guards, much like any other business or state enterprise, has its own political economy.

119. K. Subrahmanyan, 'The trial of terror', *Sunday Times of India* (3 September 1995), p. 17.

III

GANDHIAN HERMENEUTICS/HERMENEUTIC GANDHIISM

Five

NAKEDNESS, NON-VIOLENCE, AND BRAHMACHARYA: GANDHI'S EXPERIMENTS IN CELIBATE SEXUALITY

The life of Mohandas Karamchand Gandhi is certainly as well-documented as any life of modern times. There are nearly 1000 biographies of him in English alone, and Gandhi himself was extraordinarily prolific, judging from the 100 volumes of his collected writings. Given the monumental nature of the record of his life, and the scrutiny to which it has been subjected, it is all the more surprising that one of the most critical, and from a certain standpoint most disturbing, events in what is sometimes seen as a saintly life should have received so little attention. In the last few years before his assassination in January 1948, but most certainly no earlier than the death of his wife in 1944, Gandhi began the practice of taking naked young women to bed with him at night. Gandhi, who never wore many clothes to begin with, would himself be naked on such occasions. Three women—his grandnieces Abha and Manu, and his personal physician of sorts, Sushila Nayyar—were involved in this 'experiment' in brahmacharya, which with erroneous simplicity is rendered as 'celibacy'. Gandhi described brahmacharya as the 'search [for] Brahma [truth]', and thus, in its most ordinarily accepted sense, the 'control in thought, word and action, of all the senses at all times and in all places.'[1] Brahmacharya, the elimination of all desire, was to be obtained by diving into, and realizing, the inner self: and it is this spiritual discipline that furnished the non-violent resister with true armour. 'Without Brahmacharya the Satyagrahi will have no lustre,' wrote Gandhi, 'no inner strength to stand unarmed against the whole world . . . . His strength will fail him at the right moment.'[2]

Many years after Gandhi's death, Sushila Nayyar provided an account of Gandhi's brahmacharya experiments. It is she who first shared Gandhi's bed, but as she was to recall, she never experienced any sexual desire, and felt the same way as she would with her mother. At the outset it was no more than a part of Gandhi's programme of 'nature cure'. Gandhi might ask her to lie on his back if his back ached, and Nayyar reports that Gandhi would even go to sleep while she was perched on his back. Subsequently, more often that not, it was Manu who shared Gandhi's bed with him. At first Manu had slipped under the covers with her clothes on, and apparently 'was snoring within minutes of getting into his bed.' Then, Nayyar says, Gandhi told Manu that their purity had to be subjected to the 'ultimate test', and they were to offer the 'purest of sacrifices'. He suggested that they 'now both start sleeping naked.'[3] Manu, reports Nayyar, readily consented.

There was never any suggestion that Gandhi made any improper advances towards Manu or the other two women who on occasion had slept with him, or that the encounter was in the remotest matter sexual, or even that he had entertained 'impure' thoughts towards Manu and the other women. Gandhi himself eventually made this matter public knowledge and was to write voluminously on the nature of his experiment, though in this matter there appears to have been some unusual dissimulation on his part, insofar as initially he kept the matter of his sharing a bed with a fully-clothed woman a secret. 'She often used to sleep with me to keep me warm', Gandhi said of a fellow ashramite by the name of Prabhavati, 'even before I was conscious that I was making an experiment.'[4] He may have suspected that this narrative would seem quite implausible to others, as indeed it did, the common rejoinder being that Gandhi had merely to take recourse to more blankets to keep himself warm. Later, Gandhi would admit that he had erred only in not publicly divulging his practices: this not only allowed others to place on his actions whatever constructions they thought desirable, but the principle that the seeker of truth can have nothing to hide had also been violated.[5]

In late 1946, then, when Gandhi's brahmacharya experiment came to the fore, he was 77 years old, and it was 40 years since he had engaged in a sexual relationship with any woman, his own wife not excepted. Independence was on the horizon, and Gandhi had already, by some portion of the population, been assimilated into the pantheon not merely of the immortals, but of renowned saints and even gods. It is not for nothing that he had been christened a 'mahatma' by his great countryman, Rabindranath Tagore, three decades ago; and as the eminent philosopher and cultural critic Ananda Coomaraswamy reminds us, mahatmas or 'great souls' are those who, though having become liberated in this life, *jivan-mukta*, undergo acute suffering to bring succour to ordinary men and women.[6] Yet, in the waning years of his life, as he was receiving in some respects the greatest accolades that had ever been showered on him, and as he honourably stood aside from the struggles for power that engaged the attention of the political leaders who were about to condemn the country to vivisection, Gandhi was prepared to face the public ignominy that knowledge of his sexual experiments was bound to produce. Indeed, in an instant he lost many of his friends, and many of his most trusted disciples and colleagues were to forsake him. Many Indian women, who have expressed intense admiration for Gandhi, construe the Mahatma's practice of taking naked young women to bed as an unaccountable blot on an otherwise noble life, and he has not been forgiven this massive indiscretion. The author of the earliest, and what remains to this day the most exhaustive, account of Gandhi's experiments in sexuality was to note much later that he had to publish his account at his own expense, as 'after Gandhiji's death everyone wanted to suppress all further discussion of the brahmacharya experiments.'[7] Many of the acclaimed biographies of Gandhi of recent years have nothing to say of this matter,[8] and the most detailed monograph to explore Gandhi's relations with women, though authored by an Indian woman activist and scholar,[9] is stunningly silent on this question while being quite profuse in its delineation and critique of Gandhi's views on sexuality and sexual conduct.

One might have expected that Gandhi's detractors,[10] of whom there are many, would have pounced upon the Mahatma for harbouring sexual fantasies in the ripe years of his life while proclaiming himself to be a celibate, for compromising the lives of very young women, and for exploiting the vastly iniquitous power relationship that obtained between him and the young women. However, even his critics, whether it be the Marxists, Indian liberals, or Hindu militants such as his assassin, Nathuram Godse, have always understood that though agreement with Gandhi's political and economic views was never to be expected, and that though his political conduct may be open to question, his personal life was unimpeachable.[11] Gandhi would appear to present an extraordinarily easy target to his critics, but in his death, as much as in his life, he continues to confound his opponents regardless of the shade of their opinion. Indeed, neither Gandhi's advocates, nor his detractors, have had an easy time of him. The upholders of tradition thought they had found in Gandhi, who was opposed to violent revolutionary change and even declared himself to be a follower of the sanatan dharma, or the eternal faith, a reliable ally. But Gandhi had little use for institutional religion, paid little or no heed to caste practices, and unequivocally declared that the authority of the scriptures was to be abrogated whenever the scriptures advocated positions reprehensible to the conscience.[12] It is Gandhi's contribution to social reform, his efforts to improve the position of women and 'backward classes', and his advocacy of religious harmony that endeared him to the modernizers; and yet these very modernizers are compelled to castigate Gandhi for his refusal to endorse modern industrial civilization, his critique of scientism, his supposed naiveté about the nature of the modern world and realpolitik, and his seemingly ineffective and conciliatory insistence on persuasion, faith, discipline, and the adherence to non-violence and truth as the preconditions for radical change.

Gandhi has, to modernizers such as his own 'disciple' Jawaharlal Nehru and the Nobel Laureate Amartya Sen, too much semblance to a relic of some bygone age.[13] His opposition to industrialization, and his purported defence of the bourgeois order, always made him an abhorrent figure to the Marxists,[14] but lately Indian Marxists are discovering that Gandhi was more attuned to the problems of caste and class in India than their own revolutionary theorists, and that India's deeply syncretistic traditions may be more effective in combating the resurgence of Hindu militant ideologies than secularism of the Western variety. This same dilemma has confronted the feminists. While berating Gandhi for holding to conventional views about the relative duties of men and women, for his failure to recognize female sexuality, and for his apparent willingness to have women be confined to the prescribed realms of marriage, wifehood, motherhood, and domesticity, Indian feminists nonetheless concede that Gandhi was, paradoxically, instrumental in bringing women into the nationalist movement and allowing them a significant public space, much as he laid the groundwork for the Indian women's movement by stressing the equality of men and women, rendering respectable the decision of women to forego marriage for other ends, and holding men to the same standards of moral conduct and responsibility to which women were bound.[15]

Gandhi has never been, in consequence, easily appropriable, and both his admirers and critics have found that wrestling with the Mahatma generates acute anxiety. What is, in many respects, the most extraordinary episode in his life must present even graver problems of interpretation, just as it produces a great deal of unease. That, however, can be no warrant for not examining the nature of Gandhi's experiment, its political consequences and moral implications, and the complicated cultural history and logic that informed his practices. It is not pleasing to the self-appointed guardians of his memory and reputation, particularly those who have devoted their lives to what they perceive to be Gandhian causes, or who have for long been associated with various Gandhian institutions, that Gandhi should be associated with what, at least in ignorance, may be taken as unsavoury incidents, just as his status as Father of the Nation appears to demand that only a hagiographic portrait of Gandhi should be allowed to circulate. One American journalist who knew Gandhi well maintains that 'probably we shall never know the whole truth about Gandhi's "experiments" with lying naked with naked women in the evening of his life,'[16] while a renowned Indian scholar who was Gandhi's associate in 1946-47 feels that the wall of silence will never be brought down, as 'the wish to be truthful died in our country with Gandhiji. It was never very strong, even among his disciples.'[17] As Gandhi himself argued, it is not given to humankind ever to know the 'whole truth'; nonetheless, an understanding of Gandhi's experiment in what may be called 'celibate sexuality' allows us to probe the extent of his engagement with Indian sexual, political, and spiritual traditions, and to consider how far his insights into sexuality extend beyond parameters that have seldom been conceived even by the proponents of free love. As I will argue, Gandhi takes us into that realm of the politics of the body where 'woman' and 'man' must be reconfigured, and in this sense he provides a striking illustration of the manner in which the post-modern is already prefigured in the pre-modern.

I

THE VOW OF BRAHMACHARYA AND THE COMPANY OF WOMEN

On 22 February 1944, Kasturba Gandhi died in the Aga Khan's Palace in Poona as a prisoner under British custody. A well-known photograph of the Mahatma taken at this time shows a forlorn and utterly dejected Gandhi sitting by his wife's deathbed, almost unable to comprehend the enormity of his loss.[18] Through sixty-two years of a long and, what was at first, a tumultuous married life the two had developed a friendship, association, and political companionship unusual in the annals of Indian marriage. Their early years of married life were spent largely in separation, as Gandhi left for London to pursue his studies, and then took up a career in South Africa. Nevertheless, five years after his marriage at the age of thirteen, Gandhi was already a father; and over the course of the next thirteen years, Kasturba was to give birth to three more sons.

In 1906, when he was thirty-seven years old, Gandhi, the father of four children, took a lifelong vow to abjure from all sexual relations with his wife and indeed any other woman. He had first decided upon this course of action in 1901, and it may have been, as one scholar has conjectured, his reason for not wanting Kasturba and their children to join him in South Africa upon his return to that country.[19] The presence of his wife, Gandhi might have felt, would weaken his desire to abjure any sexual contact with her. But Gandhi was unable to keep to his resolve, and at least intermittently must have continued to maintain sexual relations with Kasturba. Finally, in 1906, as he was about to launch a major non-violent campaign to resist the 'harassing and degrading restrictions in South Africa' to which Indians were subject,[20] Gandhi decided to embrace brahmacharya, or complete celibacy. Gandhi's autobiography suggests that Kasturba was of the same mind as her husband, but it is not quite clear how far Kasturba was consulted before Gandhi reached his monumental decision. He might not have thought her acquiescence to his decision as critical, as at this point in his life he appears to have held the view that 'husband and wife do not have to obtain each other's consent for practicing brahmacharya': 'mutual consent is essential for intercourse, but no consent is necessary for abstention.'[21] The author of an eight-volume biography of Gandhi, who aims at sketching a hagiographic profile of the Mahatma as the man who was destined to free India from the servitude of British rule, is extraordinarily laconic about Gandhi's assumption of celibacy. He notes that Gandhi discussed 'the vow of brahmacharya with his intimate co-workers and conveyed his resolution to Kasturbai.' One might have thought that Gandhi would discuss the matter with Kasturba and convey his resolution, insofar as it had to be conveyed to anyone else, to his fellow workers. His biographer adds: 'Thus brahmacharya which Gandhi had been observing "willy-nilly" since 1900 was sealed with a vow in the middle of 1906.'[22] An American biographer states, likewise, that Gandhi told Kasturba of being 'irrevocably determined to live in perfect chastity. An obedient wife, she accepted this decision as she accepted all the other demands he made on her.'[23]

Gandhi's close association with his wife would henceforth take different forms. Kasturba never acceded to her husband's wishes easily, and Gandhi's autobiography itself furnishes a remarkable testimony to her tenacity and independence of judgment, and the sharp disagreements she came to have with him when, in the first two decades of their marriage, he unreasonably sought to bring her under his control.[24] But Kasturba gave Gandhi her support in his quest for social, economic, and political equality for Indians in South Africa and India, and she was among the first batch of satyagrahis, or non-violent resisters, sent from Phoenix into the Transvaal to protest against the decision of the South African government to declare all non-Christian marriages as null and void.[25] After their permanent return to India in 1914, and Gandhi's entry into the Indian political scene in 1917, Kasturba was to become even more of a political actor. She would take his place at political meetings which he was unable to attend, and was particularly active in the long periods of his various imprisonments. In time she acquired a political personality of her own,[26] though in a short introduction Gandhi provided to a biography of Kasturba after her death, he described the 'root cause which attracted the public to Kasturba' as her ability to lose herself in him. Gandhi says that he 'never insisted on this self-abnegation. She developed this quality of her own. At first I did not even know that she had it in her. According to my earlier experience, she was very obstinate. In spite of all my pressure she would do as she wished. This led to short or long periods of estrangement between us. But as my public life expanded, my wife bloomed forth and deliberately lost herself in my work.' Most significantly, Gandhi was to add: 'What developed the self-abnegation in her to the highest level was our Brahmacharya.' Gandhi says that he made a resolve to become a brahmacharya 'and Ba, as she was affectionately called, accepted it as her own': indeed, he admits, brahmacharya was 'more natural for her than for me', and so he arrives at the formulation of 'our brahmacharya.' It is from this time that they became 'true friends', and ceased to live as a married couple in the conventional sense of the term; and correspondingly Kasturba 'had no other interest in staying with me', says Gandhi, 'except to help me in my work.'[27]

Though Gandhi took the vow of brahmacharya, he did not thereby cease to mix in the company of women. Quite to the contrary, he adored their presence, and was almost always surrounded by many women disciples and initiates. Gandhi had a very considerable female entourage, and conducted a number of what in the West would be understood as 'platonic' relationships. After Madeleine Slade, the daughter of an English admiral, arrived in India in 1925 to serve Gandhi and, in her words, 'the cause of oppressed India', she rapidly assumed Kasturba's duties, and would henceforth be Gandhi's cook, nurse, and helpmate.[28] It was Madeleine, or Mirabehn as she was called,[29] who accompanied Gandhi on his trip to London in 1931 to attend the Round Table Conference, and who ministered to his daily needs. Mirabehn was exceedingly possessive of the Mahatma, demanded his constant attention, and felt a need for close physical proximity to him at all times. Gandhi had to send her away often, and described the many missives they exchanged during these periods of separation, which Mirabehn found agonizingly painful and which Gandhi himself described as full of 'spiritual agony', as 'love messages'.[30] Gandhi recognized, as on one occasion in 1927, that he had been 'very severe' with Mirabehn, but said he 'could not do otherwise. I had to perform an operation and I steadied myself for it.' In the same vein, he wrote a few days later: 'I have never been so anxious as this time to hear from you, for I sent you away too quickly after a serious operation. You haunted me in my sleep last night and were reported by friends to whom you had been sent, to be delirious, but without any danger.'[31] Mira was to write in her autobiography that 'the pain of our parting would not leave me', but Gandhi, while acknowledging that she was besides herself with the pain of separation, nonetheless insisted that she should cultivate the detachment that would make her a 'perfect woman': 'You must not cling to me as in this body. The spirit without the body is ever with you. And that is more than the feeble embodied imprisoned spirit with all the limitations that the flesh is heir to. The spirit without the flesh is perfect, and that is all we need. This can be felt only when we practice detachment. This you must now try to achieve.'[32]

In taking the position that a detached and yet intense relationship with women in his married state constituted no abrogation of his conjugal vows, and that a true spiritual relationship could not be predicated on the ephemeral attachments of the flesh, Gandhi was doubtless also drawing on the teachings of the *Bhagavad Gita*, which dwells on the manner in which the soul merely inhabits the body, and counsels the cultivation of a frame of mind whereby one renounces not so much action as the fruits or rewards of one's actions.[33] It is not women who were to be renounced by a man aspiring to master his senses and conquer the ego, which would have been the way of Indian sages, but that attachment to sex which makes impossible the selfless passion of which the *Gita* sings. Mirabehn was only one of many women with whom Gandhi, as a married man, had an extraordinarily close relationship. The Indian psychoanalyst, Sudhir Kakkar, has described the intensely possessive feelings towards Gandhi entertained by another young woman, Prema Kantak, who came to stay in Gandhi's ashram in her twenties. Kakar hazards the opinion that 'in the ashram, the competition among women for Gandhi's attention was as fierce as it is in any guru's establishment today.'[34] But Gandhi's relationships to women can by no means be confined to this category of experience. His personal physician for some years was to be another woman, Sushila Nayyar: she was to be a party to his future experiments. One of his closest political associates, and perhaps the only friend who took the liberty of playfully mocking Gandhi, was Sarojini Naidu. It is she who, adverting to Gandhi's long ears, nicknamed him 'Mickey Mouse',[35] and coined the famous quip that 'it takes a great deal of money to keep Bapu living in poverty'.[36] Thus, though Kasturba clearly stood apart from all the other women in Gandhi's life as his wife, women such as Mirabehn and Sushila Nayyar were no less dear to him, and in certain respects they occupied a niche in Gandhi's life that no one else could fill.

How soon after Kasturba's death in February 1944 Gandhi commenced his experiments in brahmacharya remains uncertain. The photographs from the last four years of his life show that his two grandnieces, Abhabehn and Manubehn, and more particularly the latter, were henceforth to be his constant companions. One year before her death, Kasturba induced the prison governor at the Aga Khan's Palace in Poona to allow Manu, then 15 years old and suffering a term of imprisonment in Nagpur for her part in the Quit India movement, to join Kasturba as her nurse companion. Manu arrived at the palace in March 1943 and soon established her place as the devoted servant to both Kasturba and Gandhi. As Kasturba lay dying, she entrusted Manu to Gandhi's care.[37] Six weeks after Kasturba's death, Gandhi himself fell seriously ill, and was prostrated by a serious attack of malaria. Kasturba's death had debilitated him: as Gandhi himself put it, 'I cannot imagine life without Ba . . . . Her passing has left a vacuum never to be filled. . . .' But Manu was there to nurse Gandhi back to health; and she came to have a special place in his affections. In a touching and remarkable testament that Manu was to pen a few years later, she described the manner in which Gandhi brought her up as his daughter, and the interest he took in her mental growth, health, nutritional needs, and physical and spiritual development. Gandhi washed and oiled her hair, taught her spinning, and even cooked for her, though he himself usually ate little more than nuts, fruits, and boiled vegetables. Manu, let it be noted, called her little testament *Bapu—My Mother*.[38]

II

SLEEPING WITH THE VIRTUOUS

Manu was eighteen years old when, in early December 1946, she joined Gandhi in the remote villages of Noakhali in East Bengal. The tortuous road that led Gandhi to Noakhali cannot be traced here, but suffice to note that some of its Muslim inhabitants had taken it upon themselves to empty Noakhali of its minority Hindu population. (In Bihar, not much later, the Hindu community would mindlessly enact its revenge, but that is another story.) The massacres in Noakhali commenced on 10 October 1946, and slowly the stories of the orchestrated orgies of violence, the brutal murder of men, the abduction and rape of women, and the torching of entire villages made their way into the media and the portals of power in Delhi. No sooner had Gandhi received reliable information of these monstrosities that he decided to make his way to Noakhali. That mantra, 'Do or Die', which he had given to the nation in 1942, as he launched the final movement against British rule in India, now beckoned him to proceed to the violence-torn and malaria-stricken Noakhali in a demonstration of his deeply-held belief that Hindus and Muslims were perfectly capable of living together in harmony. His fellow satyagrahis and companions were each dispatched to various Muslim villages, to take up residence there, and Gandhi, after moving from village to village, set himself up in the village of Srirampur.

Gandhi's entourage, this time unusually small, consisted of Parasuram, who served as his typist, and Nirmal Kumar Bose, a Bengali scientist on the faculty at Calcutta University. For some years, Bose had been interested in Gandhi's work and thought, and had been waiting for an opportunity when he might observe him at first hand; Gandhi, on his part, required the services of an able interpreter, as he was without knowledge of Bengali. Bose also came to serve as Gandhi's secretary and personal assistant, and it was he who prepared Gandhi's meals, helped him bathe and shave, and attended to all his other personal needs. As Bose understood, Gandhi had never been 'physically so alone' since his return to India in 1915: he was without trusted friends and associates, his wife had passed away, and his women companions were scattered in Noakhali and elsewhere. To Bose it appeared as though 'Gandhiji was bent upon putting up with as much inconvenience as possible, if thereby he could somehow gain access into the hearts of the Muslim peasantry of Noakhali.'[39] Now, as negotiations for India's independence were taking place, Gandhi might have well thought that his teachings had been abandoned, and that his trust in the efficacy of non-violence was highly misplaced.

A month after Gandhi's arrival in Srirampur on 20 November 1946, however, Manu came to join him,[40] and started sleeping in Gandhi's bed at once. Bose had taken to keeping a diary, and recorded the following entry for 20 December: 'When I reached Gandhiji's room even before 4 in the morning, I heard him talking to Manu in a low voice in his own bed, where she had gone to sleep at night.'[41] Bose reports Gandhi as telling Manu that 'he personally felt that he had reached the end of one chapter in his old life and a new one was about to begin. He was thinking of a bold and original experiment, whose "heat will be great."'[42] One can reasonably surmise that by the 'bold and original experiment' Gandhi meant his recourse to testing himself as a brahmachari. Before long Parasuram had approached Gandhi to unburden his mind on 'certain private matters', and Bose likewise discussed with Gandhi his relations with women. On 31 December, Gandhi informed Bose that it was 'indeed true that he permitted women workers to use his bed, this being undertaken as a spiritual experiment at times. Even if there were no trace of passion in him of which he was conscious, it was not unlikely that a residue might be left over, and that would make trouble for the girls who took part in his experiment. He had asked them [the girls] if, even unconsciously, he had been responsible for evoking the least shade of evil sentiment in their heart. This "experiment", as he called it, had been objected to by distinguished co-workers like Narahari (Parekh) and Kishorelal (Mashruwala); and one of the grounds of their complaint had been based on the possible repercussions which the example of a responsible leader like him might have upon other people.'[43]

As this excerpt from Bose's diary shows, a number of Gandhi's associates were unhappy with his 'experiment', and expressed their view that someone in Gandhi's position should have shown a keener sense of moral responsibility. Gandhi's stenographer, Parasuram, evidently found it impossible to stay any longer with him, for on 2 January Gandhi wrote a briefly reply to what must have been a very lengthy letter: 'I have read your letter with great care. I began it at 3 a.m.; finished reading it at 4 a.m. It contains half-truths which are dangerous.' While complimenting him on his 'frankness and boldness', Gandhi averred that Parasuram had wronged him and the girls by suppressing his opinions for so long; and as there was a 'conflict of ideals', Gandhi would not prevent him from exercising his wish to be relieved of his responsibilities. In keeping with his view that the practice of non-violence was in no manner compatible with secrecy, Gandhi told Parasuram that he was 'at liberty to publish whatever wrong you have noticed in me and my surroundings.'[44] The same day, Gandhi dictated another letter to Mirabehn, who appears to have sent him an anxious query, adumbrating the spiritual meaning and context of his experiment. 'Everything depends', he told Mira, 'upon one's purity in thought, word and deed, using the word "purity" in its widest sense. Then there may be no cause for even so much as a headache. Only get hold of this fundamental fact.' Gandhi described his objective as wanting to 'empty' himself 'utterly', the condition whereby God would then 'possess' him. In the most telling passage, Gandhi wrote: 'Then I know that everything will come true but it is a serious question when I shall have reduced myself to zero. Think of "I" and "O" in juxtaposition and you have the whole problem of life in two signs.'[45]

Parasuram left him, Gandhi wrote to a friend, because 'he did not believe in my ideals . . . . The immediate cause I think was that Manu shared the same bed with me.'[46] While recognizing that Manu was like a granddaughter to Gandhi, and that their relationship was nothing but innocent, Parasuram thought that the impropriety of the action lay in it constituting a bad example for other men, who were without Gandhi's purity, nobility of purpose, and spirituality of discipline. His departure did not prevent 'fresh objections' from pouring in, and now some of Gandhi's closest and most respected associates stepped up their criticism.[47] Kishorelal Mashruwala, who was then editing Gandhi's weekly magazine, *Harijan*, relinquished charge and Gandhi acknowledged that his 'agony is difficult to bear. He is so upset that he is on the verge of breaking down.'[48] Gandhi wondered whether the women at his ashram in Sevagram were 'suffering', but in Noakhali he was unable to see any signs of the women having been affected. As he admitted, 'Maybe that prevents me from feeling the full impact of people's reactions.' Yet his own resolve had become 'firmer than ever', for that could not be 'true brahmacharya', he was to write to his disciple and fellow brahmachari Vinoba Bhave, which required hedges.[49]

Nonetheless, over the course of the next two months, Gandhi entered into a conversation with many of his friends and relatives over the issue of his experiment, and in a characteristic vein apprised the audiences at his prayer meetings of the fact that, at his behest, his granddaughter was sharing his bed with him. On the evening of 1 February 1947 at the village of

Amishapara, he referred to the 'small-talks, whispers and innuendoes' of which he had become aware. Saying that he did not wish 'his most innocent acts to be misunderstood and misrepresented', he adverted to the Prophet's saying that he wanted not those eunuchs in his service who had become so by an act of operation, but those who became such by prayer to God. Gandhi described this as his aspiration: 'It was in the spirit of God's eunuch that he had approached what he considered was his duty. It was an integral part of the yajna he was performing and he invited them to bless the effort. He knew that his action had excited criticism even among his friends. But a duty could not be shirked even for the sake of the most intimate friends.'[50] The same day, in a letter to his son Manilal, Gandhi described his ahimsa, or belief in non-violence, as 'being severely tested', and pleaded with him to remain indifferent to the public criticism of Gandhi's actions: 'Do not let the fact of Manu sleeping with me perturb you. I believe that it is God who has prompted me to take that step. If, however, you cannot understand, do not get upset and bear with me.'[51] In the mean time, Gandhi continued with his experiment, and it is only as an unexpected sequel to a conversation on 25 February 1947 between Gandhi and Amritlal Thakkar, a very prominent Indian social reformer whose advice Gandhi often sought, that Manu ceased to go to bed with Gandhi. Thakkar appears to have convinced Manu that, while he did not doubt her 'perfectly innocent and undisturbed sleep' as she lay beside Gandhi, it would be prudent to give up the experiment. Manu consented to Thakkar's request, provided Gandhi agreed, and with the understanding that in doing so, 'she had renounced nothing, surrendered not an iota. The concession was only to the feelings and sentiments of those who could not understand his (Gandhiji's) stand and might need time for new ideas to sink into their minds.'[52] Thereafter, Gandhi appears to have suspended his experiment, and though Manu and Abha would continue to be by his side for the remainder of his life, being his constant companions and serving as his 'walking sticks',[53] it is possible that he never went to bed with either of them again, or indeed with any other woman.

III

CONTINENCE AND THE BLOT OF LUST

Gandhi's experiment in 'sexual celibacy', or 'celibate sexuality', paves the way, as I shall argue, for an enhanced understanding of his relations to women, his simultaneous reliance on, and defiance of, Indian traditions of sexuality and sexual potency, his advocacy of androgyny, and his articulation of the relationship of non-violence to sexual conduct. Though it would be wholly erroneous to speak of the sexlessness of Gandhi, who appeared to many of his friends, associates, and visitors as possessed of a 'strong sexuality',[54] it is quite transparent that he sought to cultivate the ideal of brahmacharya, and more specifically its component of celibacy understood as voluntary abstinence from sex, while decrying the tendency, particularly pronounced among those with spiritual aspirations, to segregate the sexes. Gandhi evidently relished the company of women, and his life and writings are a striking testimony to his willingness to reject emphatically varying standards of sexual mores for men and women, and to persuade women to give up false standards of modesty which ironically undermined the true capacities of feminine power. Gandhi's brahmacharya experiment also enables us to pose some questions, which have been most inadequately addressed, about Gandhi's renunciation of power, his understanding of the nature of political power in the twentieth century, his conception of indigenous knowledges, and his view that the ontology of the female is superior to that of the male.

'The core of the Gandhian teaching', wrote T. K. Mahadevan in a seminal piece on Gandhi's political philosophy, 'consists of one piece— and no other. It is truth.'[55] The primacy of satya or truth in Gandhi's thinking is widely accepted and Mahadevan was surely right in pointing to the folly of ascribing greater interpretive importance to ahimsa. Gandhi is, in the popular conception, the Prophet of Non-Violence, and it is the various non-violent campaigns which he waged in the struggle to free India from British rule that have won him a place in the common imagination. But Gandhi himself termed his movement of non-violent resistance satyagraha, the force of truth, and as Mahadevan has so persuasively argued, he can be located within an Indian tradition which has accorded an extraordinarily privileged place to the quest for truth, oftentimes in ways that cannot be reconciled with Western epistemological frameworks. 'He is a satyagrahi', Gandhi was to say, 'who has resolved to practice nothing but truth, and such a one will know the right way every time.'[56]

Though the cardinal principle in Gandhi's thought may well be satya, it is nonetheless revealing that Mahadevan should not have considered the place of brahmacharya, alongside satya and ahimsa, in Gandhi's conception of the ethical and political life. To a very large extent, his views on sexuality and brahmacharya have been an embarrassment to his admirers, while provoking outrage among his detractors. 'I cannot imagine a thing as ugly as the intercourse of man and woman',[57] averred Gandhi with scarcely a trace of any misgiving, and such frequently voiced sentiments, though less harshly expressed in his later years, were not calculated to earn him the goodwill of those who took a more 'modern' and 'healthy' view of sex. Having taken the vow of brahmacharya, which is commonly understood as abstinence from sex, Gandhi counselled others to become celibate as well; moreover, celibacy was to be observed, not merely by the young and the unmarried, but also by married couples. Though sexual intercourse outside marriage was unpardonable, even within marriage it had no place, in Gandhi's view, except as a regrettably unavoidable means to create progeny. The observance of celibacy among the unmarried was scarcely a matter for congratulation, for Gandhi held that the true meaning of celibacy could only be realized within a marriage. The institution of marriage provided a legal sanction to the sexual intercourse of man and woman, husband and wife, and celibacy could only be constituted as a worthy sacrifice when sexual intercourse, though construed as a natural right and a pleasure in which indulgence could legitimately be sought, was forsaken. Brahmacharya commanded married people to behave as though they were unmarried.[58]

While some of Gandhi's associates took heart in his teachings, and emulated their leader, the greater number of the men and women who worked with him considered his views, in the words of Jawaharlal Nehru, 'unnatural and shocking'. Gandhi 'has gone to the extreme limit of his argument', Nehru added prosaically, 'and does not recognize the validity or necessity of the sexual act at any time except for the sake of children; he refuses to recognize any natural sex attraction between man and woman.' Describing Gandhi as 'absolutely wrong in this matter', Nehru thought it likely that his advice, if followed, could only lead to 'frustration, inhibition, neurosis, and all manner of physical and nervous ills.'[59] More recent assessments, scholarly and journalistic alike, adopt almost entirely the same argument: thus Bhikhu Parekh, critiquing Gandhi for subscribing to a 'dualist ontology' that made him hold steadfast to the distinction between the 'physical' and the 'spiritual', finds Gandhi incapable of making a distinction between the sexual act involved in rape and the sexual act that takes place between a loving couple.[60] Gandhi's 'ideas and preachments' on the subject of sex seemed to one of his most intense admirers to be 'outlandish and almost inhuman', and Nehru appears to have encapsulated a fairly common view that Gandhi was 'obsessed' with sex.[61]

Insofar as Gandhi's espousal of brahmacharya has been taken seriously, then, it is deemed to be nothing more than a zealous advocacy of celibacy, and Gandhi's insistence on recommending celibacy even to married couples is construed as evidence of his irrational and almost monstrously insensitive view of 'human nature'. The most generally accepted interpretation of Gandhi's acute difficulties with sex, and his refusal to recognize any 'legitimate' sexual desire, traces the origins of Gandhi's views to a calamitous incident that took place in the early years of his marriage.[62] As recounted by Gandhi himself, he was sixteen years old, and his father was bedridden, indeed on the verge of death. Gandhi was one of his father's principal attendants, and every night he massaged his legs, gave him medication, and ministered to all his needs. 'I loved to do this service', Gandhi wrote, and throughout his life he was to retain this extraordinary capacity of nursing sick people and animals to health: much before men had to demonstrate their 'feminist' credentials by showing themselves possessed of the qualities of nurturing and caring, Gandhi was an avid male nurse and feminine healer. One evening, as he was nursing his father, Gandhi was consumed by lust for Kasturba. Though she was pregnant, Gandhi could not contain himself, and left his father's side to consummate his desire—as he adds, 'that too at a time when religion, medical science and commonsense alike forbade sexual intercourse.' Gandhi had not been with Kasturba, rudely woken from her sleep, for more than 'five or six minutes' when the servant announced that Gandhi's father was dead. Had not 'animal passion' blinded him, Gandhi wrote, he would have been by his father's side in the last moments of his life: he should have been rendering his father 'wakeful service', not indulging in 'carnal desire'. The 'shame' of his desire was not to be forgotten, and in his autobiography of 1927, Gandhi characterized it as a blot 'I have never been able to efface or forget, and I have always thought that, although my devotion to my parents knew no bounds and I would have given up anything for it, yet it was weighed and found unpardonably wanting because my mind was at the same moment in the grip of lust. I have therefore always regarded myself as a lustful, though a faithful, husband. It took me long to get free from the shackles of lust, and I had to pass through many ordeals before I could overcome it.'[63] The child born of that lustful moment, moreover, was to die within a few days. 'Nothing else could be expected': the laws of compensation cannot be arrested, and Gandhi added for good measure: 'Let all those who are married be warned by my example.'

Though Gandhi's own assessment of the indelible shame left by his 'carnal desire' is not to be doubted, it behooves the imagination to suppose, as might some psychoanalyst, that Gandhi's view of brahmacharya was shaped primarily by an incident from his adolescent years, and that henceforth he was to construe the sexual life as distasteful, merely a form of gross material existence. Gandhi had, almost from the outset, found the most narrow and widely accepted conception of brahmacharya as the abstinence from sexual intercourse woefully inadequate, nor did he think that the practitioner of brahmacharya was to be judged by the moral conventions of the day. No one who desired, but merely failed to realize the desire, could be considered celibate: 'So long as the desire for intercourse is there, one cannot be said to have attained brahmacharya. Only he who has burned away the sexual desire in its entirety may be said to have attained control over his sexual organ.'[64] As Gandhi was to stress repeatedly over the course of many years, 'Brahmacharya means control of the senses in thought, word and deed.'[65] Brahmacharya was not to mean that one could not touch a woman 'in any circumstances whatsoever.' But, in so touching a woman, it was implied 'that one's state of mind should be as calm and unruffled during such contact as when one touches, say, a piece of paper. . . . He [the brahmachari] has to be free, as free from excitement in case of contact with the fairest damsel on earth, as in contact with a dead body.'[66] Gandhi had so averred in 1926, but this formulation late in his life must have appeared to him as somewhat tentative, for in a letter to his female friend Amrit Kaur on 18 March 1947, the capacity to partake of the private company of naked women was to constitute an integral part of his definition of brahmacharya. Gandhi now described the 'meaning of brahmacharya' thus: 'One who never has any lustful intention, who by constant attendance upon God has become proof against conscious or unconscious emissions, who is capable of lying naked with naked women, however beautiful they may be, without being in any manner whatsoever sexually excited.' The richer meaning of being able to lie 'naked with naked women' without having any sexual thoughts would then flower into the more sublime teachings of the scriptures: a 'full brahmachari', Gandhi noted, is 'incapable of lying, incapable of intending or doing harm to a single man or woman in the whole world,' and such a person remained 'free from anger and malice and detached in the sense of the *Bhagavad Gita*.' Gandhi's definition of brahmacharya in an instant takes us away from celibacy towards self-realization, and a brahmachari correspondingly is described as a 'person who is making daily and steady progress towards God and whose every act is done in pursuance of that end and no other.'[67]

No less important than that dark night of his youth, when Gandhi abandoned his dying father for his pregnant wife (and so, on a different reading, embraced life over death), was an experience from the eve of his life where too he was awakened to the possibility that his spiritual discipline was seriously wanting. One evening in 1936, as he was recovering from a physical breakdown induced by long hours of work, Gandhi was given a jolting and painful reminder of the inadequacy of his brahmacharya, which he said he had been 'trying to follow . . . consciously and deliberately since 1899.' He dreamt of some woman and, as a consequence, experienced an erection which caused a seminal emission. There had been only 'one lapse' previously in his '36 years' constant and conscious effort' to remain pure in thought and deed, he wrote, and only on that occasion had he experienced such 'mental disturbance'. He felt utterly 'disgusted' with himself, and at once acquainted his 'attendants and the medical friends' with his 'condition.' But this was a matter where others could only be sympathetic listeners: 'They could give no help. I expected none.' Nonetheless, he adds, 'the confession of the wretched experience brought relief to me. I felt as if a great load had been raised from over me. It enabled me to pull myself together before any harm could be done.'[68] Gandhi, doubtless, took the view, not uncommon in India, that a true brahmachari experiences no sexual passion even in the dream state.[69] Towards the end of the year, he was to advert to this matter again in his weekly newspaper *Harijan*, this time in more characteristically ominous and even apocalyptic tones. He says that his 'darkest hour' came to him when, in his sleep, he felt as though he wanted to experience the body of a woman. That was not pleasing to him, for a man who had tried to rise superior to the instinct for nearly forty years was bound to be intensely pained when he had this frightful experience. I ultimately conquered the feeling, but I was face to face with the blackest moment of my life and if I had succumbed to it, it would have been my absolute undoing.[70]

The 'path of self-purification', as Gandhi would readily concede in his autobiography, is 'hard and steep', and from his own standpoint he had faltered once too often. His political triumphs seemed rather easier than the conquest of 'subtle passions', and he acknowledged that since his return to India he had had 'experiences of the dormant passions lying hidden within [him].'[71] In May 1924, Gandhi had reported having had 'bad dreams',[72] but the intensity of his wet dream of 1936, a recurrence of which on 14 April 1938 once again left him shocked and repulsed,[73] gave him other reasons for alarm. Many commentators hold that Gandhi ascribed to the view, said to be especially prominent in India, that a man must preserve his 'vital fluid', most particularly because, as common wisdom had it, semen is not easily formed: indeed, as the anthropologist Morris Carstairs was to say of the widely-held belief of his informants, 'it takes forty days, and forty drops of blood to make one drop of semen.'[74] The 'ascetic longings of Yogis who seek to conquer and transform' sexuality 'into spiritual power', opines Kakar, 'has been a perennial preoccupation of Hindu culture',[75] and Erik Erikson thought that Gandhi's conduct late in his life could be reasonably rooted in a 'deeply Indian preconception with seminal continence and mental potency.'[76] Writing on sexual matters for his newspaper *Harijan* in 1936, pursuant to his own nocturnal troubles, Gandhi himself adverted to a discussion of the 'vital fluid', insisting that any expenditure of it other than for the purpose of procreation constituted a 'criminal waste', the 'consequent excitement caused to man and woman' being an 'equally criminal waste of precious energy.' 'It is now easy to understand', wrote Gandhi, 'why the scientists of old have put such great value upon the vital fluid and why they have insisted upon its strong transmutation into the highest form of energy for the benefit of society.'[77] 'If a man controls his semen except on the occasion of such purposeful cohabitation,' Gandhi wrote elsewhere, 'he is as good as an avowed brahmachari', but for 'an avowed brahmachari' of his aspirations no such indulgence was permitted.[78] To this one can add the observation, whose more extended and ripe meanings cannot here be explored, that in both mythological and folkloric Indian traditions, the semen retained by a yogi is thought to turn into milk, and such a yogi is said to develop breasts. 'The yogi thus becomes', writes Wendy O'Flaherty, 'like a productive female when he reverses the flow of his male fluids.'[79]

In various Indian schools of spiritual ecstasy encapsulated under the term 'tantrism', or in otherwise obscure religious cults, the retention of semen is considered vital as well, and one scholar has argued that Gandhi first commenced his experiment 'only a few years' after he had read Sir John Woodruffe's writings on the tantra tradition.[80] In all other respects, however, Gandhi's doctrines bear little resemblance to the theories of tantra, and he would have unequivocally condemned tantra's advocacy of passionless sexual intercourse as a means of attaining spiritual prowess. Gandhi was nothing if not passionate, and sexual intercourse was not his chosen medium to express his eroticism. There are also evident similarities in Gandhi's ideas to Freud's theory of sublimation, and such anxiety about the loss of semen as has been recorded by psychologists and social workers, however pronounced in India,[81] is commonly experienced in other cultures as well. More to the point, the belief that loss of semen was weakening to the male, depriving him of the energy that was required for him to sustain the family and uplift society, was widely prevalent in nineteenth-century Britain, and some scholars have been inclined to the view that Gandhi's views on sexuality may also have been shaped by what are purported to be Victorian norms,[82] and most certainly by some kind of loathing for the body. Thus some feminists, while admiring Gandhi's efforts to bring women into the political life of the country, have thought that Gandhi's relations with Kasturba may have been informed by this disgust for the body, and that had he shared a more equitable life with Kasturba, he would have learned from her that 'our bodies are gifts, not hindrances.'[83]

IV

GANDHI'S VAGINA: A POLITICAL ACCOUNT OF SEMEN

Whatever Gandhi's own pronouncements about the imperative to preserve the 'vital fluid', any interpretation which fixates on this aspect of his thought, or on what is taken to be his troubled view of the body as an obstacle to spiritual enlightenment, does not offer a compelling insight into the more striking relationship between Gandhi's advocacy of brahmacharya, his political life, and his espousal of femininity. For even as enthusiastic and careful a student of Gandhi's life as the Indian political scientist Bhikhu Parekh, the whole matter of Gandhi's 'bizarre' sexual life can virtually be dispensed with the observation that his 'theory of sexuality rested on a primitive approach to semen'. Working almost entirely within a positivist framework, Parekh has nothing much to say except that Gandhi's ideas about the 'production and accumulation' of semen were 'untrue', and that the old man was 'wrong' to 'mystify' semen by ascribing it with 'life-giving power', just as he was 'wrong to associate it with energy'; indeed, 'the very concept of *ojas* or spiritual energy is largely mystical and almost certainly false.' Yet, as is amply clear, there are innumerable mystical traditions and sexual practices around the world for which there is no 'evidence' or 'basis in facts',[84] and this ought not to compel us to confine our explorations to the most common forms of heterosexual love. Likewise, the supposition that to Gandhi his own body was a 'foreign' object, for which any person of intense spiritual inclination could have nothing but fear and loathing, can scarcely be reconciled with everything we know about Gandhi's relation to his own body. Few men could have been as finely attuned to the rhythms of their bodies as Gandhi was with his own, and accounts of ashram life suggest his remarkable ease with his nakedness. Far from avoiding all contact with women, as we have previously observed, Gandhi revelled in their company, and it is pre-eminently through the sense of touch that he consorted with the men and women around him. He would dictate letters to his secretaries, or conduct other important business, while his body was being massaged, and he thought nothing of putting his arms around the shoulders of friends, associates, and even visitors. He kept a minute record of the food ingested by him, and his bowel movements were of as much concern to him, as indeed they should have been, as the negotiations for Indian independence. Gandhi's attentiveness to matters of sexuality, hygiene, nutrition, and the presentation of the body was his way of injecting the body into the body politic, and nowhere does he show the brahman's disdain for the polluting body, or the exaggerated modesty of the Indian female, which he decried, towards her body.

If the physiological account of semen loss has little to commend to our attention, can we profitably render what we might call a political account of semen? In his next life, Gandhi had often said, he would liked to have been reborn as an untouchable, the most exploited element of Indian society, and numerous times he gave the impression of wanting to be reborn as a woman: in either case, one would be positioned to gain a more complex phenomenological understanding of the nature of oppression. In his arduous quest for mastery over his sexual desires, Gandhi appears to have found masculinity a nearly insuperable obstacle, and he may have thought that women had, in this respect, an envious advantage. It is almost plausible to speak of Gandhi's vulva envy. Among Indian renunciates, as the psychoanalytical investigations of one Indian brahmachari's dreams suggests, is prevalent the idea that 'as long as the penis remains, one cannot be a true ascetic.'[85] It is not sufficient to curtail the activities of the penis, or to prevent it from achieving a state of excitability; it must be made to disappear within the body. When the sexual passions are subdued, and the mind is prepared by means of a rigorous discipline for the exercise of abstinence, the penis begins to shrink; gradually it becomes inverted and 'draws itself within the body in such a way that its very root enters into the body. By this process its appearance becomes that of a female sexual organ, while really it is the disappearance of the male sexual organ from outside the body.'[86] In their own perverse way, Gandhi's militant detractors such as his assassin and members of the Hindu paramilitary organization RSS [Rashtriya Swayamsevak Sangh], who held him responsible for India's Partition and the inability of the Indian government to protect Hindus even in the nation's capital, may have been signifying their fear that Gandhi was not quite a man when they threw at him the epithet hijra, which in common parlance stands for a castrated or intersexed man who takes on the identity of a woman.[87]

Though it can only be speculated how the women who partook in Gandhi's experiment 'experienced' his body, the preponderant portion of the biographical and anecdotal literature suggests that the women who were intimate with him may have ceased to think of Gandhi as a man. Manu's aptly named book, *Bapu—My Mother*, points to that as much as the frequently noted observation that women felt entirely at ease in his company. Consequently, when Manu, Abha, and Sushila Nayyar agreed at various times to share Gandhi's bed with him, there is no reason to suppose that they felt they were lying besides anyone other than a woman, sharing as Indian women commonly do a bed amongst themselves. No one so far has quite been prepared to suggest that Gandhi was in this manner another Ramakrishna,[88] an unlettered Indian saint whose androgyny was striking, but this may only be from a reluctance to concede that someone who immersed himself as much in politics as did Gandhi could have been so suffused by spirituality. Ramakrishna counselled men that they were to 'assume the attitude of women' if they wished to conquer passion.[89] It is said of Ramakrishna that from his childhood he could take on, whenever he willed, the characteristics of the female sex. He was allowed in the company of women not merely because he could readily assume a woman's voice: as one of his women devotees was later to write, 'To us [women devotees] Sri Ramakrishna did not usually seem to be a man at all. It seemed that he was one of us. That is why we did not feel the slightest shyness or hesitation in his presence, as we normally do in the presence of men.'[90] When he assumed the *madhura bhava*, or the position of the lover as she approaches God, Ramakrishna would dress in feminine attire and imitate feminine behaviour: he would be the Radha to Krishna. Witnesses furnished accounts of Ramakrishna 'menstruating': he would sit in samadhi, absorbed in the divine, and blood would ooze out from the pores of his skin.[91] 'As soon as he was dressed as a woman,' writes his biographer Christopher Isherwood, Ramakrishna's mind became more and more deeply merged in the mood of womanhood. Those who saw him were amazed at the physical transformation which seemed to take place; walk, speech, gestures, even the smallest actions were perfectly in character. Sometimes, Ramakrishna would go to the house in the Janbazar district which had belonged to Rani Rashmoni and live there with the women of the family, as a woman. They found it almost impossible to remember that he was not really one of themselves.[92]

Gandhi may not have been similarly merged into womanhood, but it is in this spirit that we should take his oft-expressed remark that he was 'half a woman'; and if the testimony of his women associates and friends is any reliable guide, they expressed themselves before him as they would before other women. Moreover, if Manu and his women devotees had placed themselves under his tutelage, Gandhi might also have thought of his obligation to train them as brahmacharis, to bring them to that point of concentrated awareness where they each ceased to think of themselves as inhabiting the body of a woman.[93]

   In his aspiration to embody femininity, then, Gandhi may have been relying upon familiar idioms of Indian thought, though it is instructive how far he departed from Indian textual and customary traditions as well. It has often been overlooked that Gandhi's brahmacharya experiment had reached a more advanced state when he was conducting, according to Bose, an 'active campaign against untouchability',[94] and the trip to Noakhali had been undertaken in the endeavour to snap the barrier that had arisen between Muslims and Hindus and so restore the inextricable bonds that had served as the basis of an Indian civilization. He had fought long against these two forms of untouchability, to which was conjoined a third form: to an old man like himself, with a public reputation to protect, young women would have become sexually untouchable. However, he roundly ignored those traditions which enjoined upon their male followers to keep at a physical remove from women. 'A brahmachari, it is said,' wrote Gandhi in 1938, 'should never see, much less touch a woman. Doubtless a brahmachari may not think of, speak of, see or touch a woman lustfully. But the prohibition one finds in books on brahmacharya is mentioned without the important adverb', that is 'lustfully'. Recognizing that observance of brahmacharya was difficult 'when one freely mixes with the world,' Gandhi nonetheless added that 'it is not of much value if it is attainable only by retirement from the world.'[95] In all domains of life, Gandhi rejected the segregation of the sexes, even preferring (unusual for Indians of his time) co-educational schools to single-sex schools. He thought that Indian women's refusal to be attended by male gynaecologists or surgeons originated from a false sense of shame, though he recognized that there were 'unscrupulous doctor[s]' who took advantage of their patients.[96] Writing to the young Muslim daughter of a friend on the subject of an enema, in whose efficacy Gandhi reposed much trust, he put the matter quite candidly: 'Whether the person who helps you with the enema is a man or a woman, it should make, and I am sure it will make, no difference to you at all.'[97] To a brahmachari, in the event, this could be no important consideration.

Most tellingly, though, Gandhi appears to have found some sustenance in certain strands of Vaishnava theology and literature. During the course of one long exposition of his views on brahmacharya, Gandhi had remarked: 'When the Gopis were stripped of their clothes by Krishna, the legend says, they showed no sign of embarrassment or sex-consciousness but stood before the Lord in rapt devotion.'[98] Subsequent to disclosures about his experiment, this story was to find its way into his public speeches. The reference here is to a famous scene in Krishna's life where the gopis or milkmaids, having stripped at the banks of the river Yamuna to take a bath, are about to emerge from the water when they find their garments missing. When they look around them, they find Krishna dangling them from a tree upon which he is perched; the gopis implore him to return their clothes, while Krishna reminds them that since each of them had set their hearts on him, uttering a prayer that would grant them Krishna as their husband, they should be prepared to walk into his presence without a trace of shame.

The *Bhagavata Purana*, the pre-eminent text of Krishna devotion, states explicitly that 'bashfully they [the gopis] looked at each other and smiled, but none came out of the water.' When eventually they do so, notwithstanding their most earnest pleas that they should be spared this indignity, they cover 'their private parts with the palms of their hands'. But Krishna is not so easily appeased: since in entering the water in a naked state after taking a religious vow the gopis had committed a transgression, they were to expiate their sin by raising their folded palms to their heads and prostrating themselves on the ground. Each gopi attempts to comply with Krishna's injunction by raising one of her hands, while her other hand continues to cover her genitals; this only provokes Krishna to the observation that such a mode of rendering obeisance constitutes a gross violation of the ethics of worship, and that the Lord cannot be satisfied other than by a complete fulfillment of religious observances. In this manner the gopis, now aware of the nature of their transgression, submit in a state of complete nudity, and their clothes are returned to them.[99]

Their obeisance has been rendered, and now they can reasonably await its fulfillment: it is also characteristic of Krishna that, recognizing the longing each gopi has for him, the longing that each one of us has to be merged into the absolute and to receive the favours of the divine lover, he exercises the power within him to satisfy each gopi. Thus, in the received versions of the Krishna legend, he can be with nearly 20,000 gopis simultaneously, though each lives in the illusory state that she alone is the object of his affections.[100] Yet this 'satisfaction' has no necessary, or even any, referent to sexual intercourse: indeed, one of Krishna's myriad names is Acyuta, 'the one whose seed does not fall', since once sexual orgasm has been achieved, the erotic play is over.[101] This interpretation is unequivocally echoed in a Hindi proverb, where it is said of Krishna, *'Solah sahasra nari phir bhi brahmachari'* ('He has sixteen thousand women but still remains a celibate'). It is perhaps against this backdrop that we should view Gandhi's comment to his disciple Vinoba Bhave: 'My mind daily sleeps in an innocent manner with millions of women, and Manu also, who is a blood relation to me, sleeps with me as one of these millions.'[102]

Whatever liberty Gandhi appears to have taken in suggesting that the gopis showed no embarrassment in appearing before Krishna in a state of nakedness, what is particularly illustrative is the manner in which Gandhi sought to deploy the trope of nakedness in the service of a philosophical and political conception of 'truth'. Though no detailed thoughts can be entertained here over Gandhi's sartorial politics, it is germane that over the course of a lifetime Gandhi came increasingly to shed clothes. In the early years of his youth, as a law student in Britain, he had endeavoured to dress as an English gentleman, and it was not until he thrust himself into the struggle to procure Indians political rights in South Africa that he simplified his dress. It was around the time of the non-cooperation movement of 1920-22, by which time Gandhi had already initiated a daily regimen of spinning and also urged it upon the nation as part of a programme of national rejuvenation, that he further shed himself of clothes, choosing to move around only in a simple loincloth, a shawl thrown over his chest during the winter months.[103] This is the image with which he would henceforth be associated, captured nowhere better perhaps than in his remark to a English reporter in 1930, as he was questioned about whether he proposed to go dressed in this manner to have tea with His Royal

Highnesses at Buckingham Palace, that the King-Emperor was wearing enough for both of them. In a similar vein, while taking note of Churchill's insulting remark that the prospect of direct negotiations between the British government and a 'half-naked seditious fakir of a type well known in the Orient' was too nauseating to be contemplated, Gandhi had expressed the hope that he might become completely naked.

V

NAKED BEFORE GOD: THE INFINITE PLAY OF SEXUALITY

Gandhi had set for himself the ambition to appear naked before God, which for him was nothing other than Truth, and consequently come face to face with the 'Truth'. At this particular juncture, when India was almost on the verge of independence, he was nearly tormented by the awareness that his teachings on ahimsa had been less successful than he had imagined. The tone of his statement released to the press on 20 November 1946, as he was about to proceed to the village of Srirampur in Noakhali district, reveals his deep foreboding: 'I find myself in the midst of exaggeration and falsity. I am unable to discover the truth . . . . Truth and ahimsa by which I swear, and which have, to my knowledge, sustained me for sixty years, seem to fail to show the attributes I have ascribed to them.'[104] He had striven to maintain Hindu-Muslim harmony, even fasted (oftentimes with grave consequences to his health) whenever there had been a major recrudescence of communal violence, and no issue since the mid-1920s had occupied more of his attention; and yet, well more than twenty years after his attainment of Mahatmahood, he now seemed to have little control over the unfolding of events. This is scarcely to say that Gandhi subscribed to the view that his Mahatmahood conferred on him powers which were rightfully his, or that his word should have had, as it apparently once did, the force of law. If his utterances no longer commanded obedience, that was a sure sign that his voice did not carry very far into the public sphere. However, everything in Gandhi's own philosophical leanings, and most particularly his conception of truth, disposed him to the belief that the violence and untruth which pervaded the public domain were reflections of some profound shortcomings in his own practice of ahimsa and brahmacharya. Satyagraha implies that the individual carries within himself or herself the burden of social failings, and that one reads from social developments as from a mirror the history of one's own thought and practices. 'Ever since my coming to Noakhali', Gandhi reported to Bapa Thakkar in 1947, in his endeavour to explain why he commenced upon his experiment, 'I have been asking myself the question "What is it that is choking the action of my ahimsa? Why does not the spell work? May it not be because I have temporized in the matter of brahmacharya.'[105] If his teachings of ahimsa had failed to avert communal rioting, Gandhi was prone to think that there was something profoundly amiss in his own practice of ahimsa. 'There must be some serious flaw deep down in me which I am unable to discover', he wrote, and again he adds with insistent, even compulsive, force: 'There must be something terribly lacking in my ahimsa and faith which is responsible for all this.'[106]

That 'serious flaw' deep down inside him which he had 'failed to discover' might have set Gandhi on the trajectory of the last great albeit troubled experiment of his life, but in this trajectory of reasoning there appears at first sight to be more than a faint trace of an almost furtive attempt by Gandhi to recoup the power that he had exercised with unrivalled authority for over two decades. While profoundly committed to the democratic ethos, to the point where he refused to distinguish between intellectual elites and common workers, much as he thought the labour of the hands to be at least as productive and worthy as the labour of the mind, Gandhi's methods were nonetheless often autocratic. In 1939, for example, he had suffered an unprecedented defeat when his candidate for the presidency of the Congress received fewer votes than Subhash Chandra Bose, who was later to flee India and offer Germany and Japan the services of the Indian National Army; not accustomed to having his wishes defied, Gandhi made it impossible for Bose to function as President, and within a few months had procured his resignation. When he commenced his experiments in brahmacharya sometime after his release from jail in mid-1944, he had to make some effort to reestablish his pre-eminent presence on the Indian political scene, and in the negotiations for independence he was only one of several leaders with whom the British parleyed; at the same time, witnessing the carnage taking place (and which would accelerate greatly in the last year before his death), his loss of moral authority must have struck him with even greater force. In consonance with Indian teachings, one of his biographers suggests, Gandhi was under the circumstances particularly prone to accept the view that his power to influence events would be enhanced if he could test himself as a brahmachari.[107] Stretching this argument yet further, it appears not unreasonable to conclude that, forsaking the position that Gandhi had advocated since his early days in South Africa that the ends never justify the means, he was even prepared to make the young women who idolized him the instrument of his quest for political power.

Any such interpretation, as I have throughout been attempting to argue, cannot really be sustained. That Gandhi would now resort to the vulgar, not to mention reprehensible, notion that any means were permissible in order to enhance his political fortunes can scarcely be reconciled with anything we know of Gandhi's political philosophy, his decisive rejection of instrumental rationality, his practices of satyagraha, and—as even his critics concede—his willingness to endure the most dangerous risks to his own life in his resolve to bring the violence to an end. Alone among Indian leaders, Gandhi entirely repudiated the trappings of power, and understood that in the visible sovereignty and display of power reside the seeds of its destruction. He was, as I have argued in a previous chapter, more attuned to the nature of power in the modern age than the politicians, who more than fifty years after his death, consider the number of security guards attached to them as the index of their power and prestige. By this yardstick, Gandhi, who refused protection even after an attempt on his life, was a mere commoner. It is instructive that he never held office after having established a decisive moral authority over the Congress in 1920, and that from the mid-1920s onwards he was not even a member of the party over whose destiny he presided and which had been charged with liberating India from British rule. Gandhi was most certainly perturbed, indeed mortified, by the communal violence that had broken out, but this in no manner leads inescapably to the conclusion that unable to accept the loss of his influence, he was now prepared to abandon his convictions and the principles of satyagraha in the pursuit of his political ambitions. He had committed, in his own language, 'Himalayan blunders' before,[108] most particularly during the 1920-22 non-cooperation movement which he had felt compelled to suspend when it had degenerated into violence, and his political difficulties from 1945 to 1947 can easily be overstated. Then, in 1922, he had faced, with remarkable equanimity, a prison term designed to prevent him from preaching sedition, and had so embraced a form of powerlessness that would have the curative and rejuvenative effect of launching him into the next stage of the struggle for India's spiritual, political, and social revival. In the last years of his life, Gandhi again seems to have been seized with the desire to be stripped clean, and such was his disdain for power that he was altogether prepared to face calumny and approbation. As a brahmachari, he had put limits upon himself with respect to 'contacts with the opposite sex', but these limits now struck him as unacceptable, as constraints placed upon his constant engagement with the truth.[109]

On more than one occasion Gandhi had described his life's endeavour as nothing but a concerted effort to reduce himself to 'zero'. This is the note on which he concludes his autobiography of the mid-1920s, and a year before his death he was to put the matter in similar terms in a letter to Mirabehn: 'If I succeed in emptying myself utterly, God will possess me. Then I know that everything will come true but it is a serious question when I shall have reduced myself to zero. Think of "I" and "O" in juxtaposition and you have the whole problem of life in two signs.'[110] To empty oneself is not only to render oneself into a vehicle for something else, to become capable of being possessed, but to lead life to the fullest. Gandhi's nakedness needed no adornment, and any adornment would have been an effrontery to his nakedness. Appearing naked before the world, Gandhi would yet scarcely have championed nudity: he had no 'private parts', not even, despite his (near) androgyny, a penis-vagina. Having renounced sex, Gandhi had by no means abjured sexuality; quite to the contrary, he was to embrace it in the amplest measure. In the language of James Carse, Gandhi was an exponent of infinite rather than finite sexuality. Where players at the finite game of sexuality view persons as the expressions of sexuality, Gandhi was interested in sexuality as the expression of persons; and where finite players relate to the body, infinite players relate to the person in the body. 'Finite sexuality is a form of theatre in which the distance between persons is regularly reduced to zero', writes Carse with extraordinary prescience, 'but in which neither touches the other.' Gandhi had not the power of touch, for he was no miracle-maker, but he had the vision of touch: 'Finite players play within boundaries', adds Carse, but 'infinite players play with boundaries'; infinite players of sexuality play not *within* sexual boundaries, as do heterosexuals, bisexuals, lesbians, and homosexuals, but *with* sexual boundaries.[111] Gandhi, who abhorred sex, was yet the most consummate player at the game of sexuality.

Notes

1. Gandhi, 'What is Brahmacharya?', *Young India* (5 June 1924), reprinted in Anand T. Hingorani ed., M. K. Gandhi, *The Law of Continence: Brahmacharya*, Pocket Gandhi Series, no. 7 (Bombay: Bharatiya Vidya Bhavan, 1964), p. 18.

2. Quoted by Pyarelal, *Mahatma Gandhi: The Last Phase* (Ahmedabad: Navajivan Publishing House, 1956; 2nd ed., 1966), vol. I, Book Two, p. 210.

3. Ved Mehta, *Mahatma Gandhi and His Apostles* (New York: Penguin Books, 1977), p. 203.

4. *Collected Works of Mahatma Gandhi* [hereafter cited as CWMG], 100 vols. (New Delhi: Government of India, Ministry of Information and Broadcasting, Publications Division, 1954-95), vol. 79, p. 213.

5. CWMG, vol. 87, p. 90; cf. vol. 86, p. 423.

6 Ananda K. Coomaraswamy, 'Mahatma', in S. Radhakrishnan ed., *Mahatma Gandhi: Essays and Reflections on His Life and Work* (London: George Allen & Unwin, 1939; 2nd enlarged ed., 1949), pp. 63-67. As Coomaraswamy pointedly notes, Mahatma (from the Sanskrit maha: great + atma: soul) is rendered literally as 'Great Soul', but that is far from the meaning it truly implies. A Mahatma is 'one who is "in the spirit", and more than man'; such a Mahatma abandons 'the "petty self" and lives only in his "great self"'. (p. 64).

7. Nirmal Kumar Bose, as quoted in Mehta, *Mahatma Gandhi and His Apostles*, p. 193.

8. Even the biography by Catherine Clement, a French feminist and psychoanalyst, devotes just two sentences to this matter. The caption accompanying a photograph of Gandhi with Manu and Abha, who were his constant companions after Kasturba's death, states: 'He had brought up the two orphans and shared a bed with Manu, his favourite, as a way of testing their virtue. The ensuing scandal was deeply mortifying to Gandhi.' See her *Gandhi: Father of a Nation* (London: Thames and Hudson, 1996), p. 113. The English translation of the French original of 1989 appears in a series called 'New Horizons.' The most notable exception to the silence on this matter is William L. Shirer's *Gandhi: A Memoir* (New York: Simon and Schuster, 1979), pp. 230-38, though Shirer's account is largely descriptive.

9. Madhu Kishwar, 'Gandhi and Women', *Economic and Political Weekly* 20, nos. 40

and 41 (1985), reprinted as *Gandhi and Women* (Delhi: Manushi Prakashan, 1986).

10. Gandhi has had many detractors and critics over the years, among them Marxists, liberals, dalits, Hindu militants, and modernizers. The best treatment of this subject, though far from adequate, is to be found in B. R. Nanda, *Gandhi and His Critics* (Oxford: Delhi University Press, 1985).

11. The real exception here would be American and English critics, such as Richard Grenier and Michael Edwardes, to whom Gandhi was not merely an eccentric, but a 'humbug' and, in the words of the popular English historian Paul Johnson, a 'consummate sorcerer's apprentice'. See his article 'Gandhi Isn't Good For You', *Daily Telegraph* (16 April 1983). On Edwardes, see Mark T. Berger, 'Gandhi and the Guardians—Michael Edwardes and the Apologetics of Imperialism', *Bulletin of Concerned Asian Scholars* (1989).

12. M. K. Gandhi, 'Why I am a Hindu', *Young India* (20 October 1927), also anthologized in Raghavan Iyer, ed., *The Moral and Political Writings of Mahatma Gandhi*, vol. I: *Civilization, Politics, and Religion* (Oxford: Clarendon Press, 1986), pp. 26-27.

13. Nehru's profound unease with Gandhi, commingled with intense admiration for the 'miracles' that Gandhi was able to work in India, is palpably felt in all his writings on Gandhi: a good example is his autobiography, *Toward Freedom* (1941; reprint ed., Boston: Beacon Press, 1961), pp. 47-53, 65-85, 309-26; for Amartya Sen's predictable reading of Gandhi, see 'Tagore and His India', *New York Review of Books* (26 June 1997), pp. 55-63.

14. For critical Marxist views of Gandhi, see M. N. Roy, *Selected Writings of M. N. Roy*, 3 vols. (Delhi: Oxford University Press, 1989), vol. 2, pp. 152-57, 180-4, 310-5; vol. 3, pp. 457-58, 566-71; and Sudarshan Chattopadhyaya ed., *Against the Stream*: *An Anthology of Writings of Saumyendranath Tagore*, 2 vols. (Calcutta: Saumyendranath Memorial Committee, 1975).

15. See Kishwar, *Gandhi and Women*, and Ketu H. Katrak, 'Indian Nationalism, Gandhian "Satyagraha," and Representations of Female Sexuality', in Andrew Parker, Mary Russo, Doris Sommer, and Patricia Yaeger eds., *Nationalisms and Sexualities* (London: Routledge, 1992), pp. 395-406.

16. Shirer, *Gandhi*, p. 238.

17. Nirmal Kumar Bose, as quoted in Mehta, *Mahatma Gandhi and His Apostles*, p. 194. Gandhi was never addressed as Gandhi, except by British officials, newspaper editors, and strangers. To most Indians he was 'Bapu', or Father; and then he was 'Bapuji', the suffix 'ji' being an honorific. At other times he was 'Mahatmaji'. He is now spoken of as 'Gandhiji.'

18. This photograph is reproduced in, among other works, Clement, *Gandhi*, p.

99; Robert Payne, *The Life and Death of Mahatma Gandhi* (1969; reprint ed., New York: Smithmark Publishers, 1995), following p. 416; and D. G. Tendulkar, *Mahatma: The Life of Mohandas Karamchand Gandhi*, 8 vols. (new ed., New Delhi: Publications Division, Ministry of Information and Broadcasting, Government of India), vol. 6, between pp. 32-33.

19. Sudhir Kakkar, *Intimate Relations: Exploring Indian Sexuality* (New Delhi: Penguin Books, 1989), p. 94.

20. Tendulkar, *Mahatma*, vol. 1, pp. 75.

21. CWMG, vol. 30, pp. 143. Much later in life, Gandhi held a contrary view: responding to a query from a married man who wished to observe brahmacharya in opposition to his wife's wishes, he said, 'A husband or wife can strive for any aim which was not present in the minds of both at the time of marriage, only with the consent of the other party. In other words, a husband cannot take the vow of brahmacharya without the consent of his wife.' See CWMG, vol. 66, p. 70.

22. Tendulkar, *Mahatma*, vol. 1, p. 77.

23. Payne, *Life and Death of Mahatma Gandhi*, p. 160.

24. Writing to a European woman on 12 March 1928, Gandhi had this to say about his treatment of Kasturba: 'But I thought that if people recognize me as a gentle peace-loving man, they should also know that at one time I could be a positive beast even though at the same time I claimed to be a loving husband. It was not without good cause that a friend once described me as a combination of sacred cow and ferocious tiger.' See Iyer, ed., *Moral and Political Writings of Mahatma Gandhi*, vol. 1, pp. 28-29.

25. Ibid., pp. 256-58.

26. The memory of Kasturba in modern India is, unfortunately, confined to the handful of octogenarians and others who were active in the freedom movement. It is not the case that her slide into relative oblivion was inevitable, owing to the much greater presence of her husband; rather, it is the other Gandhis, Indira and her clan, who were to monopolize the public space with the name of Gandhi.

27. Introduction by M. K. Gandhi to Sushila Nayyar, *Kasturba: Wife of Gandhi* (Wallingford, Pennsylvania: Pendle Hill, 1948), p. 9. I have seen both spellings, 'Nayar' and 'Nayyar', in the literature but have retained 'Nayyar' for consistency.

28. Madeleine Slade, *The Spirit's Pilgrimage* (New York: Coward-McCann, Inc., 1960). Her description of her first meeting with Gandhi is priceless: she was ushered into Gandhi's presence, and was 'conscious of nothing but a sense of light.' Madeleine fell to her knees; then hands gently raised her up, and a voice said: 'You shall be my daughter' (p. 66).

29. Madeleine was renamed Mira in emulation of the great Mirabai, the sixteenth-century woman saint who imagined Krishna as her lover, and whose rapturous devotion to Krishna took the form of ecstatic bhajans or devotional songs, which have ever since been considered one of the greatest treasures of Awadhi-Bhojpuri-Hindi literature.

30. Gandhi's letters to Mira were published in the United States as *The Love Letters of Mahatma Gandhi*. See also Mira Behn, ed., *Bapu's Letters to Mira (1924-1948)* (Ahmedabad: Navajivan Press, 1949), p. 42.

31. Mira Behn, ed., *Bapu's Letters to Mira*, pp. 42-43.

32. Slade [Mira Behn], *The Spirit's Pilgrimage*, pp. 92-93.

33. Mahadev Desai ed., M. K. Gandhi, *Gita According to Gandhi or the Gospel of Selfless Action* (Ahmedabad: Navajivan Publishing House, 1946).

34. Kakar, *Intimate Relations*, p. 111.

35. Payne, *Life and Death of Mahatma Gandhi*, p. 277.

36. Geoffrey Ashe, *Gandhi* (New York: Stein and Day, 1969), p. 267. I advert to this saying in the following chapter as well, suggesting one link among many others between the two chapters.

37. Mehta, *Mahatma Gandhi and His Apostles*, p. 197.

38. Manubehn Gandhi, *Bapu—My Mother* (Ahmedabad: Navajivan Publishing House, 1949).

39. Nirmal Kumar Bose, *My Days with Gandhi* (Calcutta: Nishana, 1953), p. 55. Gandhi himself released a statement to the press on November 20, in which he described himself as placed in the midst of 'exaggeration and falsity', 'unable to discover the truth', and faced with 'terrible mutual distrust'. To test his belief in satya and ahimsa, Gandhi added, 'I am going to a village called Srirampur, cutting myself away from those who have been with me all these years, and who have made life easy for me.' See CWMG, vol. 86, p. 138.

40. Bose, *My Days with Gandhi*, p. 113.

41. Ibid., p. 115.

42. Ibid., p. 116.

43. Ibid., p. 134.

44. CWMG, vol. 86, pp. 299-300; also published in Bose, *My Days with Gandhi*, pp. 135-36.

45. CWMG, vol. 86, p. 314.

46. Bose, *My Days with Gandhi*, p. 136.

47. Ibid., p. 154.

48. Gandhi, letter to Vinoba Bhave, 10 February 1947, in CWMG vol. 86, p. 452.

49. Ibid.

50. CWMG 86:420; see also Pyarelal, *The Last Phase*, vol. I, Book II, pp. 219-20;

Bose, *My Days with Gandhi*, p. 154; *Harijan*, 23 February 1947.

51. Letter to Manilal Gandhi, 1 February 1947, in CWMG, vol. 86, p. 415.

52. Pyarelal, *The Last Phase*, vol. I, Book II, p. 226; CWMG, vol. 87, pp. 14-16.

53. Gandhi leaned, in the last years of his life, on the shoulders of Manu and Abha, who walked and stood on either side of him. Nathuram Godse, Gandhi's assassin, pushed aside the two girls when he shot the Mahatma point-blank. Manu died in 1969, the centenary year of Gandhi's birth. Abha is still alive: a recent, albeit short, account of her life with Gandhi and her activities is found in S. Theodore Baskaran, 'Witness to history', *The Hindu* (29 January 1995), Sunday Magazine, p. 2. I am grateful to my friend Henry Ranjeet of Kolam Travels, Madras, for bringing this article to my attention.

54. Shirer, *Gandhi*, p. 230.

55. S. C. Biswas ed. , T. K. Mahadevan, 'An Approach to the Study of Gandhi', in *Gandhi, Theory and Practice* (Simla: Indian Institute of Advanced Study, 1969), p. 46.

56. Ibid., p. 49, citing a letter by Gandhi, 9 June 1914.

57. CWMG, vol. 23, p. 102.

58. Gandhi, *Law of Continence*, p. 55.

59. Jawaharlal Nehru, *Toward Freedom: The Autobiography of Jawaharlal Nehru* (Boston: Beacon Press, 1958), pp. 316-17.

60. Bhikhu Parekh, 'Gandhi's Theory of Non-violence: His Reply to the Terrorists', in Noel O'Sullivan ed., *Terrorism, Ideology and Revolution* (Boulder, Colorado: Westview Press, 1986), pp. 193-94. This is also the opinion of Gandhi's respected biographer Geoffrey Ashe, who attributes Gandhi's shortcomings on the subject of sex to the inability of Hindus through the centuries to strike a 'balance'. Gandhi 'never grasped', says Ashe, 'that a sexual companionship might be ennobling and generous. Myopia in this quarter was his tragic flaw, all the more tragic because he was free from vulgar prudery.' Ashe views Gandhi's position on sex, having in it the 'shadow of something pallid and life-denying', as unfortunate, more particularly as it obfuscates his otherwise extraordinary insights into human nature (*Gandhi*, pp. 181-82).

61. Shirer, *Gandhi*, p. 119; Nehru, *Toward Freedom*, p. 317.

62. Shirer, *Gandhi*, p. 232; Kakar, *Intimate Relations*, pp. 86-91; see also Lynne Shivers, 'An Open Letter to Gandhi', in Pam McAllister ed., *Reweaving the Web of Life: Feminism and Nonviolence* (Philadelphia: New Society Publishers, 1982), pp. 181-94 at pp. 189-91.

63. M. K. Gandhi in Mahadev Desai tr., *An Autobiography or The Story of My Experiments with Truth* (Ahmedabad: Navajivan Publishing House, 1927; reprint of 2nd ed., 1959), Book I, Chapter IX, 'My Father's Death and My Double Shame', pp. 21-3. Since there are many editions of the autobiography, references to book

and chapter are provided.

64. M. K. Gandhi, *Key to Health* (Ahmedabad: Navajivan Publishing House, 1948), p. 44.

65. Gandhi, *Law of Continence*, p. 45; cf. also p. 21, 53, 56, 58, passim.

66. Navajivan, 26 February 1925, in Gandhi, *The Law of Continence*, p. 25.

67. Letter to Amrit Kaur, 18 March 1947, CWMG, vol. 87, pp. 107-8.

68. Gandhi, 'Nothing Without Grace', *Harijan* (29 February 1936), reprinted in Tendulkar, *Mahatma*, vol. 4, p. 52. The previous 'lapse' was in 1924: see the discussion below, and CWMG, 40, p. 312.

69. CWMG, vol. 62, p. 247; cf. Sarasi Lal Sarkar, 'A Study of the Psychology of Sexual Abstinence from the Dreams of an Ascetic', *International Journal of Psycho-Analysis* 24 (1943), pp. 170-75 at p. 170.

70. *Harijan* (26 December 1936), cited by Shirer, *Gandhi*, p. 233, and in part by Ashe, *Gandhi*, p. 329.

71. Gandhi, *Autobiography*, 'Farewell', p. 371.

72. Ashe, *Gandhi*, p. 254.

73. CWMG, vol. 62, p. 30.

74. Morris Carstairs, *The Twice-Born* (London: The Hogarth Press, 1968), p. 83; see also Bhikhu Parekh, *Colonialism, Tradition and Reform: An Analysis of Gandhi's Political Discourse* (New Delhi: Sage Publications, 1989), pp. 177-78. The fear of semen loss is described by some scholars as being particularly prominent in India: see Joel Paris, 'Dhat: The Semen Loss Anxiety Syndrome', *Transcultural Psychiatric Research Review* 29, no. 2 (1992), pp. 109-118, and A. Bottero, 'Consumption by semen loss in India and elsewhere', *Culture, Medicine and Psychiatry* 15 (1991), pp. 303-320. An Indian psychiatrist reports a belief held by many of his patients that 40 meals produce one drop of blood, 40 drops of blood are required to produce one drop of bone marrow, and 40 drops of bone marrow yield one drop of semen: consequently, it requires no great imagination to surmise why the preservation of semen should so forcefully be insisted upon! See S. Akhtar, 'Four culture-bound psychiatric syndromes in India', *International Journal of Social Psychiatry* 34 (1988), pp. 70-74.

75. Kakar, *Intimate Relations*, p. 118.

76. Erik H. Erikson, *Gandhi's Truth: On the Origins of Militant Nonviolence* (New York: W. W. Norton and Co., 1969), p. 404.

77. Tendulkar, *Mahatma*, vol. 4, p. 59.

78. CWMG, vol. 62, p. 247.

79. Wendy Doniger O'Flaherty, *Women, Androgynes, and Other Mythical Beasts* (Chicago: The University of Chicago Press, 1980), p. 44.

80. Parekh, *Colonialism, Tradition and Reform*, p. 200. Gandhi's secretary in later

years, Pyarelal, says that Gandhi recommended the study of tantra: *Gandhi, The Last Phase*, 2 vols. (Ahmedabad: Navajivan Publishing House, 1956), vol. 1, p. 589. This appears to be corroborated by Gandhi's remarks to his interlocutors on 15-16 March 1947 that he had read works on Tantra (CWMG, vol. 87, p. 91).

81.   Cf. James W. Edwards, 'Semen Anxiety in South Asian Cultures: Cultural and Transcultural Significance', *Medical Anthropology* 7, no. 3 (Summer 1983), pp. 51-68

82.   For a brief comparison between Victorian and Gandhian ideas of sexuality, see Pat Caplan, 'Celibacy as a solution? Mahatma Gandhi and Brahmacharya', in Pat Caplan, ed., *The Cultural Construction of Sexuality* (London: Tavistock, 1987), pp. 271-95 at pp. 278-79, 286-87. It is no longer widely accepted that there was nothing much more to Victorian sexual mores than repression, and Foucault's hypothesis that the nineteenth and twentieth centuries share an uncommon concern for sex has been influential. See Michael Mason, *The Making of Victorian Sexuality* (Oxford: Oxford University Press, 1995).

83.   Judy Costello, 'Beyond Gandhi: An American Feminist's Approach to Nonviolence', in McAllister ed., *Reweaving the Web of Life*, p. 179.

84.   Parekh, *Colonialism, Tradition and Reform*, p. 182.

85.   Sarkar, 'A Study of the Psychology of Sexual Abstinence', p. 174.

86.   Ibid., p. 175.

87.   See Chapter VII.

88.   Of all his biographers, Ashe comes closest to viewing Gandhi as akin to Ramakrishna, though he ultimately disavows any such comparison: see his *Gandhi*, pp. 130-32, 260-63.

89.   Mahendranath Gupta [known as 'M'] in Swami Nikhilananda tr., *The Gospel of Sri Ramakrishna*, 2 vols. (Mylapore: Sri Ramakrishna Math, 1980), vol. 2, p. 595.

90.   Swami Chetanananda, ed. and tr., *Ramakrishna as We Saw Him* (St. Louis: Vedanta Society, 1990), pp. 357-59.

91.   Swami Saradananda in Swami Jagadananda tr., *Sri Ramakrishna the Great Master* (Mylapore: Sri Ramakrishna Math, 1952), pp. 233-34.

92.   Christopher Isherwood, *Ramakrishna and His Disciples* (1950; reprint ed., New York: Simon and Schuster/Touchstone Books, 1965).

93.   *Harijan*, 14 November 1936; C. Shukla, ed., *Gandhi As We Know Him* (Bombay: Vora and Company, 1945), p. 47.

94.   Bose, *My Days with Gandhi*, p. 170. The discussion of this point in Amrit Srinivasan, 'The Subject in Fieldwork—Malinowski and Gandhi', in Meenakshi Thapan, ed., *Anthropological Journeys: Reflections on Fieldwork* (Delhi: Orient

Longman, 1996), p. 77, is incisive and has been helpful.

95. CWMG, vol. 67, pp. 194-95.

96. Joshi, *Gandhi on Women*, pp. 209-11.

97. Letter to Amtul Salaam, 2 January 1947, in CWMG vol. 86, p. 300.

98. Pyarelal, *The Last Phase*, vol. 1, p. 224.

99. Ganesh Vasudeo Tagare, ed and tr., *The Bhagavata Purana* (Delhi: Motilal Banarsidass, 1978), Part IV, Book X, Chapter 22, pp. 1395-99.

100. The amorousness and frivolity of Krishna do not sit easily with many modernizing Indians, obsessed as they are with demonstrating that Krishna, much like Muhammad or Christ, was a historical, rational, and sombre figure. Typical of this profound unease is Asha Goswami's *Krnsa-Katha and Allied Matters* (Delhi: Y. R. Publications, 1994), where the author remarks that the puranic and epic accounts of Krishna's 16,108 wives ought to be discounted, since Krishna 'surely could not have been so fickle and frivolous about his marriage which in fact is a very important social event in human life' (p. 174).

101. The temple-dancers of Orissa, the subject of a study by the anthropologist Frederique Apffel-Marglin, offered her an extended account of why Krishna must not spill his seed: see 'Types of sexual union and their implicit meanings', in J. S. Hawley and D. M. Wulff, eds., *The Divine Consort: Radha and the Goddesses of India* (Berkeley: University of California Press, 1982), pp. 298-315 at pp. 306-7. The god Shiva, who is often represented as a yogi, likewise has the ability to hold an erection without spilling his seed, and indeed his erect phallus is symbolic not only of his power to impregnate but also of his chastity. See O'Flaherty, *Women, Androgynes, and Other Mythical Beasts*, esp. II.2.B.

102. Gandhi to Vinoba Bhave, 10 February 1947, CWMG vol. 86, p. 453.

103. Gandhi, 'My Loin-Cloth', *The Hindu* (15 October 1921), reprinted in CWMG, vol. 21, pp. 225-27.

104. CWMG, vol. 86, p. 138.

105. CWMG, vol. 87, p. 14.

106. CWMG, vol. 86, p. 302. On 10 January 1947, Gandhi addressed his son Ramdas on the same subject, and after informing him of the experiment he had undertaken of sharing his bed with Manu, added: 'I am still surrounded by darkness. I have no doubt whatever that it indicates a flaw somewhere in my method. Take it as though I had confined myself to this place [Noakhali] to detect that flaw. It must lie somewhere in my practice of ahimsa. Could it be that I am nurturing only weakness in the name of non-violence!' (CWMG, ibid., p. 335).

107. Ashe, *Gandhi*, p. 377.

108. Payne, *Life and Death of Mahatma Gandhi*, p. 333.

109. CWMG, vol. 67, pp. 194-98.

110. CWMG, vol. 86, p. 314; *Autobiography*, p. 371: 'Farewell'.

111. James P. Carse, *Finite and Infinite Games: A Vision of Life as Play and Possibility* (New York: Ballantine Books, 1987), pp. 12, 91-103.

Six

GANDHI AND THE ECOLOGICAL VISION OF LIFE:
TOO DEEP FOR DEEP ECOLOGY

I

GANDHI AND THE INDIAN ENVIRONMENTAL MOVEMENT

In a lecture given in 1993, the Indian historian Ramachandra Guha proposed to inquire whether Gandhi could be considered an 'early environmentalist'.[1] Though Gandhi was a vociferous critic of modern industrial civilization, he had, when one considers the sheer range and volume of his writings, relatively little to say about nature or its representation, whether in art, literature, or science. No doubt his writings are littered with remarks on man's exploitation of nature, and his views about these matters can reasonably be inferred from his famous pronouncement that the earth has enough to satisfy everyone's needs but not everyone's greed. He had strong views about 'human nature', as does everyone else, and some circles seek to remember him for nothing more than his radical advocacy of 'nature cure'. Still, when 'nature' is viewed in the conventional sense, Gandhi was rather remarkably reticent on the relationship of humans to their external environment. His name is associated with innumerable political and social reform movements, extending from his famous satyagraha campaigns in defiance of British rule to his efforts to abolish untouchability and open Hindu temples to what were then known as the 'depressed classes', but it is striking that he never explicitly initiated an environmental movement, nor does the word 'ecology' ever appear in his writings. Again, though commercial forestry had commenced well before Gandhi's time, and the depletion of Indian forests would persistently provoke peasant resistance, Gandhi himself was never associated with forest satyagrahas, however much his name was invoked by peasants and rebels.

Guha observes also that 'the wilderness had no attraction for Gandhi.'[2] His writings are singularly devoid of any celebration of untamed nature or rejoicing at the chance sighting of a wondrous waterfall or an imposing Himalayan peak; and indeed his autobiography remains utterly silent on his experience of the ocean, over which he took an unusually long number of journeys for an Indian of his time. A Melville, Conrad, or Jack London would have been, one might justifiably surmise, unintelligible to him. In Gandhi's innumerable trips to Indian villages and the countryside—and seldom had any Indian acquired so intimate a familiarity with the smell of the earth and the feel of the soil across a vast land—he almost never had occasion to take note of the trees, vegetation, landscape, or animals. As we shall see, he was by no means indifferent to animals, but he could only comprehend them in a domestic capacity. Students of Gandhi certainly are aware not only of the goat that he kept by his side and of his passionate commitment to cow-protection, but of his profound attachment to what he often described as 'dumb creation', indeed to all living forms.

The modern environmental movement was, of course, still several decades distant from being inaugurated in Gandhi's time, and it may be no more than wishful thinking to expect that Gandhi could have been an environmentalist a generation before that became a political possibility. But it is indubitably certain that Gandhi at least cannot be constrained or exculpated by that conventional and tedious yardstick with which so much scholarship sadly contents itself: namely, that he was a man of his times, and that an environmental sensibility was not yet positioned to intervene significantly in the shaping of society. Gandhi was an ardent exponent of vegetarianism, nature cure, and what are today termed 'alternative' systems of medicine well before these acquired the semblance of acceptability in the West; he was a dedicated practitioner of recycling before the idea had crept into the lexicon of the liberal consciousness; he was a trenchant critic of modernity before the Frankfurt school, not to mention the post-modernism of Lyotard, had provided some of the contours of modern thought; and he was, needless to say, an advocate of non-violent resistance long before uses for such forms of resistance were found in the United States, South Africa, and elsewhere. No one suspects that Gandhi was merely a man of his times: so it is not unlikely that Gandhi could have been an environmentalist and more, anticipating in this respect as in many others, modern social and political movements.

Indeed, the general consensus of Indian environmentalists appears to be that Gandhi inspired and even perhaps, in a manner of speaking, fathered the Indian environmental movement. He cannot, however, be likened to John Muir or Aldo Leopold, and much less to Thoreau: Gandhi was no naturalist, and it is doubtful that he would have contemplated with equanimity the setting aside of tracts of land, forests, and woods as 'wilderness areas', though scarcely for the same reasons for which developers, industrialists, loggers, and financiers object to such altruism. The problems posed by the man-eating tigers of Kumaon, made famous by Jim Corbett, would have left less of a moral impression upon him than those problems which are the handiwork of men who let the brute within them triumph. It is reported that when the English historian Edward Thompson once remarked to Gandhi that wildlife was rapidly disappearing in India, Gandhi replied: 'wildlife is decreasing in the jungles, but it is increasing in the towns.'[3] Though Ramachandra Guha has noted some limitations in viewing Gandhi as an 'early environmentalist', such as his purportedly poor recognition of the 'distinctive social and environmental problems' of urban areas, Guha readily acknowledges, as do most others, that the impress of Gandhian thinking is to be felt in the life and works of many of India's most well-known environmental activists.[4] It was Gandhi's own disciples, Mirabehn and Saralabehn, who came to exercise an incalculable influence on Chandi Prasad Bhatt, Vimla and Sunderlal Bahuguna, and others who have been at the helm of the Chipko agitation, a movement to ensure, in the words of women activists, that Himalayan forests continue to bear 'soil, water and pure air' for present and future generations.[5] Similarly, Medha Patkar and Baba Amte, the most well-known figures associated with the more recent Narmada Bachao Andolan, a movement aimed at preventing the construction of one of the world's largest dam projects and the consequent dislocation and uprooting of the lives of upwards of 100,000 rural and tribal people,[6] have been equally generous in acknowledging that their inspiration has come in great part from Gandhi. It may be mistaken to speak of these movements as 'Gandhian', since any such reading perforce ignores the traditions of peasant resistance, the force of customary practices, and the appeal of localized systems of knowledge, but the spirit of Gandhi has undoubtedly moved Indian environmentalists.

Thus far, then, it appears that Gandhi presents something of a difficulty to those who would propose to describe him as the author or father of Indian environmentalism. It is undoubtedly possible to see the environmentalist in him, particularly if one is willing to engage in certain hermeneutic exercises, but one hesitates in describing him as an environmentalist. Similarly, if I may multiply the layers of this anomaly, Gandhi was a lover of animals without being a pet-lover, a warrior who absolutely forsook arms, an autocrat deeply wedded to democratic sentiments, an admirer of the Ramayana who rejected the dogmatism of many of its verses, a follower of the sanatan dharma or eternal faith who in his later years would only bless inter-caste weddings, and a traditionalist whose apparent allegiance to hideous traditions led him to counsel the rejection of all authorities except one's own conscience. His close friend and associate, the renowned poet and rebel Sarojini Naidu, pointed to this seemingly enigmatic aspect of Gandhi's personality when she once quipped that 'it takes a great deal of money to keep Bapu living in poverty'.[7] Though his pronouncements spoke of the conventional division of labour between men and women as 'natural', in his own ashrams he insisted that all its members were to partake equally of all the tasks, and no differentiation was permitted, in matters of either labour or morality, between men and women; moreover, the kitchen, the toilet, the Viceroy's palatial residence, and the prison were all equally fertile arenas for testing the truth of one's convictions. These circumstances constitute the grounds, as I shall endeavour to argue, for viewing Gandhi as a man with a profoundly ecological view of life, a view much too deep even for deep ecology.

II

WHAT IS DEEP ECOLOGY?

Gandhi's own views would perhaps be deemed to have the closest resemblance, among the various strands of radical ecology encountered today, to the philosophical presuppositions of deep ecology. It is no coincidence that the Norwegian philosopher Arne Naess, with whose name 'deep ecology' is pre-eminently associated, was an ardent student of Gandhi's thought and work before he turned his attention to the problems of the environment, and that in Gandhi he found a political philosopher who most clearly shows the way to the resolution of group conflicts.[8] In an extended interview that he gave a few years ago, Naess described himself as having fallen under the 'influence' of Gandhi in 1931; and as war came to Europe some years later, Naess was to counsel non-violent resistance to his pacifist friends.[9] From Gandhi Naess divined the importance of all work as a form of self-realization, and it is Gandhi who, as he was to write in a study of Gandhi's mode of conflict resolution, provided him with the assurance that 'the rock-bottom foundation of the technique for achieving the power of non-violence is belief in the essential oneness of all life . . . . More than a few people, from their earliest youth, feel a basic unity with and of all the human beings they encounter, a unity that overrides all the differences and makes these appear superficial. Gandhi was one of these fortunate people.'[10]

In a short paper published in 1973, Naess was to distinguish between the 'shallow' and 'deep' approaches to environmentalism, and so pave the way for the 'deep ecology' movement.[11] The exponents of the shallow view of environmentalism, Naess maintained, are bound to an anthropocentric view of the universe. They have no intrinsic commitment to the preservation of nature, but are only interested in nature insofar as it affects the interests of humans. Their world view has room enough for viewing nature as something other than merely the repository of wealth to be extracted and exploited for use and profit; but if nature is not merely an instrument to some better end, it is emphatically not an end in itself. While not necessarily beholden to an economistic framework, they are by no means averse to cost-benefit analyses: thus they would deplore pollution not only on the grounds that it fouls the air, contaminates the soil and the food that is put on the table, and renders unsafe our supply of drinking water, but because it leads to numerous other costs that outweigh any benefits that might be generated by industries that release pollutants in the air. Thus the shallow environmentalists would insist on factoring in the costs of treatment for respiratory and skin diseases, the expenditure on research aimed at providing solutions to problems created by pollution, and so on. They would be sensitive to the fact that smoke from industries in the vicinity of the Taj Mahal has eroded the pristine quality of the marble and rendered somewhat obscure the marvellous hues of the inlaid gems and stones, and they would undoubtedly have agreed with the judge who ordered the relocation of these industries. But they may too readily ignore the fact that such relocation jeopardizes the livelihood of many people and introduces a new set of class relations. As Naess notes, 'if prices of life necessities increase because of the installation of anti-pollution devices, class differences increase too.'[12] Moreover, if I may hazard the proposition in this provocative form, shallow environmentalists prize museums more than they do living cultures.

Shallow environmentalists, as can now be surmised, have no intrinsic objection to industrialism, but only to its excesses: they are advocates, in the clichéd phrase, of 'development with a human face', or 'sustainable development' as it is known in the scholarly literature, though this perhaps slightly overstates their compliance with bourgeois models of human engineering. Naess has also objected to shallow environmentalists on the grounds that they are largely concerned with the fate of the affluent or post-industrial nations, this concern having arisen as a consequence of the rapid depletion of non-renewable natural resources. Though shallow environmentalists are not without democratic sentiments, they have always envisioned an upward levelling: the rest of the world was to be raised to a higher standard of living, but no decrease in their own standards of living was to be contemplated. Thus, when faced with an oil crisis and increased pollution, the shallow environmentalists would not necessarily have countenanced the elimination of automobiles, but only their more efficient use. The shallow environmentalists are among those who would support research on battery-powered automobiles, but their enthusiasm for mass-transport systems, such as battery-powered trains, is less frequently expressed. They are agreed that the problems created by technology are best resolved by improved technology. The ingrained presupposition is that technology can invariably resolve, if necessary with the aid of ethics, sociology, and the applied sciences, its own shortcomings.[13]

In contrast to 'shallow' environmentalism, Naess and his supporters posit an ecological view of the world that is less wedded to technocratic and managerial solutions, short-term panaceas, and an instrumentalist (though not necessarily exploitative) view of nature. What is distinctive about 'deep ecology', quite simply, is that it asks 'deeper questions.' Where shallow environmentalism, or what may be termed (after Kuhn) normal ecology, is reticent about asking 'what kind of society would be the best for maintaining a particular ecosystem',[14] since such a query is seen as falling within the provenance of politics, ethics, value theory, and sociology, deep ecology is intrinsically committed to the proposition that it is not possible to alter man's relationship to nature without altering man's relation to man and even the relationship to self.[15] Deep ecology entails, in Naess's words, the 'rejection of the human-in-environment image in favor of the relational, total-field image':[16] man is viewed as being not merely 'in' the environment, but 'of' it; and where the environment takes precedence, man and all other species receive their just due. The elaboration of the deep ecology movement is to be found in what are called the 'platform principles'. These principles command us to recognize that the 'well-being and flourishing of human and non-human Life on Earth have value in themselves', and that these 'values are independent of the usefulness of the non-human world for human purposes.' Human beings are enjoined to respect the 'richness and diversity of life forms', which are not to be compromised 'except to satisfy vital needs'; the 'quality of life', rather than a 'higher standard of living', is to be accorded primacy'; and this 'quality of life', for human and non-human species alike, is described as not being achievable except through a 'substantial decrease of the human population.' The platform principles decry the increasing interference of humans with the non-human world, and call for policy changes that would affect the 'basic economic, technological, and ideological structures' that are today widely accepted.[17]

Deep ecology, unlike shallow environmentalism, recognizes the intrinsic worth of the non-human world, just as it recognizes the importance of conserving resources for the use of all species, not only human beings. Domestic animals are valued not merely because they make for good pets and serve as companions in increasingly fragmented societies, or because they satisfy our aesthetic impulses or desire to nurture those who are weaker than us, but because they have an invaluable place in the moral order. Deep ecology celebrates wilderness and an untethered nature. If the principles of diversity, symbiosis, and 'biological egalitarianism' undergird deep ecology,[18] no less important is its insistence on spiritualism and religious values: as Gandhi might have put it, we are only God's trustees on earth. Deep ecology rejects the claim that growth is an intrinsically good economic end, but unlike the 'growth specialists' who claim to take the long-term view but are interested in no more than resource management and profit maximization, deep ecologists feel responsible for future generations. Thus deep ecology recognizes that overpopulation in so-called advanced countries is no more acceptable than overpopulation in developing countries;[19] and it would even go so far as to acknowledge that the vastly higher per capita consumption, whether of goods or resources, in industrialized countries places greater pressures on the environment than does overpopulation in the developing world.[20] To this extent, deep ecology can be said to have sensitivity to issues of class, and it certainly does not appear to countenance a world order where the health and well-being of the affluent nations become the predominant criteria by which policies are framed.

The proponents of deep ecology would, then, go far beyond the shallow environmentalists in the manner in which they address problems posed by the degradation of nature. If the most radical proponents of shallow environmentalism would be prepared to go no further than to advocate exclusive spending on mass-transit systems, deep ecologists must be prepared to offer a critique of automobile pollution of an altogether different ontological order. Such a critique must begin with the complex social history of the automobile, its relationship to the design and planning of American megalopolises such as Los Angeles and Houston, and the culture of fast food, drive-in theatres, and shopping malls that emerged from automobiles. This social history would also encompass the relation of the automobile to the creation of the American suburb and the rise of advertisements: 'pollution' itself must be seen as taking on new meanings. All this and a great deal more, however, falls as much within the expertise of any accomplished sociologist, cultural geographer, or student of urban planning, and the deep ecologist must go even further in expounding a different world-view. If analytically one might ask how the automobile alters conceptions of time and space, and how it gives rise to new ideas of leisure and changing conceptions of 'home', the deep ecologist must also enquire what inverse relation the automobile has to the ethos of walking. What does the decline of walking as a once widely recognized activity for the mind and body portend for our culture, and what different conception of self does the peripatetic mode suggest? Must we go only as far as our hands and feet take us, as Gandhi was to argue in *Hind Swaraj,* and what sort of transgression of limits is entailed by the automobile?[21] Have our bodies, as a consequence of automobiles, become unfit for experiencing other modes of reality?

There is something self-evidently ecological about walking, no doubt, but here common-sense understanding, or even the interpretive framework of the 'expert', will not suffice to suggest why it is that the peripatetic mode signifies a different symbolic and cultural order of being. It is a telling fact that, in the English language at least, politicians run (or even stand)—but do not walk—for elections; and it is equally significant that no Indian had walked across the breadth and length of India as much as did Gandhi, just as he never ran for office. With the attainment of independence and the creation of the nation-state, the space for those who would rather walk than run had appeared to narrow. Gandhi's life was marked by an extreme regularity, and prominent in his daily regime of subversive discipline—if I may so entertain an oxymoron which has never been explored—was the daily walk of 10 kilometres. It is on these walks that Gandhi encountered the poverty of a nation, and so came face to face with the village India that had all but disappeared from nationalist discourse;[22] it is on these walks that Gandhi was flanked on both sides by his secretaries, who took down his dictation and so enabled him to reply to each and every one of the tens of thousands of letters that he received; and it is on these walks that Gandhi kept pace with the time of India and the rhythms of his own body.[23]

From the perspective of deep ecology, the whole can never be encompassed by the sum of the parts. It requires no great imagination to critique technology on the grounds that it displaces human labour and so leads to anomie, just as it is transgressive of limits, but it does require an ecological vision to be able to hint at the principle of compensation that underlies the moral universe we inhabit. When the gain is easily perceived, the heart must be moved to apprehend the loss; and when the loss is patently before our eyes, we must train ourselves to perceive the gain. How many of us have even momentarily thought, as the typewriter collapsed before the onslaught of the computer, that the typewriter required a spirited defence on the grounds that the computer surrenders possession of the primal sound? What relation does the aesthetics of sound bear to the flow of ink and the stream of thought? And what of the typewriter's own predecessors, the writing brush or the humble lead pencil which no one other than Henry David Thoreau did more to develop before he moved to the next phase of his adventure in the woods?[24] The novelist Junichiro Tanizaki wonders what the history of Japan might have been if the fountain pen had been invented by the Chinese or Japanese. 'The ink would not have been this bluish color but rather black, something like India ink,' he writes, 'and it would have been made to seep down from the handle into the brush.' Japanese paper would still have been in vogue; and Japanese literature and thought might not have been so imitative. 'An insignificant little piece of writing equipment, when one thinks of it,' Tanizaki concludes, 'has had a vast, almost boundless, influence on our culture.'[25]

It is no less than the 'vast, almost boundless, influence on our culture' that a pencil exercises on us that Gandhi had in mind on the occasion when he misplaced a two-inch stub of a pencil. One of Gandhi's associates, Kaka Kalelkar, has noted that at an annual session in Bombay of the Indian National Congress, the pre-eminent body of nationalist opinion, he found Gandhi frantically searching for something one evening. When his enquiry revealed that it was no more than a pencil, he offered Gandhi his own pencil and pleaded with him not to waste his time. But Gandhi insisted that he could not have any other pencil, and added: 'You don't understand. I simply must not lose that little pencil! Do you know it was given to me in Madras by Natesan's little boy? He brought it for me with such love! I cannot bear to lose it.'[26] If today we effortlessly substitute one pencil for another, what prevents us from substituting something else in its place tomorrow? What are the limits of substitutability? If we recognized that we hold even a pencil in trust, would we not treat the earth more gently? And when this trust is betrayed, how do we calibrate the nature and extent of that betrayal? Another one of Gandhi's associates, Jehangir Patel, tells us, to evoke a yet more complex pencil story, that one morning he found him examining the tiny stub of a pencil 'which had been put ready for his use'. Gandhi commented that whoever had sharpened the pencil was 'very angry. See how roughly and irregularly the wood has been scored and cut.' Jehangir replied that he didn't find much wrong with it, but if Gandhi was so particular about this matter, he could perhaps make an enquiry. At breakfast, Gandhi looked around the table, and as soon as his eyes fell on Manu, he asked her: 'Manu, you sharpened my pencil this morning, didn't you, and you were feeling angry when you did it?' 'Yes, I was', she replied. 'Well,' said Gandhi, 'please don't sharpen my pencil while you are angry, it distresses me.'[27] To deep ecology's concern for spiritualism and idolization of 'value', Gandhi would no doubt have added, in the fullest sense of these terms, the insistence on truth and non-violence.[28]

III

THE CRITIQUE OF DEEP ECOLOGY

So far 'deep ecology' has appeared as a movement that might receive our sympathetic if not unequivocal assent, though I have already hinted at the beginning of a critique. As is now well known, it has been subjected to more systematic criticisms by exponents of social ecology and, more recently, ecofeminists. In keeping with my endeavour to pave the way for Gandhi from deep ecology, with which its proponents believe he would have had considerable affinity, I will suggest only the outlines, and that too briefly, of the principal critiques of deep ecology, since one can imagine that Gandhi would have shared in these critiques to some extent. A more exhaustive study of the critiques of deep ecology, or of the numerous variants of the ecological movement, such as bioregionalism, is well beyond the scope of this chapter. From there I will move, finally, to a discussion of how Gandhi might be seen as having an ecological view of life, though perforce that does not make him an environmentalist.

The critics of deep ecology have described it as an ideology and movement that, in its resolute ecocentrism, expects human beings to reorganize their societies around the laws of nature. They have pointed to deep ecology's misanthropic tendencies, and it has not helped that such prominent ecologists as Dave Foreman, who has been prominent in the Earth First! movement, have described humans as a 'cancer on nature.'[29] The principal organ of the Earth First! movement, *Earth First! Journal*, has frequently been known to espouse neo-Malthusian positions, and in the early years of the AIDS crisis, its pages aired the view that this epidemic was a blessing in disguise, since it promised to diminish human population and so relieve the pressure on the earth's resources. Deep ecology's agenda to contain the human population has been even less favourably received, as one can imagine, by some feminists. They perceive this objective, to put the matter simply, as yet another patriarchal attempt to take control of women's reproductive powers, and in particular to render Third World women subservient to the interests of both indigenous and First World elites. Though the celebration of nature's fertility receives fulsome expression in the writings of deep ecologists, they seem considerably less enthused by human fertility. This tendency points to more than what feminists axiomatically assume to be the male fear of female sexuality, and to the declining emphasis on female fertility: it suggests the continuing inability of Western culture to treat children with dignity, as something other than incomplete or miniaturized versions of adults, and to exult in the joy of children.

It is the same ecocentrism of deep ecology that, as some scholars and critics have suggested, renders it oblivious to the fact that its agenda cannot be transplanted to Third World countries without aggravating the social inequities that exist in those societies. The establishment of wilderness areas—a widely agreed upon objective of the American ecological and conservation movement—in India, it has been argued, often involves the displacement of local populations and the loss of traditional homelands; elsewhere, as among the Ik people of Uganda, who were expelled to make way for the Kidepo National Park, the consequences have been more catastrophic, including famine, begging, the rise of prostitution, and the total collapse of traditional societies.[30] The American model of national parks, many of them set up in areas which are very sparsely populated, and where in any case there was comparatively little conflict between people and resources, was transplanted wholesale to countries such as India where the relationship between people and their environment has been much closer, and where animals and people continue to have a symbiotic, though scarcely conflict-free, relationship with each other.[31] All of this was opaque to the members of the Indian 'conservation establishment', who are inclined to see ' "ordinary people" and "conservation" [as] irreconcilably opposed', and who hold to the view that, unless one wishes to surrender to the experience of peasants and tribals, only 'experts' are qualified to speak on this matter.[32]

Even the much applauded Project Tiger, which is among the more successful conservation projects in India,[33] has come in for this criticism, and as Ramachandra Guha writes, 'the emphasis on wilderness is positively harmful when applied to the third world.'[34] Guha suggests that such an emphasis amounts, in effect, to a transfer of wealth from the poor to the rich, just as it ignores the more pressing problems of environmental degradation that affect the poor, from scarcity of key natural resources to air and water pollution. If there is an intellectual poverty in deploying the conservation ethos of industrialized nations in countries that have not similarly been able to fatten themselves on the exploited wealth of others, there is perhaps also a failure in the deep ecology movement as a whole to recognize adequately the 'structural' nature of environmental problems. The brunt of the Marxist critique is none other than the assertion that it is the logic of capitalism which leads to environmental degradation, and that the establishment of a 'wilderness cult' not only creates rifts between environmentalists and all those who are involved in innumerable other social and political struggles, but that it signals a descent into reactionary politics. 'The moral cant that marks the recent reworking of the ecology movement into a wilderness cult,' writes the vitriolic Murray Bookchin, 'a network of wiccan covens, fervent acolytes of Earth-Goddess religions, and assorted psychotherapeutic encounter groups beggars description. For all their talk about "self-empowerment", theistic "immanence", "care", and "interconnectedness", such mystics actually manage to navigate themselves away from the serious social issues that underlie the present ecological crisis and retreat to strategies of personal "self-transformation" and "enrichment" that are predicated on myths, metaphors, rituals, and "green" consumerism.'[35]

Though Bookchin's own denigration of what may be termed poetic modalities, his caricature of certain strands of feminism, and similarly his equation—which he has rendered explicit elsewhere—of deep ecology with gnosticism and witchcraft, sheer woolliness about pre-literate man's supposed oneness with nature, and Oriental forms of 'mysticism'—which are better recognized in the West than they are in the East—all equally point to the acute limitations in his own thinking, the force of his criticism cannot but be acknowledged by those who are conversant with the history of how radical movements and philosophies are almost invariably denuded of their political force in the United States. Indeed, Bookchin and many others have gone much further in denouncing deep ecology for its fascistic tendencies. It is alleged that deep ecology's valorization of 'rootedness in the soil', its excessive biocentrism, and its undifferentiated love of animals make it the companionable mate of the 'nature mysticism' of National Socialism. It is Nazi Germany that, in November 1933, passed the first law in the Western world calling for the explicit protection of animals as beings-in-themselves—in other words, a law which 'would recognize the right which animals inherently possess to be protected in and of themselves'.[36] One philosopher finds in Nazi legislation and deep ecology 'a shared revalorization of the *primitive* state against that of (alleged) civilization', the 'same *romantic and/or sentimental* representation of the relationship between nature and culture'.[37] Of course this criticism is little more than the tiresome rejoinder that we all are, or ought to be (barring the reticence of some obdurate primitives), the children of the Enlightenment, and that no critique of modernity is to be permitted except in categories and terms rendered permissible by the Enlightenment's own structures of thought. Those critiques which seek to lay bare the purported fascism of deep ecology seem woefully unaware of their own oppressive parochialism.

By far the most sustained critique of deep ecology, however, has emanated from within ecofeminism. Where social ecology finds deep ecology inadequately grounded in an awareness of the nature of modern social relations, ecofeminism finds deep ecology deeply embedded in the same patriarchal assumptions which men generally hold, and which as a consequence render them sharply deficient in political awareness. The outlines of the feminist critique were first noted in a short albeit powerful paper by the Australian feminist Ariel Kay Salleh. She observed that the formulations of deep ecology use 'the generic term *Man* in a case where use of a generic term is not applicable.' This is no minor matter, for women's experiences of menstruation, pregnancy, childbirth, lactation, and menopause already ground their consciousness 'in the knowledge of being coterminous with Nature.' What the deep ecologist seeks to introduce as an 'abstract ethical construct', namely the desirability of a communion with nature on the principle of shared living, already constitutes part of women's experiences.[38] Though deep ecology purports to celebrate life-affirming values, its advocacy of strict population control constitutes an intervention in natural life processes, and to this extent it partakes of the same rationalist and technicist world-view that it otherwise critiques. While deep ecology recognizes the fact of oppression, and deplores man's exploitation of man and of nature, it does not recognize man's oppression of woman. It is attuned to the suffering and oppression of animals, but the everyday oppression of women escapes its watchful attentiveness.[39] Salleh insists, quite rightly, that to assimilate man's oppression of woman into a general class of exploitative acts perpetrated by man upon man is to overlook the political meaning of violence against women and the iconic meanings attached to 'woman' in various discursive formations. The ecofeminist is reserved about deep ecology's otherwise commendable anti-class postures because 'in bypassing the parallel between the original exploitation of nature as object-and-commodity resource and of nurturant women as object-and-commodity resource, the ecologist's anti-class stance remains only superficially descriptive, politically and historically static. It loses its genuinely deep structural edge.'[40]

Though appreciative of deep ecologists' endeavours to be more humane and caring, Salleh characterizes their objective, the 'spiritual development of "personhood"', as the 'self-estranged male reaching for the original androgynous natural unity within himself.' Deep ecology is a largely 'self-congratulatory reformist move; the transvaluation of values it claims for itself is quite peripheral'; and it represents 'a spiritual search for people in a barren secular age'.[41] It is surely no accident that it is the most secular versions of Eastern spiritual traditions, such as Zen Buddhism and the thought of Krishnamurti, that have attracted the largest followings in the West. And if deep ecology's most sustained contribution is to reject the 'instrumentalist pragmatism of the resource-management approach to the environmental crisis', even here Salleh finds deep ecology's shortcomings ominous. She makes the very pointed remark that the constant references to 'implementation of policies', 'exponential growth of technical skill and intervention', and the like betray the fact that 'the masculine sense of self-worth in our culture has become so entrenched in scientistic habits of thought, that it is very hard for men to argue persuasively without recourse to terms like these for validation.' Naess's own writings are pervaded by terms such as 'rules', 'postulates', 'hypotheses', and 'policy formulations', and his 'overview of ecosophy is a highly academic and positivized one, dressed up in the jargon of current science-dominated standards of acceptability.'[42]

It was another feminist writer who suggested that ethics has been discussed primarily in the language of the father. This is the language of fairness, justice, and rights. Perhaps, if ethics deigned to speak in the language of the mother, the language of human caring, and of the memory equally of caring and of being cared for, deep ecology might become truly deep.[43] It is this language that, as we have seen in the expression of Bookchin's outrage, hard-nosed realists will seek to mock, and not always without cause. Caring, too, in the manner of everything else, has become an industry with its management specialists, professionals, and various other staffers; it has also become, in a world saturated by the media, pop psychology, and political correctness, a substitute for thought, reflection, spiritual discipline, and equanimity. Nonetheless, the contamination of the ethic of caring by marketing and crude psychological reductionism does not entirely vitiate the possibility that we can yet render ourselves ecological in more ways than deep ecology can possibly imagine. The 'deep ecology movement will not truly happen', writes Ariel Salleh, 'until men are brave enough to rediscover and to love the woman inside themselves.'[44] No ecology, howsoever deep, can give us pregnant fathers. How far beyond deep ecology, then, does Gandhi take us?

IV

GANDHI AND THE ECOLOGICAL VIEW OF LIFE

Though Gandhi was no philosopher of ecology, and can only be called an environmentalist with considerable difficulty, he strikes a remarkable chord with all those who have cared for the environment, practised vegetarianism, cherished the principles of non-violence, resisted the depredations of developers, or accorded animals the dignity of humans. It is useful to recall that the word 'ecology' is derived from 'economy' (from Greek *oeconomy*) which itself has little to do, in its primal sense, with inquiries made by those who are now styled economists; rather, economy was understood to pertain to the most efficient and least costly management of household affairs. It is largely an application of this meaning that Thoreau had in mind when, in titling the opening chapter of *Walden* 'Economy', he described the manner in which he reduced his needs as much as his wants to the bare minimum, and so lived life to the fullest. It is the same economy of lifestyle—and indeed of conduct, speech, and thought—that Gandhi ruthlessly put into practice in his various ashrams. From there, then, one can follow the trajectory from 'economy' to 'ecology'. The *Oxford English Dictionary* defines ecology as the 'science of the economy of animals and plants', and this implies the imperative to look after animals, plants, and the environment to which they bear a relation. Ecology consequently means, in the first instance, that we are commanded to economize, or render less wasteful, our use of the earth's resources. To do so, we have to use our own resources, howsoever narrowly conceived, with wisdom and with the utmost respect for economy. On no other grounds can we explain the many apparently enigmatic, and some would say bizarre or idiosyncratic, practices of thought and conduct in which Gandhi engaged.

A recent study of Gandhi, which describes him as 'a practicing ecological yogi', makes the point that Gandhi bound himself to the observance of a certain set of rules of conduct.[45] Some of these rules or *niyamas* prescribe what a human being should do, while others (*yamas*) are injunctions to abstain from forms of conduct harmful to humans and, in some cases, other living beings. Khoshoo suggests that it is from these environmental and ethical principles, which variously counsel us to practice austerity, introspect on the self, cultivate contentment, learn self-reliance, renounce possessions beyond our needs, and always keep in mind the interests of the weakest and the poor, that Gandhi derived his political movement; and it is from these same principles, argues Khoshoo, that Gandhi worked to develop his ideas of 'sustainable development'.[46] It is doubtful, however, that Gandhi spoke at all in the language of 'development', much less in the language of 'sustainable development', since the very idea of development owes a great deal to the politics of knowledge in the post-World War II period.[47] Besides, ethics, ecology, and politics were all closely and even indistinguishably interwoven into the fabric of his thought and social practices. If, for instance, his practice of observing twenty-four hours of silence on a regular basis was a mode of conserving his energy, entering into an introspective state, and listening to what he called the still voice within, it was also a way of signifying his dissent from ordinary models of communication with the British and establishing the discourse on his own terms. Similarly, Gandhi deployed fasting not only to open negotiations with the British or (more frequently) various Indian communities, but to cleanse his own body, free his mind of impure thoughts, feminize the public realm, and even to partake in the experience of deprivation from which countless millions of Indians suffered. Gandhi deplored the idea of waste, and fasting was a sure means of ascertaining the true needs of the body and preserving its ecological equanimity.

In considering Gandhi in relation to ecology, then, his entire life opens up before us, a life documented, moreover, in almost excruciatingly minute detail. One is confronted at once with the anomaly that, whatever Gandhi's propensity to be ecological in thought and conduct, he was an extraordinarily prolific writer. Admittedly, by far the greater majority of the pieces collected together in the gargantuan 100-volume set of his collected writings are models of brevity, and Gandhi did not waste a word. To write poorly was to do violence to the language and to the recipient of one's missives, and Gandhi chose his words with great care. At the same time, he was quite adamant that nothing was to remain of his writings upon his death. 'My writings should be cremated with my body', he wrote, adding: 'What I have done will endure, not what I have said or written.'[48] Indeed, what is remarkable about Gandhi's life is that, unlike most public figures with a political career, whose social practices are tradition-bound even when their pronouncements are radical, Gandhi was extremely conservative in his pronouncements while being radical in his conduct. As I have noted previously, though he thought that men would continue to be the principal breadwinners for the family, his ashrams were run firmly on the principle that women and men would share equally in all the work. For someone who ate very modestly, Gandhi himself spent an inordinate amount of time in the kitchen. Though spinning might in village India be a task undertaken by women, Gandhi himself spun every day, and made of it, and the respect that it implied for bodily labour as the source of one's daily bread, a religion to be followed by all those who aspired for independence. If he was insistent that women were to remain chaste, he was even more adamant that such chastity was incumbent on men, who had rendered women into sexual objects.[49] The profoundly ecological impetus of his style here demands recognition: promising little, he was generous in the fulfilment of his word. Nature may appear to be niggardly, but its rewards are rich and deeper than we habitually imagine.

Moving from Gandhi's writings to his social practices and conduct, to which anecdotes from his life are perhaps the best guide, suggests innumerable ways, of which I shall mention only a few, in which Gandhi can be seen as having an ecological vision of life. First, as nature provides for the largest animals as much as it provides for its smallest creations, so Gandhi allowed this principle to guide him in his political and social relations with all manner of women and men. Gandhi's close disciple and attendant, Mirabehn, wrote that while he worked alongside everyone else in the ashram, he would carry on his voluminous correspondence and grant interviews. 'Big people of all parties, and of many different nations would come to see Bapu, but he would give equal attention to the poorest peasant who might come with a genuine problem.'[50] In the midst of important political negotiations with senior British officials, he would take the time to tend to his goat. It is this aspect of Gandhi's personality that his contemporary, the short-story writer Acharya Chatursen Shastri, captured when, in a story about Gandhi, he showed him peeling potatoes while in conversation with a little boy.[51] He remained supremely indifferent to considerations of power, prestige, and status in choosing his companions; similarly, he was as attentive to the minutest details as he was to matters of national importance. One of his associates has reported—and such stories are legion—that when news reached Gandhi of the illness of the daughter of a friend, he wrote to her a long letter in the midst of an intense political struggle in Rajkot, detailing the medicines that she was to take, the food that she was to avoid, and the precautions she was to exercise. Though he was notoriously thrifty, writing even some of his letters on the back of envelopes addressed to him, he did not begrudge spending a large sum of money to send her a telegram.[52] His own grandniece, pointing to the meticulous care with which Gandhi tended to her personal needs, all the while that he was engaged in negotiations for Indian independence, perhaps showered him with the most unusual honour when, in writing a short book about him, she called it *Bapu—My Mother*.[53] The interpreters of Gandhi

have chosen to describe his equanimity as an illustration of the teachings of
the Gita, which counsels us to perform our duty and remain equally
indifferent to joy and sorrow, praise and censure; but his life here can just
as well be seen as illustrative of the working of laws of nature. The banyan
tree gives its shade alike to the prince and the commoner, the vendor and
the businessman, the saint and the crook. [54]

Secondly, without being an advocate of wilderness as that is
commonly understood today, Gandhi was resolutely of the view that nature
should be allowed to take its own course. Arne Naess has written that he
'even prohibited people from having a stock of medicines against poisonous
bites. He believed in the possibility of satisfactory coexistence and he
proved right. There were no accidents . . .' [55] His experiments in nature care
are well-known, as is his advocacy of enemas and mud baths, but there is
more to these narratives than his rejection of modern medicine. Mirabehn
has reported that one day as Gandhi worked in a tent in the afternoon heat
of 110 degrees, she and some other workers became exasperated at their
inability to keep away the hordes of flies. 'I'm told they have come down
from the tree tops for shade, Bapu,' said Mirabehn, whereupon he replied:
'Yes. It is not for me to blame them. If God had made me one such, I
should have done exactly the same.' [56] Gandhi scarcely required the verdict
of the biologist, wildlife trainer, or zoologist to hold to the view that
nature's creatures mind their own business, and that if humans were to do
the same, we would not be required to legislate the health of all species.
On occasion a cobra would come into Gandhi's room: there were clear
instructions that it was not to be killed even if it bit Gandhi, though Gandhi
did not prevent others from killing snakes. 'I do not want to live', wrote
Gandhi, 'at the cost of the life even of a snake.' [57] In some rendering of these
stories, the cobra would often be described as rearing itself up before
Gandhi and placing its hood above his head, as if in homage to the Emperor. [58]
The hagiographic tone of these accounts does not, however, detract from
the fact, for which there is ample evidence, that Gandhi was quite willing
to share his universe with animals and reptiles, without rendering them
into objects of pity, curiosity, or amusement. He described himself as wanting
'to realize identity with even the crawling things upon earth, because we
claim descent from the same God, and that being so, all life in whatever
form it appears must essentially be so', [59] but it is altogether improbable

that he would have followed some deep ecologists in treating animals, insects, and plants as persons.

Though it may be reasonable to infer that it was Gandhi's adherence to non-violence that would have prevented him from taking the life of a snake, such an interpretation ignores the critical primacy accorded to satya over ahimsa in Gandhian thinking, much as it overlooks the fact that Gandhi was an advocate of the mercy killing of animals. The incident when he had a young calf in his ashram put to death with an injection when she could not be saved from an extreme illness is well-known; less known is the incident of the stray dogs.[60] In 1926 Ambalal Sarabhai, a textile magnate in Ahmedabad and friend of Gandhi, rounded up sixty rabid dogs on his properties and had them shot; subsequently, feeling repentant, he approached Gandhi to share his anguish with him. Gandhi comforted him with the remark, 'What else could be done?'[61] When the Ahmedabad Humanitarian Society came to know of this, it sought an urgent explanation from Gandhi; and thereafter, for the next three months, as Gandhi himself took this issue to the public, he was bombarded with letters accusing him of cruelty to animals and of forsaking his commitment to ahimsa. Throughout, while admitting that he might have erred, Gandhi explained his position with consistency and clarity. There was no course open to Sarabhai 'but the destruction of rabid dogs. At times we may be faced with the unavoidable duty', wrote Gandhi, 'of killing a man who is found in the act of killing people.'[62] Roving dogs, particularly a swarm of them, were a 'menace' to society; the multiplication of them was quite unnecessary; and those who now counselled their protection on the grounds of religion, even at cost to the life and safety of humans, were to be reminded that to practice 'the religion of humanity' required also the recognition that 'we offend against dogs as a class by suffering them to stray and live on crumbs or savings from our plates that we throw at them and we injure our neighbours also by doing so.'[63] Gandhi unequivocally rejected the argument that protection must always entail 'mere refraining from killing'; quite to the contrary, 'Torture or participation, direct or indirect, in the unnecessary multiplication of those that must die is *himsa* [violence].'[64] As he was to reiterate in another rejoinder, 'Merely taking life is not always *himsa*, one may even say that there is sometimes more *himsa* in not taking life.'[65] He advised those who had become agitated about this matter to learn from the

West, where the people had 'formulated and perfected' a 'regular science of dog-keeping.' It was mistaken to believe that people in the West were lacking in humanity: as Gandhi put it trenchantly, 'The ideal of humanity in the West is perhaps lower, but their practice of it is very much more thorough than others. We rest content with a lofty ideal and are slow or lazy in its practice. We are wrapped in dark darkness, as is evident from our paupers, cattle and other animals. They are eloquent of our irreligion rather than of religion.'[66]

Thirdly, Gandhi transformed the idea of waste and rendered it pregnant with meanings that were the inverse of those meanings invested in it by European representational regimes. As the complex scholarship around the practices of colonialism has now demonstrated, almost nothing was as much anathema to European colonizers as the idea that the vast lands lying before their gaze, whether in largely barren areas of Australia and Canada, or in the densely inhabited parts of India, were entirely unproductive or certainly not as productive as they thought desirable. To render them fertile, they had to first render them productive of meaning, as something other than realms of emptiness (and hence of nothingness), which was only possible by construing them as wastelands which required the brain, will, and energy of white men to effect their transformation. Gandhi, on the other hand, was inclined to the view that man was prone to transform whatever he touched, howsoever fertile, fecund, or productive, into waste. His close disciple and associate, Kaka Kalelkar, narrates that he was in the habit of breaking off an entire twig merely for four or five *neem* leaves he needed to rub on the fibres of the carding-bow to make its strings pliant and supple. When Gandhi saw that, he remarked: 'This is violence. We should pluck the required number of leaves after offering an apology to the tree for doing so. But you broke off the whole twig, which is wasteful and wrong.'[67] He also described himself as pained that people would 'pluck masses of delicate blossoms' and fling them in his face or string them around his neck'.[68] Yet this alone was not wasteful: there was also human waste, around the disposal of which an entire and none too savoury history of India can be written. While it was a matter of shame that Indian society had set apart a special class of people to deal with the disposal of human excrement, whose occupation made them the most despised members of society,[69] Gandhi found it imperative to bring this matter to the fore and make it as much a subject of national importance as the attainment of political independence and the reform of degraded institutions. Unlike the vast majority of caste Hindus, Gandhi did not allow anyone else to dispose off his waste. His ashrams were repositories for endeavours to change human waste into organic fertilizer. Moreover, during the course of the last twenty years of his life, he was engaged in ceaseless experiments to invent toilets that would be less of a drain on scarce water resources.

Fourthly, and this is a point that cannot be belaboured enough, Gandhi did not make of his ecological sensitivities a cult or religion to which unquestioning fealty was demanded. His attitude towards meat is illustrative in this respect. Though he was himself a very strict vegetarian, he was not insistent that everyone else, even in his presence, should be forbidden from eating meat. Khoshoo credits him with the saying, 'I am a puritan myself but I am catholic towards others', and rightly rejects the notion that Gandhi might have been a 'puritanical vegetarian.'[70] But this is a testimony only to Gandhi's liberality, not to that ecumenical feature of his thinking which is based on a different notion of largesse. Once, when he had an European visitor at his ashram who was habituated to meat at every meal, Gandhi had meat served to him. He himself partook of milk and milk products, unlike those who style themselves 'vegans' in the United States, and his reverence for life and respect for animals did not border on that fanaticism which is only another name for violence. One of his disciples, Jehangir Patel, has written that one day Mirabehn came running to him in an agitated state of mind. 'Bapu won't be able to eat his breakfast', she said. 'Someone has put meat into the fridge where his food is. How could you allow such a thing?' The cook, Ali, explained that he had got the meat for the dogs, and offered to remove it at once. Jehangir asked him to let the meat remain there, and Gandhi himself was fetched. Jehangir then apologized to Gandhi: 'I did not think of speaking to Ali. I did not realise that this might happen.' Gandhi replied, 'Don't apologise. You and Ali have done nothing wrong, so far as I can see.' Gandhi took some grapes lying next to the meat, and popped them into his mouth; turning then to Mirabehn, he said: 'We are guests in our friend's house, and it would not be right for us to impose our idea upon him or upon anyone. People whose custom it is to eat meat should not stop doing so simply because I am present.' Similarly, though Gandhi championed prohibition, he would not prevent anyone from drinking alcohol, and he condemned altogether the principle of drinking on the sly; as he told Jehangir, 'I would much rather you were a drinker, even a heavy drinker, than that there should be any deceit in the matter.'[71]

Gandhi's entire life, I would submit, constitutes an ecological treatise, and it is no exaggeration to suggest that he left us, in his life, with the last of the Upanishads or 'forest books'. He dispelled wisdom, but not from a mountain-top; he even waded through human waste as he walked around riot-torn villages, but he retained his equanimity. The grounding for his own ecological vision was clearly furnished by what he understood, perhaps with some naiveté, as the ecological wisdom of India's epic and religious literature,[72] just as it is amply clear that in his practice of simple living and non-violence, and advocacy of satya and brahmacharya, Gandhi sought to put the principles of an ecologically aware life into motion. But these are truisms that shall have to be inflected in more than the ordinary fashion, and yield more than the clichéd observations that Gandhi was the 'prophet of non-violence' or an astute political campaigner unusually interested in moral questions, if we are to be fully cognizant of the profound manner in which Gandhi's entire life functioned much like an ecosystem. This is one life in which every minute act, emotion, or thought was not without its place: the brevity of Gandhi's enormous writings, his small meals of nuts and fruits, his morning ablutions and everyday bodily practices, his periodic observances of silence, his morning walks, his cultivation of the small as much as of the big, his abhorrence of waste, his resort to fasting—all these point to the manner in which the symphony was orchestrated. Though the moralists, non-violent activists, feminists, journalists, social reformers, trade union leaders, peasants, prohibitionists, nature-cure lovers, nudists, critics of Western medicine, renouncers and scores of others will all find in Gandhi something to sustain them in their aspirations and objectives, Gandhi will remain elusive unless the deeply ecological foundations of his life are recognized.

Notes

1.   Ramachandra Guha, *Mahatma Gandhi and the Environmental Movement*, The Parisar Annual Lecture 1993 (Pune: Parisar, 1993), p. 2.

2.   Ibid., p. 20.

3.   Cited by T. N. Khoshoo, *Mahatma Gandhi—An Apostle of Applied Human Ecology* (New Delhi: Tata Energy Research Institute, 1995), p 18.

4.   Guha, *Mahatma Gandhi and the Environmental Movement*, p. 20.

5.   For a short account of the Chipko movement, that highlights in particular its Gandhian impetus, see J. Bandyopadhyay and Vandana Shiva, 'Chipko', *Seminar*, no. 330 (February 1987), pp. 33-39; a more systematic account is furnished by Anupam Mishra and Satyendra Tripathi, *Chipko movement: Uttarakhand women's bid to save forest wealth* (New Delhi: People's Action for Development with Justice, 1978). For a short account by Bahuguna, which acknowledges the inspiration he received from Gandhi's life, *see The Chipko Message* (Silyara Tehri, Garhwal: Chipko Information Centre, 1987, esp. pp. 22-26; also useful is Sunderlal Bahuguna, 'The Crisis of Civilization and the Message of Culture in the Context of Environment', *Gandhi Marg* 9, no. 8 (November 1987), pp. 451-68, though Bahuguna reads much better in Hindi. These might well be considered 'partisan' accounts of the Chipko movement; for a more scholarly and detached treatment, the reader would do well to turn to Ramachandra Guha, *The Unquiet Woods: Ecological Change and Peasant Resistance in the Himalaya* (Delhi: Oxford University Press, 1991), pp. 153-84. Mirabehn's work in the Himalayan region is ably and touchingly evoked in Krishna Murti Gupta, *Mira Behn: Gandhiji's Daughter Disciple*, Birth Centenary Volume (New Delhi: Himalaya Seva Sangh, 1992). On the women of Chipko, see Vandana Shiva, *Staying Alive: Women, Ecology, and Survival in India* (New Delhi: Kali for Women, 1988), pp. 67-77.

6.   The figure of 100,000 displaced people is based, as Madhav Gadgil and Ramachandra Guha have noted, on the 'outdated 1981 census', and others have furnished much higher numbers. See their book, *Ecology and Equity: The Use and Abuse of Nature in Contemporary India* (Penguin Books, 1995), p. 73. The literature on the subject is voluminous.

7.   Cited by Geoffrey Ashe, *Gandhi* (New York: Stein and Day, 1968), p. 267. Some attribute the saying to Gandhi himself: see David Rothenberg, *Is It Painful to Think? Conversations with Arne Naess* (Minneapolis: University of Minnesota Press, 1993), p. 170.

8.   Arne Naess, *Gandhi and the Nuclear Age* (Totowa, New Jersey: Bedminster Press, 1965).

9.   David Rothenberg, *Is It Painful to Think?*, pp. 103-5. Elsewhere Naess wrote of himself as a 'student and admirer since 1930 of Gandhi's non-violent direct actions in bloody conflict', 'inevitably influenced by his metaphysics'. See Naess, 'Self-Realization: An Ecological Approach to Being in the World', *The Trumpeter* 4, no. 3 (1987), pp. 35-42, reprinted in Alan Drengson and Yuichi

Inoue eds., *The Deep Ecology Movement: An Introductory Anthology* (Berkeley, California: North Atlantic Books, 1995), p. 22.

10. Arne Naess, *Gandhi and Group Conflict: An Exploration of Satyagraha—Theoretical Background* (Oslo: Universitietsforlaget, 1974), cited by Rothenberg, Introduction to *Is it Painful to Think?*, p. xix.

11. Idem, 'The Shallow and the Deep, Long-Range Ecology Movement: A Summary', in Drengson and Inoue eds., *The Deep Ecology Movement*, pp. 3-10.

12. Ibid., p. 5.

13. For an engaging critique of 'technicism', see Ashis Nandy, 'From Outside the Imperium: Gandhi's Cultural Critique of the West', in his *Traditions, Tyranny, and Utopias: Essays in the Politics of Awareness* (Delhi: Oxford University Press, 1987; Oxford India Paperbacks, 1992), pp. 127-62.

14. Stephen Bodian, 'Simple in Means, Rich in Ends: An Interview with Arne Naess', in George Sessions ed., *Deep Ecology for the 21st Century: Readings on the Philosophy and Practice of the New Environmentalism* (Boston: Shambhala, 1995), p. 27.

15. I have used the expression 'man's relationship to nature' deliberately, since the brunt of ecofeminist criticism, which I shall consider at greater length subsequently, is precisely that deep ecology is just as patriarchal as environmentalism or the other philosophies that it critiques.

16. Naess, 'The Shallow and the Deep, Long-Range Ecology Movement', in Drengson and Inoue eds., *The Deep Ecology Movement*, p. 3.

17. Arne Naess and George Sessions, 'Platform Principles of the Deep Ecology Movement', in Drengson and Inoue eds., *The Deep Ecology Movement*, pp. 49-50.

18. See Ariel Kay Salleh, 'Deeper than Deep Ecology: The Eco-Feminist Connection', *Environmental Ethics* 6, no. 4 (Winter 1984), p. 340.

19. Bodian, 'Simple in Means, Rich in Ends', p. 29.

20. Arne Naess, 'The Deep Ecological Movement: Some Philosophical Aspects', in Sessions, ed., *Deep Ecology for the 21st Century*, pp. 72-73.

21. M.K. Gandhi, *Hind Swaraj or Indian Home Rule* (1909; new ed., 1938; reprint ed., Ahmedabad: Navajivan Publishing House, 1982), pp. 44-46.

22. I merely wish to call attention to the criticism, without considering it at length, that Gandhi idealized 'village India', and consequently endorsed the caste system which has historically been the basis of village life. The further extrapolation, namely that the eradication of untouchability, which cannot be understood other than in relation to the caste system and village life, demands the embrace of all that stands in opposition to 'village India'— urbanization, industrialization, scientific planning, technological growth—

suggests how fundamentally at odds Gandhi's world-view may be with the position advocated by radical dalits. Doubtless, the dalits (formerly known as the Untouchables, described in official reports as the 'scheduled' or 'depressed' castes, and 'christened' as 'Harijans', or 'children of God', by Gandhi) appear as ardent advocates of modernization and industrialization. A proper consideration of the issues at stake here would take us far astray into more detailed readings of Gandhi's views on science, modernity, and development, as much as into the heated debates surrounding Indian developmental politics. It is also erroneous to suppose that, because the dalits are hostile to the idea of 'village India' and to Gandhi's thinking, they lack an ecological sensibility. Oppressed people who have survived on as little as have the dalits are extraordinarily ecological in their habits and thinking. For an interesting illustration of some of these debates, which have made their way into Indian newspapers, see Gail Omvedt, 'Why Dalits dislike environmentalists', *The Hindu* (24 June 1997), p. 17, and a rejoinder of sorts by A. Ranga Rajan, 'Why Dalits should become "environmentalists"', *The Hindu* (22 July 1997), p. 17.

23.   The cultural politics of walking has not received any attention, and the huge literature on Gandhi has singularly failed to comprehend the place of this phenomenon in Gandhi's life; as might be expected, however, Gandhi's famous march to the sea at Dandi has been the focus of many scholarly studies, and also of major artistic representations, such as the portraits of Gandhi by the Bengali painter Nandalal Bose. Rabindranath Tagore had a glimpse of what it meant for Gandhi to walk from one village to another when he wrote of him: 'He stopped at the threshold of the huts of the thousands of dispossessed, dressed like one of their own. He spoke to them in their own language. Here was living truth at last, and not only quotations from books. For this reason the Mahatma, the name given to him by the people of India, is his real name.' See his 'The Call of Truth', *Modern Review* (October 1921); there are slight variants in this widely reproduced article. A unique study by Anne D. Wallace, *Walking, Literature, and English Culture: The Origins and Uses of the Peripatetic in the Nineteenth Century* (Oxford: Clarendon Paperbacks, 1994), points to some of the ways in which a study of Gandhi's association with walking might be attempted.

24.   For an arresting account of the history of the pencil and the part played by Thoreau in creating what is essentially its modern shape, see Henry Petroski, *The Pencil: A History of Design and Circumstance* (New York: Alfred Knopf, 1990).

25.   Jun'ichiro Tanizaki, *In Praise of Shadows*, tr. Edward G. Seidensticker (New Haven, Connecticut: Leete's Island Books, 1977), pp. 7-8.

26.   Kakasaheb Kalelkar, *Stray Glimpses of Bapu* (Ahmedabad: Navajivan Publishing House, 1950; 2nd rev. ed., 1960), pp. 26-7. G. A. Natesan, founder and editor

of the *Indian Review*, became a firm supporter of Gandhi, and it is his publishing house that released the first major anthologies of Gandhi's writings.

27. Jehangir P. Patel and Marjorie Sykes, *Gandhi: His Gift of the Fight* (Rasulia, Madhya Pradesh, India; Friends Rural Centre, 1987), pp. 107-8.

28. Few people in the deep ecology movement, apart from Naess himself, appear to have studied Gandhi's works and life; and among those who have, they seem to have gone no further than Naess's own books on Gandhi. One of the principal figures in the movement, Bill Devall, admits that the 'term *nonviolence* creates problems for some supporters of deep ecology because they equate nonviolence with passivity or non-resistance. Nothing could be further from the meaning of nonviolence as used by Gandhi, Martin Luther King, Jr., and by Greenpeace.' See Bill Devall, *Simple in Means, Rich in Ends: Practicing Deep Ecology* (Salt Lake City: Gibbs Smith Publisher, 1988), p. 141. His own discussion of Gandhi, under the heading 'Direct Action, Monkeywrenching and Ecotage', betrays considerable ignorance of the complexity of Gandhi's thought and the common susceptibility to sloganeering and impoverished classificatory schemes (pp. 138-150). 'Ecotage', presumably from ecology+sabotage, would not likely have met with Gandhi's approval; and fancy neologisms do not go very far towards making a non-violent revolution.

29. Dave Foreman, 'Beyond the Wilderness', *Harper's Magazine* (April 1990), p. 48. Murray Bookchin, in the revised edition of *The Ecology of Freedom: The Emergence and Dissolution of Hierarchy* (Montreal and New York: Black Rose Books, 1991), says of deep ecology and other 'mystical ecologies' that they 'often view the human species as an evolutionary aberration—or worse, as an absolute disaster, a "cancer" on the biosphere' (p. xxi).

30. See Ashish Kothari, Saloni Suri, and Neena Singh, 'People and Protected Areas: Rethinking Conservation in India', *The Ecologist* 25, no. 5 (September-October 1995), pp. 188-94 at p. 190.

31. On the Sundarbans Tiger Preserve, which has the largest tiger population in the world, see the charming book by Sy Montgomery, *Spell of the Tiger: The Man-Eaters of Sundarbans* (Boston: Houghton Mifflin Co., 1995). I by no means wish to suggest that conflicts over resources between animals and humans are unknown in India; indeed, they are all too common, and widely reported in Indian newspapers and specialized magazines, such as *Sanctuary* and *Down to Earth*. Nor is my observation of the 'symbiotic' relationship of animals to humans based on the Hindu reverence for the cow, or on the fact that cows roam Indian streets with abandon. The question partly revolves around understanding how far animals are or are not invested with distinct identities, their place in the cultural imaginary, and the dependence of animals and

humans on each other and the closeness of their relations. In Hinduism, animals are important to deities, and are seen as having the mark of divinity within them—a notable example being Hanuman.

32. Kothari, Suri, and Singh, 'People and Protected Areas', p. 190.

33. The recent deaths of thirteen white tigers at the Nandankanan Zoo in Orissa, as well as of a thirteen-month-old tigress in the Hyderabad Zoo, shown skinned on Indian television, have once again cast doubts about the future of India's tiger population and its wellbeing. Bittu Sahgal offers a sharply critical view of India's zoos, 'Is the Tiger a Burden?', reprinted in *The International Indian* 8, no. 6 (December 2000), p. 48.

34. Ramachandra Guha, 'Radical American Environmentalism and Wilderness Preservation: A Third World Critique', *Environmental Ethics* 11, no. 1 (Spring 1989), p. 75.

35. Bookchin, *Ecology of Freedom*, p. il.

36. Cited by Luc Ferry in Carol Volk tr., *The New Ecological Order* (Chicago: University of Chicago Press, 1995), pp. 91-100.

37. Ibid., p. 93. See also the discussion in Michael Zimmerman, *Contesting Earth's Future: Radical Ecology and Postmodernity* (Berkeley: University of California Press, 1994), pp. 170-83.

38. This paragraph draws on Ariel Kay Salleh, 'Deeper than Deep Ecology: The Eco-Feminist Connection', *Environmental Ethics* 6, no. 4 (Winter 1984), pp. 340-41.

39. The argument is reinforced in Ariel Salleh, 'The Ecofeminism/Deep Ecology Debate: A Reply to Patriarchal Reason', *Environmental Ethics* 14, no. 3 (Fall 1992), p. 204.

40. Salleh, 'Deeper than Deep Ecology', p. 341.

41. Ibid., pp. 344-45.

42. Ibid., pp. 342-43.

43. Patsy Hallen, 'Making Peace with Nature: Why Ecology Needs Feminism', in Drengson and Inoue, eds., *The Deep Ecology Movement*, p. 208, citing Nel Noddings, *Caring: A Feminine Approach to Ethics and Moral Education* (Berkeley: University of California Press, 1984), p. 1.

44. Salleh, 'Deeper than Deep Ecology', p. 345.

45. Khoshoo, *Mahatma Gandhi—An Apostle of Applied Human Ecology*, pp. 1-2.

46. Ibid., pp. 2, 8.

47. Cf. Arturo Escobar, *Encountering Development: The Making and Unmaking of the Third World* (Princeton, New Jersey: Princeton University Press, 1995).

48. Cited by Sunil Khilnani, 'A bodily drama', *Times Literary Supplement* (8 August 1997).

49. The recent anthology by Puspha Joshi, *Gandhi on Women* (Ahmedabad: Navajivan Publishing House, 1990), provides extraordinary insights into Gandhi's views on chastity, the division of labour between the sexes, and the public role of women; for his experiments in the kitchen and thoughts on food, see M. K. Gandhi in Sushila Nayar tr., *Key to Health* (Ahmedabad: Navajivan Publishing House, 1948), pp. 10-24.

50. Gupta, *Mira Behn: Gandhi's Daughter Disciple*, pp. 286-87.

51. Acharya Chatursen Shastri, 'Lauhapurusha' (in Hindi), tr. Vinay Lal as 'The Iron Man', unpublished ms.

52. Kalelkar, *Stray Glimpses of Bapu*, pp. 165-66.

53. Manubehn Gandhi, *Bapu—My Mother*

54. It has been suggested to me by an anonymous reviewer of this chapter, when it was accepted for publication as a paper by *Environmental Ethics*, that the image of the 'banyan tree' is 'unfortunate', 'as nothing grows under it.' As the reviewer noted, however, the image is not entirely inapposite, since Gandhi did not give birth to a 'new generation of leaders' who truly were cast of the same clay. Some of the political leaders who style themselves 'Gandhian' are an embarrassment, and even crooks have profited by deploying Gandhi's name towards the achievement of ends that stand distinctly in opposition to his teachings and ideas. Shahid Amin's masterful analysis in Ranajit Guha ed., 'Gandhi as Mahatma', *Subaltern Studies III: Writings on South Asian History and Society* (Delhi: Oxford, 1984), pp. 1-61, suggests how the 'Mahatma' became a floating signifier, in whose name even violence could be committed by the votaries of nationalism.

   After much deliberation, and with full knowledge of the fact that historians appear to have a predilection for metaphors of 'seed' and 'tree' in their work, I have decided to retain the image of the 'banyan' tree: it resonates in Indian culture in myriad ways, and points the way to more semiological, hermeneutic, and nuanced readings of the trope of the banyan tree in the study of Indian culture.

55. Naess, 'Self-Realization: An Ecological Approach . . .', p. 28.

56. Gupta, *Mira Behn: Gandhi's Daughter Disciple*, p. 120.

57. M.K. Gandhi, *Truth is God* (Ahmedabad: Navajivan Publishing House, 1959), p. 102.

58. Kalelkar, *Stray Glimpses of Bapu*, pp. 54-55. See also Mukulbhai Kalarthi in H. M. Vyas tr., *Anecdotes from Bapu's Life* (Ahmedabad: Navajivan Publishing House, 1960), pp. 22-23.

59. Gandhi, *Truth is God*, p. 50.

60. Louis Fischer, *The Life of Mahatma Gandhi* (New York: Harper and Brothers, 1950), p. 239.

61.   *CWMG*, vol. 31, p. 486. Gandhi penned eight articles on this subject under the title 'Is This Humanity?'; all citations are from these articles. A short account of the exchange between Gandhi and his correspondents is furnished in Fischer, *Life of Mahatma Gandhi*, pp. 236-39.

62.   CWMG, 31:487.

63.   Ibid., pp. 505-6

64.   Ibid., p. 505.

65.   Ibid., p. 525.

66.   Ibid., 32:16.

67.   Kalarthi, *Anecdotes from Bapu's Life*, p. 31. Mirabehn has recounted having had a similar experience and being reprimanded by Gandhi for plucking too many leaves, that too at night when trees are resting (see Gupta, *Mira Behn: Gandhiji's Daughter Disciple*, p. 130).

68.   Gupta, *Mira Behn: Gandhiji's Daughter Disciple*, p. 130.

69.   This subject is given a moving and poignant treatment in the 1935 novel by Mulk Raj Anand, *Untouchable* (reprint ed., Harmondsworth: Penguin Books, 1995).

70.   Khoshoo, *Mahatma Gandhi—An Apostle of Applied Human Ecology*, p. 19.

71.   Patel and Sykes, *Gandhi: His Gift of the Fight*, pp. 103-4.

72.   The subject of what India's epic and religious literature has to say about the environment, and how far early texts can be viewed as documents encompassing an 'ecological wisdom', is far too complex to entertain in this chapter. It is even possible to adopt a contrary position and argue that the epics are not merely indifferent to ecological thinking, but hostile to the ecological vision of life. The Ramayana begins with the wanton killing of a bird engaged in love-play with its mate; in the other epic, the Mahabharata, the Khandava forest is burned down so that the Pandavas can make good their escape. My own view is that these are not very nuanced readings of the epics, which I am inclined to consider as repositories of ecological insight; and I would refer the reader to Ramchandra Gandhi, *Sita's Kitchen: A Testimony of Faith and Inquiry* for an ecologically radical and inspired reading of the Ramayana.

IV

THE CATEGORIES OF KNOWLEDGE:
A CIVILIZATIONAL PERSPECTIVE ON INDIA

Seven

NOT THIS, NOT THAT: THE HIJRAS OF INDIA AND
THE CULTURAL POLITICS OF SEXUALITY

As is well-known to students and observers of Indian society, there has been in existence for some time in India (or since 'time immemorial' in the language of the Orientalist) a community of people known as the hijras, described variously in scholarly and popular literature alike as eunuchs, transvestites, homosexuals, bisexuals, hermaphrodites, androgynes, transsexuals, and gynemimetics; and if this multiplicity of terms was not enough, they are also referred to as a people who are intersexed, emasculated, impotent, transgendered, castrated, effeminate, or somehow sexually anomalous or dysfunctional. The hijras themselves most often distinguish between those who are born hijras, that is with ambiguous genitals, and those, an undoubtedly much larger number, who are made such through castration, though other distinctions, which we shall have occasion to consider, have at various times been advanced. A recent anthropological study, with the enticing title of 'Neither Man nor Woman', inclines to the view that hijras may reasonably be described as an institutionalized third gender.[1]

The plethora of definitions that purport to unravel the supposed mystery of the hijras, a mystery evoked in a recent book which paradoxically describes these ubiquitous street performers as 'invisibles',[2] testifies certainly to the ambivalence if not confusion that is rampant in the literature, and to a general incapacity, as may not unreasonably be suggested, to probe the deeper significance for a possibly emancipatory politics of knowledge signified by the community of hijras. Though there is an emerging sociological literature on their lifestyles,[3] and much curiosity and abhorrence about the manner in which the hijras replenish their numbers, we are, I would suggest, far removed from any understanding of what hijras might tell us about the nature of Indian civilization, the history of human sexuality, the relationship of the history and culture of the hijras to recent formulations and contestations about the pluralism of Indian society, and the dominance of modern knowledge systems.

While it may be a trifle too self-serving for moderns to suppose that a real revolution has taken place in our thinking on sexuality over the last two decades, it can scarcely be doubted that the notion that there are only two sexes, male and female, no longer remains uncontested. Once the first advance had been made in distinguishing between sex, or the ascription of male or female to a newborn baby, and gender, or the psychosocial attributes and conduct on the basis of which a person is described as masculine or feminine, social constructionism was bound to take us further along in our understanding that sex and gender might not coincide, and that the gamut of sex may extend far beyond male and female. Though most men will be socialized into behaving as men and exhibiting manly characteristics, just as most women will learn to conduct themselves as women and display those characteristics said to be common to their sex, that can furnish no warrant for supposing that persons of one sex, biologically speaking, always construe themselves as having a gender identity commensurate with their sex. Womanhood and manhood need not have any logically necessary relation to genitalia. The author of one recent article speaks of 'five sexes' and suggests even that sex may be 'a vast, infinitely malleable continuum': thus, moving beyond male and female, she delineates three categories of intersexed persons, namely hermaphrodites, male pseudohermaphrodites, and female pseudohermaphrodites.[4] Though medical literature has for some time recognized the existence of 'intersexed' persons, there is overwhelming evidence to suggest that physicians still harbour what one feminist researcher has described as an 'incorrigible belief in and insistence upon female and male as the only "natural" options.'[5] Howsoever incontrovertible the evidence before a physician that an infant has some combination of male and female reproductive and sexual features, an irrevocable gender assignment is made as soon as possible after birth: this is what Foucault, adverting to other institutional practices, termed as 'normalization'.[6] It is not unlike fixation on genitalia, productive of other forms of 'normalization', which has inspired prison doctors, and their supporters in various state legislative assemblies, to pursue treatment for male sex offenders that entails the monthly injections of Depo-Lupron, which obstruct the production of testosterone, or, even more drastically, castration.[7]

In this matter, as in most others, investigators have largely confined themselves to the Western tradition, which is also where the thinking on sexuality appears to have been most constrained until recently. Even Foucault's *History of Sexuality* makes no more than passing references to other traditions, and it is still only the occasional nod towards India, China, or other societies that one finds even in works which purport to move beyond sexual dimorphism.[8] It is rather surprising, moreover, that Indian scholars who have otherwise been persuaded (with consequences that I do not here propose to assess) by Foucault's narratives which delineate the oppressive structures of Enlightenment thought and the origin of modern institutions, or who have found in some variant reading of post-structuralism the necessary cues for discerning the epistemological imperatives and totalizing discourses of the state in colonial India, should have been so little attentive to the constructions of alternative sexualities engendered in the West by Foucault's work. While it has been a truism for practitioners in the field of the history of sexuality, following the work of Foucault, that 'sexuality *tout court*, freed from the excess baggage of social status, gender role, and other factors, was uniquely constructed in the modern West,'[9] the history of Indian literature and sexual practices suggests that certain pre-modern civilizations may have presaged the post-modern enchantment with transgendering and multiple sexualities without either the debilitating anxieties attendant upon such enterprises in our times or the much-vaunted celebrations of supposed pluralisms.

Zia Jaffrey's recent book on India's famed eunuchs, and the subsequent popular interest in them generated by her work, leaves no room for doubt that the old and highly serviceable tropes of Orientalism and exoticism will continue to be brought to the fore in representing hijras. In the late eighteenth century, James Forbes, a British merchant, found an opportunity, alongside the surgeon-major, to medically examine hermaphrodites then employed as cooks in the Maratha army, and forthwith declared 'the objects disgusting'; and similarly other colonial officials never disguised their profound distaste for members of a community whose practices they unequivocally declared to be 'revolting'.[10] The practices of the hijras provided yet another instantiation of the barbarous customs of the Hindus, and while the Sub-Collector of Poona, writing to his superior in 1836, found it 'lamentable to think that we are living amongst people who look upon infanticide[,] suttees[,] tuggee and hijeras without apparently a feeling of horror,' he was nonetheless hopeful that they could be induced to 'resign these ancient practices'.[11] The same 'apathy' that made Hindus indifferent to moral considerations also made them lazy in the defence of some of their barbarities: the Hindu, quite unlike the 'Moor', suffered from the congenital defect of lassitude, living in the vapour bath of indifference. Evidently, the hijras belong, to evoke the title of a recent American television programme on them which ordinarily amuses itself with all that appears to be bizarre, monstrous, and wildly incongruous, to a 'strange universe', inassimilable to the realm of normality.[12]

Since Orientalism, exoticism, and the anthropology of the primitive remain the predictable discourses through which the hijras are sought to be rendered manageable, I propose to shift our attention to a contemplation of their significance for the cultural politics of knowledge in our times. Just who are the hijras, we are tempted to ask, and in that emphatic 'just' there is more than the hint of a suggestion that with careful and painstaking investigation we may be positioned to pronounce the truth. The question is how far it is possible to hope for such an outcome when we are constrained by the categories that have been reified in modern knowledge systems.[13] It is through the axes of male and female, Hindu and Muslim, and myth and history that we have sought to assimilate the hijras to our world-view. The colonial state, for example, was predisposed to distinguishing Hindu hijras from Muslim hijras even while recognizing that they were 'alike in all respects except they did not interdine.'[14]

From the perspective of colonial sociology, which postulated the uniquely primordial place of religion in Indian society, the religious identity of the hijra had perforce to predominate. Doubtless there was a distinction to be drawn at one point between 'the religious role of the hijras, derived from Hinduism, and the historical role of the eunuchs in the Muslim courts,' but this distinction has now largely if not altogether collapsed among the Hijras themselves, however inclined some observers might be to insist on such boundaries.[15] Even though 'Hindu hijras' speak of becoming 'Muslims', and Islam is accorded great prestige in the community, with the heads of all the principal 'houses' being Muslims, it is a Hindu goddess, Bahuchara Mata, around whom hijra devotional practices take place; and as one anthropologist has written, none of the 'Muslim hijras' that she knew had any problem 'belonging to a community whose religious aspect centers on devotion to a Hindu goddess and other rituals that are contrary or even offensive to Islam.'[16] As I will suggest, there is in the tale of the hijras another tale to be told of the deep encrusting of Indian society in mythic structures, the resistance of Indian civilizational modes to the classificatory and confining imperatives of the modern nation-state, and the possibilities of being and imagining oneself that exceed what in the West are taken to be radical if not deviant forms of self-presentation.

I

THE MYTHIC DIMENSIONS OF HIJRA ORIGIN STORIES

There is in the Mahabharata itself a line to the effect that whatever is not found in the epic does not exist, and by a certain measure everything in India does appear to return to the Mahabharata, which is by common consent a vast storehouse of Indian myths, folkloric motifs, archetypes, proverbs, religious practices and beliefs, and philosophical systems. To resort to the epics is by no means to return to the framework of Orientalism and its highly textualist strategies, since the Indian epics, and more generally the vast literature encapsulated under the category of the puranas, still provide the categories through which Indians order the world around them and give shape to their lives. The stories of the epics, which exist in myriad forms in numerous oral traditions, resonate in the everyday life and practices of Indians, and not only Hindus.

Not unexpectedly, then, hijras too find sanction for their lives in the great epic of the Mahabharata, though that mythic shape is also filled and shaped by the Ramayana. Hijras are wont to describe themselves, in the words of the spokesman of the All India Hijra Kalyan Sabha, a newly created organization that purports to make the voices of the hijras heard in a democratic polity, as 'descended from Hinduism from olden times, right from the Ramayana.' As Rama prepared to go into exile with Sita and Lakshmana at the behest of his father, he was followed to the banks of the river at the edge of the forest by his adoring subjects. According to the hijras, he turned to his people, and while imploring them to wipe away their tears added the following words: 'Men and women, please go back and perform your duties.' When Rama returned to Ayodhya fourteen years later after his victory over Ravana, he found a cluster of people still gathered at the same spot, and was told that, since they were neither men nor women, they had felt themselves exempt from Rama's injunction. For this act of exemplary devotion they received the blessing of Rama.[17]

That the hijras consider an 'auspicious' beginning as critical to their account of their originary place in Indian society itself suggests how much of the texture of Indian civilization predominates in the narrative space that hijras inhabit. The idea of the 'auspicious', which speaks to almost nothing in the experience of the late twentieth-century civilization of the West, still occupies a commanding presence in the Indian imaginary. The auspicious is one of the categories that the Indian nation-state has retained from its other self, which it is eager to repudiate in its embrace of the modern, namely Indian civilization. More to the point, hijras themselves are harbingers of the auspicious. At what are traditionally held to be the two most auspicious moments in an adult person's life, namely marriage and the birth of a male child, hijras come into their own as persons possessed of the power of conferring blessings and, complementarily, inflicting curses. It is said that a bride's face must not be open to the gaze of hijras, since the curse of infertility (the stigma of which in India carries its own inestimable force) might fall upon her; on the other hand, when hijras confer blessings upon the child, this ensures that the child will have healthy progeny.[18] The presence of hijras is auspicious, and yet terrifying; and while themselves incapable of carrying or seeding children, they appear to have some inexorable power over the reproductive process. It is paradigmatic that, unable to partake experientially in what are conventionally viewed as the two most fecund and poignant moments in a person's life, namely marriage and childbirth, the hijras nonetheless leave the stamp of their own unconventionality on these life cycles: their very 'lack' makes them the most desirable witnesses to truths which they can only know vicariously.

The element of the auspicious makes an insertion into the tale of the hijras in yet more complex ways. In much of northern and western India, Ganesh is the god of auspicious beginnings, but he is also the offspring of Shiva and Parvati. It is as her attendant and guardian that Ganesh was brought into being, and when Shiva attempts to invade Parvati's privacy, the duty of chasing his own father away from his mother's chamber devolves upon Ganesh. As one scholar has noted, the story provides a stellar example of the operation of the primal oedipal triangle of son, father, and mother in India, but what is most germane in the narrative is that after a prolonged fight, Shiva emerges triumphant when he beheads Ganesh with his trident. Beheading is a 'displaced mode of castration', frequently encountered in the Hindu legends, but it is notable that the narrative ends on a note of rejuvenation: enraged at her husband's act, Parvati successfully pleads with him to restore to Ganesh his life, whereupon an elephant head is placed upon his body.[19]

Hijras simultaneously identify themselves with Shiva, who both takes and restores Ganesh's life, even though they view themselves as vehicles of the divine power of the Mother Goddess. Among the numerous Hindu creation myths, there is one in which Shiva is asked by Brahma and Vishnu to create the world. Thereupon Shiva retreats into the water: but as he remains plunged in it for a thousand years, Brahma is induced by Vishnu to create all the gods and other beings. When Shiva finally emerges from the water, and is prepared to commence with the creation, it dawns on him that the universe no longer has any vacuum. Consequently Shiva breaks off his phallus and tosses it aside with the remark that he has not much further use for his generative organ; yet as the phallus falls and breaks into pieces, it extends fertility over the entire earth. Thus, even as Shiva himself becomes a sexual renunciate and loses the power to procreate, his phallus becomes emblematic of 'universal fertility', and it is to this circumstance that one can trace the cult of lingam or phallus worship.[20] The hijras, in their own life, provide a mirror image of this scenario: while themselves impotent, they confer the blessings of fertility on others. Not less significantly, even while some hijras engage in sexual relations with men and have recourse to prostitution, they insist on being considered akin to sexual ascetics or religious mendicants. Whatever the credibility of that claim, it is pertinent that Shiva is represented in the Hindu tradition chiefly as a yogi, venerated for the *tapas* or power yielded by his practices of asceticism.

One of the other most popular representations of Shiva is as Ardhanarisvara, or 'the Lord who is half woman': in numerous miniature paintings and sculptures, one half of his body has a female breast, long hair, and anklets. It is this representation of Shiva that, not coincidentally, is evoked in the figure of Arjuna, who appears in the guise of a eunuch in the fourth book, the Virataparvan, of the Mahabharata. At this point of the narrative, the Pandavas are in the thirteenth year of their exile, which they are obliged to spend in disguise by the terms of the conditions imposed upon them by Duryodhana. Arjuna had spent a good part of the first twelve years in the Himalayas, practicing austerities, in emulation of Shiva, all the more that he might obtain celestial weapons from Indra;[21] and in the thirteenth year of exile, he takes up employment in the court of Virata disguised as a eunuch. The Pandavas are to remain incognito, or, if detected, be resigned to another thirteen-year stretch of exile: and there is something profoundly ironical in Arjuna's mode of being incognito, since as a eunuch he is already nameless and incognito, unknowable—as shall presently become clear—to all methods of cognition. Arjuna's excuse for taking up this disguise is that only the elaborate clothes and jewellery of a woman can hide the bowstring scars on his arms which are the unmistakable emblems of his extraordinary prowess as an ambidextrous archer, but he is not in this matter a free agent. Having previously rejected the sexual advances of the nymph Urvasi, he is cursed to lead forever the life of a *napumsaka*, a neutered transvestite of ambiguous sex, and it is merely on account of the goodwill of his father Indra, at whose court Urvasi resides, that the curse is modified so as to be in effect for one year. That Arjuna is not in fact a eunuch is indicated by the very name which he assumes: as the Sanskritist van Buitenen noted, 'Brhannada', a feminine noun, means 'having a large reed', or, as is quite evident, being well endowed with signs of manliness.[22]

To Virata, Arjuna appears as 'a great man wearing the adornments of a woman': he is not, however, merely a transvestite: the text speaks of him as belonging to the *trtiyam prakrtim*, that is the 'third sex', though elsewhere he is also described as *kliba*, emasculated, impotent, and neutered.[23] To the Kauravas, who fail to penetrate his disguise, 'he has something of a man, something of a woman' in his manners, again an unmistakable allusion to the *ardhnarisvara* form of Shiva. He offers dancing and music lessons to Uttara, the King's daughter: in this aspect of his disguise, too, he bears a proximity to Nataraja, the dancing form of Shiva that carries with it the two-fold overtones of auspiciousness, the triumph of knowledge over ignorance, but also cosmic destruction and dissolution.[24] When Virata eventually offers him his daughter's hand in marriage, Arjuna refuses with the words, 'I dwelt in the seraglio always seeing your daughter, secretly and in the open, and she trusted me like a father.'[25] But if Arjuna is the primordial eunuch, who has shared an asexual and parental intimacy with Uttara, he must preside (as do hijras) over a marriage and the birth of a male child. This is accomplished when Arjuna arranges for the marriage of his son Abhimanyu to Uttara, and prepares her, in a manner of speaking, for the birth of her son, Pariksit, upon whom alone will fall the burden of continuing the dynasty of the Kurus. At the conclusion of the great Bharata war, Pariksit remains the sole surviving member of the Kuru family, a testimony to the folly of humankind and to the inevitable hubris that leads human beings to reproduce themselves. This is the hubris from which hijras, however unwittingly, are spared.

II

HIJRAS AND THE PROBLEM OF CATEGORIES

Whatever the hijras may be, and howsoever they may be described, it is indubitably certain that they cannot continue their family line. As the myths from epic literature to which the hijras point as narratives about their eternal condition suggest, elements of castration, asceticism, hermaphroditism, bisexualism, and street performance are all important to their own self-definition. Yet in the most widely accepted colloquial understanding of what allows hijras to be so nominated, it is the sense of their impotence which predominates; and to abuse a man as a hijra is to proclaim loudly to the world his inability to perform sexually and to question his capacity to help a woman bear his seed. The word hijra, which is derived from Urdu, is usually rendered as either 'eunuch' or 'hermaphrodite', and, in north India at least, the two terms were once used to distinguish between those made into hijras and those born intersexed. Early twentieth-century ethnographers in the Punjab noted that hijras insisted on describing themselves as impotent, and among them was a popular saying: 'We are broken vessels and fit for nothings; formerly we guarded the harems of kings—how could they admit us into the zanana if there was the least danger? We go into the houses of all, and never has a eunuch looked upon a woman with a bad eye: we are like bullocks (castrated male cattle).'[26] An impotent man, being devoid of the desire for women, could be entrusted with entering the women's quarters. From even earlier in the literature it emerges that hijras represented themselves as impotent: thus, writing to the Collector of Poona in 1836, his inferior remarked of them that 'all state that they were incapable of copulation and that becoming Hijeras was on that account only; sterility would not have induced them; [they] seem quite unconscious of any wrong or shame.'[27] Nineteenth-century ethnographers also suggest that aspirants who sought admission into the fold of the community were required to undergo a rigorous test of impotency, being compelled to sleep for four nights or more with a prostitute, and a more recent ethnographer has noted that such a practice may not be uncommon during a hijra's probationary period.[28] This is not unlikely, when we consider that the motif of ascetics, even gods, being lured into sexual thoughts and conduct by seductive women or nymphs is rampant in mythological texts.

It is ironically in the very condition of their impotency that hijras are nonetheless able to reproduce their own kind. Anthropologists have reported hearing a belief among the hijras that an impotent man who chooses not to become a hijra is condemned to be born impotent in his next life.[29] The self-fashioning of the hijras would seem to erase the narrative of impotency: only those who have rendered themselves empty may receive the blessings of spiritual fulfilment, and only the man who is without seed can seed good fortune and progeny to others. To speak of impotency, moreover, is to conjure up the image of masculinity, however deformed, dysfunctional, or deficient: only men may be impotent. This raises the important consideration whether impotency is an appropriate, much less adequate, characteristic that one should ascribe to hijras, since such ascription would suggest that hijras should be construed merely as the defective or female pole of the male gender. As two students of queerness in ancient India remark, even Indian literature, where constructions of alternative sexualities and genders are unabashedly fecund, displays 'tendencies to assimilate the third gender', whatever that may be, 'to the male or female poles of a gender binarism.'[30] Some ethnographers have noted that a few of the hijras with whom they had contact were born female and raised as girls, but by far the greater number of hijras admit to having been born as males. Yet all strongly disavow any suggestion that they might now be considered as men, and they are united in their belief that no greater insult is possible than to describe them as males.

It is not only on the grounds that they lack a penis or possess an abnormal one that hijras decry any comparison with men. One hijra told the anthropologist Serena Nanda, 'We are not like men, we do not have the sexual desires men have', while another one remarked, 'We hijra are like *sannyasis*, we have renounced all sexual desire and family life.'[31] If hijras have no desire for women, can they reasonably be inferred as having a desire for men? 'We hijras are born as boys,' Nanda was told, 'but then we "get spoiled" and have sexual desires only for men.'[32] Indeed, the presumption that hijras are none other than homosexuals continues to pervade the literature, and Morris Carstairs, in his famous study four decades ago of upper-caste Hindus, went so far as to describe hijras as simply 'male prostitutes.' In the glossary to his work Carstairs defined hijras as 'homosexuals'; however, as he could find no one who would admit to sexual relations with hijras, he satisfied himself with the observation that 'no community admits to homosexual practices, though each accuses the other.'[33] The community of hijras, on his account, constituted a form of institutionalized homosexuality, but this institution was apparently invisible. No one else has ever accepted that hijras must pre-eminently be seen as homosexuals, and Carstairs' work has evoked angry rejoinders, as well as the reminder that the guilt associated with homosexuality was never the norm in India. In the matter of homosexuality, it is contended, the attitude of Indians has typically been healthier than that found in many other cultures.[34] Though contemporary accounts appear to display a consensus that increasing number of hijras are turning to prostitution, whether to supplement their incomes or from the point of view of personal gratification, hijras vehemently deny that prostitution forms any fundamental part of their ethos.[35] The same early twentieth-century ethnographers to whom the hijras described themselves as 'bullocks' have recorded that the hijras spoke with obvious contempt of men known as 'zenana' who, said the hijras, are 'given to sodomy': 'They are prostitutes; if we acted like them how could our [patrons] allow us to come near them? They have deprived prostitutes of their living—we are not such.'[36] In more recent years, when Zia Jaffrey broached the subject, the 'zenana' were dismissed as being different from 'hijras'.[37]

Everything thus preponderates towards the view that, considering themselves neither heterosexual nor homosexual men, the hijras may well wish to be regarded as women, or at least as having a special affinity for the female sex. This view has received a sympathetic hearing from Western scholars interested in questions of alternative and multiple genders, since it is more easily assimilated to a cross-cultural theory of transsexuality whereby it is possible to explain hijras as yet another instance of the phenomenon of a woman finding herself trapped in a man's body.[38] There is, in any case, a predisposition in Western medical practices towards assimilating intersexed persons into the female sex, since surgical procedures are capable of constructing female genitalia to much greater accuracy than the penis and restoring the intersexed person to 'normality'; moreover, historically speaking, the phenomenon of transsexuals was mainly experienced as men desirous of changing into women rather than women wanting to turn into men, though it appears that now 'about the same number of women and men approach medical providers about a sex change.'[39]

All the hijras dress in saris or the salwar-kameez, though a few have been observed in men's clothes as well, and observers are agreed that female attire is the *sine qua non* of hijra identity. The predilection for women's clothing is observed in the fact that all hijras wear a bra, which is either padded, or, as is more likely, stuffed; 'sometimes it just is there', Nanda has written, 'empty, on the flat male chest.'[40] Yet there may be a slippage here, for what is named a 'male chest' is no longer recognized by the hijra as ontologically 'male'. Hijras imitate a woman's 'swaying walk', take female names upon being initiated into the community, and affect, sometimes in a comical way, women's mannerisms; they request 'ladies only' seats on trains and buses, and stand in queues for women at railway stations and cinema halls; and they use female kinship terms, such as 'aunty' and sister, in addressing each other. They pluck rather than shave their facial hair. Yet, none of this can clinch the issue: though some hijras will readily admit to being viewed as female, they confess that they are not quite women. It is not only that their behaviour, whether it be lewd dancing or their threat to expose their genitals if their financial demands at performances are ignored, is altogether incongruous with the behaviour generally expected of women in the public realm. They make an aggressive claim upon a public space that, at least in north India, is heavily gendered, and they may be found loitering (already something of a male activity) in places where women are seldom found. Most to the point, hijras do not menstruate, and as they lack the female reproductive organs, they are without the capacity to bear children. Hijras do often tell stories which betray their desire for a child, but they recognize that wish as belonging within the realm of impossibility. Perhaps officials some generations ago meant to signify the 'not women' aspect of hijra life when they required of them that they wear male turbans with their female clothing, or a 'medley of male and female clothing.'[41]

Thus far, then, every fundamental description of hijras is seen as being inadequate. To reduce hijras to transvestites is merely to assimilate them to increasingly larger classes of people around the world who engage in cross-dressing, however complex their politics of representation,[42] just as to describe them as eunuchs or hermaphrodites is to ignore the fact that some are both, while some are neither, and that many hijras are disinclined in any case to accept this distinction. Hijras are impotent, but they replenish themselves and are believed to hold the power of fertility and infertility over others; they are born men, but they disavow the male sex; they often indulge in homosexual behaviour, but contemptuously dismiss homosexuals as not of their kind; and while construing themselves as women, they cannot experience the cycles of menstruation, pregnancy, birth, lactation, or menopause which, to greater or lesser degree, characterize the biological and cultural lives of all women. Much like the sage from the ancient philosophical texts, the Upanishads, who dismisses with the words *'neti, neti'* ('not this, not this') all attempts to endow the Supreme Being with attributes as limitations, one is tempted to reject all the characteristics commonly attached to hijras.

It is in view of these difficulties in defining hijras, then, that their characterization, which appears to meet with the approval of hijras themselves, as neither men nor women, as a 'third sex', suggests itself as most apposite. It is doubtless with respect to a class of people such as hijras that the third-century BC linguistic treatise, *Mahabhasya* [The Great Commentary, 4.1.3], noted the following: '[Q:] What is it that people see when they decide, this is a woman, this is a man, this is neither a woman nor a man? [A:] That person who has breasts and long hair is a woman; that person who is hairy all over is a man; that person who is different from either when those characteristics are absent, is neither woman nor man.'[43] The 'neither woman nor man' is designated as the *napumsaka*, which the Sanskrit dictionaries define as a neuter, 'bereft of either a masculine or feminine nature'. Significantly, texts such as the *Satapatha Brahmana* (sixth-century BC), attempt to render grammatical gender isomorphic with natural gender: thus the grammatical neuter is technically defined as emasculated, akin to a castrated bull, which is 'neither female nor male, being a male it is not a female, and being a female [that is, emasculate] it is not a male.'[44] The same relation between sexual gender and grammatical gender can be surmised by the fact that the word linga, which means sex, came around the same time to be adopted for grammatical gender; and it is also from linga that lingam, or the phallus, is derived.

Notwithstanding the valiant attempt to transcend sexual dimorphism, the third sex or *tritya prakriti*, which is neither male nor female, does not, on closer examination, appear to be a fully satisfactory designation for hijras. The literature of the Jains, where the conception of the third sex is widely prevalent, points to the same problem. Jain thinkers developed the theory of sexual orientation (*veda*), and distinguished between *striveda*, *pumveda*, and *napumsakaveda*, 'or the sexual feelings normally appropriate to a woman, a man, and a hermaphrodite respectively.'[45] They further argued that these feelings need not coincide with the biological gender of the person holding these feelings: thus, it was quite possible for a person to be biologically female, but be imbued with masculine feelings. Nonetheless, while the third sex was seen as comprised of both female and male sexualities, it was, as has been argued, 'tacitly admitted by the Jains to be the homosexual sex'—that is, sexual desire for a man was beginning to emerge from an early period as the principal element of third-sex formation.[46] This returns us to a much earlier formulation about the third sex, in our case the hijras, as an institutionalized community of homosexuals, a formulation rejected by hijras and most inadequately substantiated by the literature. There is also the more pressing difficulty that the conceptualization of hijras as neither men nor women shows a debilitating dependence on the narrow and formal system of Aristotelian logic, which works within the framework of either/or duality. Indian logic,[47] at its simplest, presents a more diverse array of possibilities: thus, where X is hijra and A is male, we can postulate that X is A; X is not A; X is not non-A; X is both A and non-A; and X is neither A nor non-A; and likewise a similar set of possibilities is conjured by rendering A as female rather than male. Thus, in this scenario, hijras may well be both male and female, non-male and non-female; and it is just as possible that they may be neither male nor non-male, nor female nor non-female.

III

TOWARDS A HIJRA POLITICS OF KNOWLEDGE

It has been argued by Serena Nanda, whose work on the hijras remains the most complete scholarly account we have of their lives, that they furnish an example of the traditional tolerance of Indian social structures for diversity and pluralism. She has argued forcefully that hijras constitute a 'gender category that cannot be understood with reference only to our own (that is, Western) gender system, with its dichotomous and permanent gender categories.' Though their conduct might appear to be 'pathological and bizarre,' it becomes 'understandable when studied from the point-of-view of the cultural system in which the hijras operate.'[48] It is only an 'accommodating society' that could have absorbed what she describes as an 'institutionalized third gender role', and likewise she puts forth a view of Hinduism as being hospitable to contradictions, allowing the hijras to survive, if not thrive, without forcing a resolution.[49]

It is possible, for instance, to take a purely instrumentalist view of the presence of hijras at births and marriage, and to suppose that they are well-versed in the art of exploitation; however, as Alf Hiltebeitel has argued, their presence at such occasions marks 'the ambiguity of those moments where the non-differentiation of the male and female is most filled with promise and uncertainty—in the mystery that surrounds the sexual identity of the still unborn child . . . and in that which anticipates the *re-union* of the male and female in marital sex.'[50] Such ambiguity is echoed in the lives of the hijras, who are at once male and female, neither-male and neither-female, eunuch and transvestite. Moving to the more material end of the argument, it is remarkable that Indian society could find a niche for those who had taken on an alternative social role: as has been noted, hijras even had 'claims on the public revenues through grants of cash and lands', and in some places they 'apparently possessed an official and codified right to beg'.[51]

Their role, Nanda says of the hijras, 'highlights many Indian cultural themes', but for the most part she does not pursue that tantalizing thought to its most promising conclusion.[52] Against her view, there stands the more conventional representation, particularly in academic scholarship, of India as a traditional, patriarchal, and misogynistic society, where gender roles have always been highly circumscribed. The American Sanskritist, Robert Goldman, has argued that the theme of a man wanting to turn into a woman is widely encountered in Indian texts as much as in the biographies of medieval and modern religious and political leaders,[53] and it is possible, on this reading, to infer that the hijras (supposing that they were only biologically male, which is not the case) merely represent the institutionalized fulfilment of that motif. But what are otherwise arresting readings of Indian myths are fatally marred by his absolute insistence on interpreting castration, in each and every instance, 'as a demeaning punishment for some kind of Oedipal transgression against a powerful and dreaded male figure,' just as the 'fantasy of a man's becoming a woman' is invariably represented 'as a deeply longed for metamorphosis that makes possible an erotic liaison with a powerful and desired male.' Consequently, Goldman has little patience for the view that there is a 'specifically Hindu ability to tolerate ambiguities', and he dismisses such reformulations of traditional hermeneutics as quite inadequate in the face of his own, somewhat absurdly, monocausal explanations.[54]

Tolerance and pluralism are, no doubt, among the troublingly familiar tropes by means of which Indians engage in self-representation, and they have even won India some respect (notwithstanding the communal riots of the last few decades) in a world that has little use for such virtues, but neither their familiarity nor predictability ought to make them sterile for those accustomed to a more harsh view of Indian civilization.[55] It would be much too easy to assimilate the hijras to the old representation of India as a land of wonders and magic, alongside fakirs, holy men, yogis, and snake charmers, and there remains the temptation to view them as mere freaks or anomalies.[56] Not everyone will be seduced by Nanda's endorsement of the hijras as a 'third gender', institutionalized or otherwise, and her insistence on the asexuality of hijras, even while she admits that a great number of them, possibly even a majority, engage in homoerotic practices, may strike some as her own disguised form of disavowal of homosexuality. Nor is this, as many modernizing middle-class Indians ashamed of the hijras argue, the only reason to be wary of narratives which purport to show the hijras as anything other than a deviant sub-group. The numerous and seemingly reliable reports of abduction of children to be recruited into the community of hijras, and their forcible castration, in obvious indifference to the strictures against mutilation in the Indian Penal Code, not to mention customary codes of ethical conduct, must not be overlooked. If indeed they are being drawn into the vortex of crime, their criminalization (and consequent elimination by the state) cannot be far away.[57]

At the same time, it must be recognized that, notwithstanding the hideously self-congratulatory impulses of modernity and post-modernism alike, modernity has been inhospitable to hijras. Doubtless the hijras have, much like other minorities, under-privileged groups, and the oppressed, begun to understand that power comes with political mobilization, and in the last two years, not only has a hijra been elected to legislative office in the state of Madhya Pradesh, but groups of hijras have lodged complaints with film censor boards about their representation in films.[58] But it is indisputably true that hijras are increasingly losing their traditional means of livelihood, they no longer enjoy the patronage of traditional elites, and their life options are in every respect narrowing; moreover, mass culture is creating its own forms of homogenization, and institutionalized forms of femininity and masculinity, which have been less predominant in Indian culture than appears to be the case from the rigid gender roles to which most Indians (particularly of the middle class) are now bound, might well render the hijras obsolete. The numerous esoteric traditions of Vaishnavite worship, in some of which male devotees affect the role of Radha, the consort of Krishna, to the point where menstruation is simulated, or the spiritual practices of Sri Ramakrishna, who is admitted as being able to 'sweat blood from the pores of his body' when, in the character of a woman, he felt the acute longing for Krishna experienced by the women of Vrindavan,[59] are among the innumerable instances known in Indian culture of the striving for androgyny and the mutability of notions of masculinity and femininity.

While it is possible to sympathize with those readings which project the hijras as fulfilling a 'third gender' role that transcends sexual dimorphism, epistemological binarism, and ontological dualism, I have suggested that even the 'third gender' designation does not convey the full promise hidden in the term 'hijra'. We shall have to venture, however tentatively, into a zone that might yield what I would describe not merely as a politics of knowledge of hijras, but as a hijra politics of knowledge. Among the most enduring of the myths available in the vast corpus of the puranas is that of Narasimha, the man-lion. The circumstances under which Narasimha descends to earth as an incarnation of Vishnu are dictated by the consideration that Hiranyakasipu, the ambitious and self-aggrandizing king of the Daityas, whose appetite for power is insatiable, has apparently rendered himself immune from destruction. Such is his *tapas*, the fire of his sacrifice and discipline, that even the gods must render him obeisance; and it is from these grateful gods that he receives a boon that he shall 'never be killed by these means: the striking and throwing weapons of my enemies, thunderbolts, dried tree-trunks, high mountains, by water or fire.' Drought, fire, earthquakes, thunder, hurricanes: from all these he shall have immunity. Most decisively, Hiranyakasipu appears to have clinched his immortality when it is conceded that he shall 'not be slain in heaven, on earth, in the daytime, at night, from neither above nor below.'[60] But Hiranyakasipu cannot be contained, his ambition grows and his enemies are decimated, and he spares not even his own son, Prahlad, whose devotion to Vishnu makes his father determined to terminate his life. Even the gods are defeated in battle; consequently, they repair to Vishnu, who is now pressed to find some way to deliver the world from the tyranny of Hiranyakasipu. Narasimha, half-man and half-lion, springs from a pillar (thus neither from 'above' nor 'below') at the exact moment of twilight, when it is neither 'day' nor 'night', and tears Hiranyakasipu apart. It is at the cusp, in the moment of liminality, that ignorance is defeated and knowledge is acquired.

In the myth of Narasimha, the story of the hijras is arguably prefigured. This is by no means to assert that the same sanctity attaches to the hijras as is commonly associated with the figure of Narasimha, the avatar of Vishnu, or that the hijras will save us from ourselves. If Narasimha is sent into the midst of the human community with a jolt to warn men (and women) of their hubris, the hijra similarly enacts more than a merely symbolic deconstruction of phallocentrism. Though I have quite deliberately steered away from a psychoanalytic and specifically Lacanian reading of hijras and the rite of castration, it is obvious that such a reading would not be entirely amiss. While Lacan's formulation that 'the phallus is the privileged signifier' or metaphor of law and desire remains hotly contested, it is more pertinent to note that much like any other sign, the phallus's function is also to represent that which is not present. As Lacan was to suggest, the phallus as signifier masks its own absence, and is invariably intertwined with its opposite, most pre-eminently castration. 'The phallus in Freudian doctrine is not a fantasy', Lacan further reminds us, 'nor is it as such an object . . . . It is even less the organ, penis or clitoris, which it symbolizes.'[61] If the penis mediates between the phallus as the signifier, and the male body as the signified, its removal points to the very disruption of patriarchal mastery. Herein lies one explanation for the ironic potency of the hijra: it is only when the penis is removed that the phallus effectively functions as a sign of generativity, that is as the receptacle of the goddess's gift of fertility. It is remarkable that the woman who wields the castrating knife is called 'dai' or midwife, that the hijra after the operation is enjoined to take the same forty days of bed-rest that are prescribed for a woman after childbirth, and that the emasculation ritual is described by the hijras as a 'rebirth'.[62] Feminists have spoken of the necessity for men to unlearn their privileges: the hijras move to a demonstrable embodiment of that political wisdom.

There is in the story and living presence of the hijras a curious power of grace and redemption, and to unravel that we will have to probe the nature of knowledge and dissent in our times. What can a census-taker do with hijras, and are we at the point where we can imagine an official census anywhere stipulating a choice beyond male and female? There is something deeply transgressive about the life choices made by hijras, just as there is a deep anxiety about their identity since they do not fall within the paradigms of classification and enumeration that are dominant in modern knowledge systems. Hijras generate for the moderns all the anxieties that, to evoke what may appear to be an anomalous comparison, are experienced by each and every nation-state in Europe when gypsies are brought into their midst. A nomadic people in a world that knows only how to cross borders rather than transgress boundaries, and where transculturalism exists in strictly prescribed modes, gypsies are the bane of the census enumerator, the enemy of the nation-state with its sacrosanct borders, the confounders of an overweening civility. Similarly, as we look into the lives of the hijras, and to the pace of globalization now overtaking middle India, we might reflect with perhaps more than a tinge of sadness upon the fact that the hijras may well be among the last few dissenters as we move into the third millennium, among the very few who, shall we dare to say it, have been chosen to defy the very models of defiance.

Notes

1.   Serena Nanda, *Neither Man nor Woman: The Hijras of India* (Belmont, California: Wadsworth Publishing Company, 1990).

2.   Zia Jaffrey, *The Invisibles: A Tale of the Eunuchs of India* (New York: Pantheon Books, 1996).

3.   See, for example, Satish Kumar Sharma, *Hijras: The Labelled Deviants* (New Delhi: Gian Publishing House, 1989), and M. D. Vyas and Yogesh Shingala, *The Life Style of the Eunuchs* (New Delhi: Anmol Publications, 1987). Neither book is satisfactory; the latter is virtually unreadable, a product of one of the numerous gutter publishing houses that have sprung up in the Indian capital in the preceding 10-15 years.

4.   Anne Fausto-Sterling, 'The Five Sexes: Why Male and Female Are Not Enough,' *The Sciences* (March-April 1993), pp. 20-21.

5.   Suzanne J. Kessler, 'The Medical Construction of Gender: Case Management of Intersexed Infants,' *Signs* 16, no. 1 (1990), p. 4.

6.   Ibid., pp. 5-8, 25; for 'normalization', see Michel Foucault in Alan Sheridan tr., *Discipline and Punish: The Birth of the Prison* (New York: Pantheon Books, 1978).

7.   For a brief discussion, see Mahin Hassibi, 'Designing Sex: Playing God, Have Doctors Gone Too Far?,' *On The Issues* 7, no. 3 (Summer 1998), pp. 13-15.

8.   Michel Foucault in Robert Hurley tr., *The History of Sexuality*, vol. I: *An Introduction* (New York: Vintage Books, 1980); see also, Richard McDougall tr., *Herculine Barbin: Being the Recently Discovered Memoirs of a Nineteenth-Century French Hermaphrodite* (New York: Pantheon Books, 1978). For an example of the conventional acknowledgment of other traditions in an otherwise intelligent piece, see Ruth Hubbard, 'Gender and Genitals: Constructs of Sex and Gender,' *Social Text*, nos. 46-47 (Spring/Summer 1996), p. 160.

9.   Leonard Zwilling and Michael J. Sweet, ' "Like a City Ablaze": The Third Sex and the Creation of Sexuality in Jain Religious Literature,' *Journal of the History of Sexuality* 6, no. 3 (January 1996), p. 359.

10.   Cited by Laurence W. Preston, 'A Right to Exist: Eunuchs and the State in Nineteenth-Century India', *Modern Asian Studies* 21, no. 2 (1987), pp. 373, 377.

11.   Cited in ibid., pp. 386-87.

12.   Programme on 'The *Hijras* [Eunuchs] in India', Channel 13 [KCOP], Los Angeles, '"Strange Universe"', broadcast on 21 January 1997.

13.   For a more extended discussion of the 'politics of knowledge', see Vinay Lal, 'Discipline and Authority: Some Notes on Future Histories and Epistemologies of India', *Futures* 29, no. 10 (December 1997), pp. 985-1000.

14.   Ibid., p. 376. Jaffrey conveys the unmistakable impression that the practices of so distasteful a group of people as the hijras cannot be other than Islamic in origin. The hijras are encountered mainly in north Indian cities, where Islamic influence has been most strongly felt, and this suggests to Jaffrey 'a more than casual link to Islamic culture' (*The Invisibles*, p. 56). Since Jaffrey's book has pretensions to being analytical, it must be held to rather more rigorous standards than the commonplace views of many middle-class Hindus, with which Jaffrey seems to be quite in agreement, that the 'institution' of hijras came to acquire force in India only with the coming of Islam. Contributing to a debate on the internet, one Hindu, Nachiketa Tiwari, gave it as his opinion that 'the number of hijras swelled by very large amounts after the Islamic invasions. The reason being, that many Islamic rulers actually forcibly made a lot [of] people hijras, and having made them impotent, gave them the charge of their large harems' (see soc.religion.hindu newsgroup, posted on 12 September 1996). When it comes to Muslims, any number of canards are

passed off as self-evident truths and historical 'facts'. No one has ever disputed that it was customary to have eunuchs at the court of Muslim kings: what is objectionable, however, is the attempt to continue to communalize the history of the hijras, and to attribute essentialistic religious identities to them. The supposition that Muslim rulers deliberately sought to render large number of Hindu men hijras is quite fantastic, and no one has advanced any evidence to render this argument plausible. For a capsule history of eunuchs in Muslim countries, see T. W. Juynboll, 'Eunuch (Muslim),' in James Hastings ed., *Encyclopaedia of Religion and Ethics* (Edinburgh:T. &T. Clark, 1914), 5:584-85.

15. Nanda, *Neither Man nor Woman*, p. 23.

16. Ibid., p. 43.

17. This story is narrated in Jaffrey, *Eunuchs*, p. 29, and Nanda, *Neither Man nor Woman*, p. 23. As might be expected, I have found no trace of this story in the Ramayana of either Valmiki or Tulsidas, and I doubt that it would be found in any of the other principal vernacular versions of the Ramayana, whether of Kamban or of Bengali writers. But there are hundreds of Ramayanas in India, and the primacy of written over oral versions is far from being universally accepted in India.

18. India still shows a marked propensity, not uncommonly found in societies that are predominantly agricultural, for male over female children. Formerly hijras only plied their skills at the birth of boys; but as times have become leaner, and the sources of patronage have dried up, they now appear at the births of female babies as well.

19. R. P. Goldman, 'Fathers, Sons and Gurus: Oedipal Conflict in the Sanskrit Epics,' *Journal of Indian Philosophy* 6 (1978), pp. 325-92 at 371-72 n. 26. The motif of transposed heads is found in numerous other contexts, and is widely prevalent in Indian folktales; it is the subject of a novella by Thomas Mann, *The Transposed Heads: A Legend of India* (New York: Vintage Books, 1959).

20. This myth is recounted in Wendy Doniger O'Flaherty, *Asceticism and Eroticism in the Mythology of Siva* (New York: Oxford University Press, 1973), pp. 130-35; for a more extended, particularly psychoanalytic, account of castration narratives in Hindu mythology, see idem, *Women, Androgynes, and Other Mythical Beasts* (Chicago: The University of Chicago Press, 1980).

21. This is brought out rather well in the re-telling of the Mahabharata by Maggi Lidchi-Grassi, *The Battle of Kurukshetra* (Calcutta: Writers Workshop, 1987), pp. 253-68; the war and its aftermath are treated in her *Legs of the Tortoise* (Calcutta: Writers Workshop, 1989).

22. J. A. B. van Buitenen, ed. and tr., *The Mahabharata* (Chicago: University of Chicago Press, 1973), vol. 3, p. 9.

23.   The most cogent discussion of the Shiva-Arjuna relation remains Alf Hiltebeitel, 'Siva, the Goddess, and the Disguises of the Pandavas and Draupadi,' *History of Religions* 20, nos. 1-2 (1980), pp. 147-174, but see in particular pp. 154-58. For definitions of *trityam prakrtim* and *kliba*, see Vaman Shivram Apte, *The Practical Sanskrit-English Dictionary*, rev. and enlg. ed. (1st ed., 1890; Delhi: Motilal Banarsidass, 1978), pp. 863, 383; Arjuna's experience of himself as belonging to the *trtiya prakrti* is to be found in *The Mahabharata*, 4.3.59.

24.   For a brief interpretative essay on Nataraja, see Ananda K. Coomaraswamy, *The Dance of Shiva: On Indian Art and Culture* (New York: The Noonday Press, 1958), pp. 66-78.

25.   Cited by Hiltebeitel, 'Siva, the Goddess, and the Disguises,' p. 165.

26.   D. C. J. Ibbetson, M. E. MacLagen, and H. A. Rose, *A Glossary of the tribes and castes of the Panjab and North-West Frontier Province* (Lahore: Civil and Military Gazette Press, 1911), 2:331, cited by Morris E. Opler, 'Further Comparative Notes on the Hijara of India,' *American Anthropologist* 63 (1961), p. 1331.

27.   Cited by Preston, 'A Right to Exist', p. 375.

28.   Ibid., and also K. Bhimbhai, 'Pavayas in Gujarat population,' in J. M. Campbell, compiler, *Gazetteer of the Bombay Presidency* (Bombay: Government Central Press, 1901), vol. 9, Pt. I, p. 506; see also G. R. Salunke, 'Cult of the Hijras,' *Illustrated Weekly of India* (8 August 1976), p. 19.

29   A. M. Shah, 'A Note on the Hijadas of Gujarat', *American Anthropologist* 63 (1961), p. 1329.

30.   Michael J. Sweet and Leonard Zwilling, 'The First Medicalization: The Taxonomy and Etiology of Queerness in Classical Indian Medicine,' *Journal of the History of Sexuality* 3, no. 4 (1993), p. 600.

31.   Nanda, *Neither Man nor Woman*, p. 16.

32.   Ibid.

33.   Morris Carstairs, *The Twice-Born: A Study of a Community of High-Caste Hindus* (Bloomington: Indiana University Press, 1958), pp. 59, 329, 321.

34.   See Morris E. Opler, 'The Hijara (Hermaphrodites) of India and Indian National Character: A Rejoinder,' *American Anthropologist* 62 (1960), p. 505. Opler was not too well-informed about the hijras himself. Though the fact of castration had been recorded in the literature, he was to state that 'males are not castrated or mutilated to supply members for the hijara group. They are "all born that way"' (p. 506). Opler is right to question the assumption that some males are castrated for no other reason than to be coerced into joining the hijras, though more recent evidence suggests that this is far from being improbable; but castration after admission into the community of hijras is not consequently precluded, and in fact appears to be widely practiced. The

assumption that all hijras are born hijras can scarcely be substantiated, and Opler would have had to do no more than to look at medical literature to arrive at the understanding that the statistical occurrence of hermaphrodites in any population is minuscule enough as to constitute a rarity. S. K. Sharma says that one gynecologist whom he consulted during his research had not encountered a single hermaphrodite child in the preceding decade (*Hijras, The Labelled Deviants*, p. 20 n. 7). One American biologist claims that as many as four percent of infants may be born intersexed, but there appears to be not a shred of evidence for such a claim: see Fausto-Sterling, 'The Five Sexes,' p. 21. On the other hand, according to Suzanne Keller, the six medical specialists she interviewed for her study 'all agreed that intersexuality is rare', and one went so far as to state that it was unlikely that an average obstetrician would encounter more than two cases in twenty years ('The Medical Construction of Gender,' p. 4 n. 4). Only one of Serena Nanda's thirty informants was 'probably born intersexed' (see her 'The Hijras of India: Cultural and Individual Dimensions of an Institutionalized Third Gender Role,' *Journal of Homosexuality* 11, nos. 3-4 (Summer 1985, pp. 35-54 at 38). It is also not the case that when a hijra says, 'I was born like this', that this is invariably to be construed as implying that the person was born intersexed or with ambiguous genitals. One hijra interviewed by Nanda, in elaborating what might have been meant when she described herself as having been born that way, appeared to indicate nothing more than the fact that from childhood, though born a boy, she preferred the company of girls, and felt much like a girl: clearly possessed of a penis, (s)he nonetheless felt herself to be of ambiguous gender. When (s)he was about thirteen, (s)he experienced the desire for a man, and came to develop a sexual relationship with a man whom she called her husband. Though this man was married, and lived with his wife, sister, mother, and brother-in-law, he took the hijra into his household. See Nanda, *Neither Man nor Woman*, pp. 85-86.

Whether hijra is rendered as 'eunuch' or 'hermaphrodite', in either case, argues Opler, 'it implies a physical defect impairing the sexual functions rather than homosexuality.' He makes the arresting suggestion, which I have not seen pursued elsewhere in the literature, that 'it was probably the emphasis on male prerogatives and the disinclination to allow women of good name to dance publicly, rather than any homosexual urge, that accounts for the hijra' (p. 507). But 'the disinclination to allow women of good name to dance publicly' can in no respect be considered distinct to India, this being a prohibition or taboo that extended widely across many cultures; nor is it clear on this account why, in the roles that hijras have performed at marriages or births, they should have had to pose as women or engage in gynemimetics.

35. For one hijra's account of a life spent in prostitution, see Nanda, *Neither Man nor Woman*, pp. 55-70.

36. Ibbetson et al, *Glossary of the tribes and castes of Punjab*, vol. 2, p. 332, cited by Nanda, *Neither Man norWoman*, p. 11.

37. Jaffrey, *The Invisibles*, pp. 107-110.

38. See Foreword by John Money to Nanda, *Neither Man norWoman*, xiv; and see also *Third Sex, Third Gender: Beyond Sexual Dimorphism in Culture and History*, ed. Gilbert Herdt (NewYork: Zone Books, 1994), in particular the essay by Will Roscoe, 'How to Become a Berdache: Toward a Unified Analysis of Gender Diversity,' pp. 329-72. For a more personal account of this phenomenon, see Leslie Feinberg, *TransgenderedWarriors: Making History from Joan of Arc to Rupaul* (Boston: Beacon Press, 1996).

39. Hubbard, 'Gender and Genitals,' p. 61.

40. Nanda, *Neither Man norWoman*, p. 17. It is uncertain what hijras would have made of bra-burning feminists in the 1960s.

41. Preston, 'A Right to Exist,' p. 373.

42. Marjorie Garber, *Vested Interests: Cross-Dressing and Cultural Anxiety* (NewYork: Routledge, 1992).

43. Cited by Zwilling and Sweet, '"Like a City Ablaze"', p. 366 n. 27; see also p. 365.

44. Cited by Sweet and Zwilling, 'The First Medicalization', p. 601. The three grammatical genders are *napumsakalinga* (neuter), *strilinga* (feminine), and *pumlinga* (masculine).

45. Foreword by Robert P. Goldman to Padmanabh S. Jaini, *Gender and Salvation: Jaina Debates on the Spiritual Liberation of Women* (Berkeley: University of California Press, 1991), p. xviii.

46. Cited by Zwilling and Sweet, '"Like a City Ablaze"', p. 374.

47. For a brief discussion of Indian logic, see M. D. Srinivas, 'Logical and Methodological Foundations of Indian Science,' in Ziauddin Sardar ed., *The Revenge of Athena: Science, Exploitation and the ThirdWorld* (London and NewYork: Mansell Publishing, 1988), pp. 261-89.

48. Nanda, *Neither Man norWoman*, p. 143.

49. Nanda, 'The Hijras of India,' pp. 49-50, 53.

50. Hiltebeitel, 'Siva, the Goddess, and the Disguises of the Pandavas,' p. 168.

51. Preston, 'A Right to Exist,' p. 372.

52. Nanda, *Neither Man norWoman*, p. 143.

53. Robert P. Goldman, 'Transsexualism, Gender, and Anxiety in Traditional India', *Journal of the American Oriental Society* 113, no. 3 (July-September 1993), pp. 374-401.

54. Ibid., p. 395.

55. The most sustained and curiously intolerant assault on tolerance and pluralism as Indian virtues, so to speak, is to be found in Achin Vanaik, *The Furies of Indian Communalism: Religion, Modernity, and Secularization* (London: Verso, 1997).

56. It is instructive that a chapter on hermaphrodites is included in Leslie Fiedler, *Freaks: Myths and Images of the Secret Self* (New York: Simon and Schuster, 1978).

57. Dilip Bobb, 'Fear is the Key,' *India Today* (15 September 1982), pp. 40-41; Charu Lata Joshi, 'Eunuchs Fight Back,' *India Today* (15 May 1994), pp. 74-75, 77; Gautam N. Allahbadia and Nilesh Shah, 'Begging Eunuchs of Bombay,' *The Lancet* 339 (4 January 1992), pp. 48-49.

58. 'Eunuch takes oath as MLA in M.P.', *Times of India* (7 March 2000), p. 12, and Papri Sen Sri Raman, 'Eunuchs seek cuts in Tamil film *Appu*', *India Abroad* (12 May 2000), p. 57.

59. Christopher Isherwood, *Ramakrishna and His Disciples* (New York: Simon and Schuster, 1965), pp. 111-115; on Krishna bhakti, see Edward C. Dimock, Jr., *The Place of the Hidden Moon: Erotic Mysticism in the Vaisnava-sahajiya Cult of Bengal* (Chicago: University of Chicago Press, 1966). See also Ch. VI

60. This version, as it appears so far, is drawn from the *Matsya Purana*, as told in Cornelia Dimmitt and J. A. B. van Buitenen ed. and tr., *Classical Hindu Mythology: A Reader in the Sanskrit Puranas* (Philadelphia: Temple University Press, 1978), pp. 76-78; for another version, see H. H. Wilson tr., *Vishnu Purana: A System of Hindu Mythology and Tradition* (London: John Murray, 1840; reprint ed., Calcutta: Punthi Pustak, 1972).

61. Jacques Lacan, 'The Meaning of the Phallus,' in Juliet Mitchell and Jacqueline Rose ed. and tr., *Feminine Sexuality: Jacques Lacan and the ecole freudienne* (New York: Norton, 1982), cited by Jane Gallup, *Reading Lacan* (Ithaca, New York: Cornell University Press, 1985), p. 136; but see pp. 133-56 for a more extended discussion of the phallus and phallocentrism.

62. Preston, 'A Right to Exist,', p. 375; Nanda, *Neither Man nor Woman*, pp. 29, 36.

Eight

THE BITTERSWEET SWEETS OF MODERNITY:
CRICKET AND THE SOUTH ASIAN SENSIBILITY

In the World Cup of cricket that concluded in the summer of 1999, Australia soundly thrashed Pakistan in the final and lifted the game's most prized trophy. Pakistan's defeat was a matter of great rejoicing in India, as if India herself had triumphed. Arriving in Delhi from Osaka the day after the final on 20 June, I heard from my friends and family that some people had even exploded firecrackers in the streets and distributed sweets. In the culture of the Indian subcontinent, sweets are distributed, as is widely known, on the most auspicious occasions, such as the birth of a child or a marriage, to mark success in examinations, or to felicitate friends and neighbours on holy days. However, some years ago, the exchange of sweets began to take on new meanings, and at the time of Prime Minister Indira Gandhi's assassination at the hands of her Sikh bodyguards in 1984, it was widely rumoured that some Sikhs, seething with the spirit of revenge for the attack launched by the Indian army upon the Sikhs' most venerable shrine, the Golden Temple, celebrated the news of her death by distributing sweets in the streets of Delhi.[1] However groundless the rumours may have been,[2] they were enough to instigate some Hindus, encouraged by political leaders, to create a reign of terror for Sikhs in the nation's capital for a few days. Not less than 2000 Sikhs, and possibly many more, were killed in that short pogrom. More than fifteen years later, less than a handful of convictions have been obtained, and the killers and their bosses are still in business. Sweet must have been that revenge which was spurred on by sweets, calamitous alike for the eaters and givers of sweets.

Of course sweets were never *just* sweets, since in any system of signification the signifier is likely to signify many things at once. Some might argue, for example, that the precedence for the distribution of sweets to mark the triumph of political vengeance was established when sweets were distributed by disgruntled refugees and the ideologues of Hindu supremacy to celebrate the assassination of Mahatma Gandhi on 30 January 1948:[3] sweets were clearly not *just* sweets. We know that sweets are tempting, but in their irresistibility is all too often a shade of the corrupt. That infernal box of mithai, which may have in it more than just sweets, has led too many policemen, civil servants, bureaucrats, politicians, or clerks who man the offices of the utility companies, down the road of bribery and corruption. But the notion of how sweets might corrupt us is rendered with far more subtlety in Premchand's short story, 'Motelal ka Satyagraha', where Motelal, who has embarked on a fast in the cause of the nation, and to provide the masses with exemplary leadership, rips—in the stealth of the night—into boxes of barfis and containers of rasgullas dripping with sugary syrup. The travails of the stomach, in the common estimation, are of greater consequence than the rumblings of the nation; and certainly Gandhian-style satyagraha demands compliance with more exacting standards of discipline than is suggested by abstention from sweets. One suspects that Gandhi would have been deeply aware of the semiotics of sugar, just as he was of the semiotics of salt. How else can we understand his march to the sea at Dandi, the grand finale of which consisted of no more than Gandhi bending down to the water, collecting some salt, and so breaking the salt laws? A pinch of salt, it is said, broke the back of the empire, and Gandhi might have ruminated on how sugar, on which the British and French empires built their wealth, became the prime killer in the 'advanced' countries of the West.[4]

Our sweets have never been just sweets, but they were that much. Alas, so deeply has the insidious politics of the nation-state system enthralled us that even our sweets are no longer sweets. We have become incapable of thinking beyond the nation-state, as if any other form of community is inconceivable. There have historically been many other ways in which people have organized their affairs, and in the scale of things, the nation-state is a relatively new form of political arrangement, an *enfant terrible*. The nation-state system arose in the conditions of internecine European warfare in the mid-seventeenth century, and was bequeathed to the colonized part of the world as the European powers beat a retreat. The transformation of a nation into a nation-state has seldom been anything but a bloody affair, and nearly everywhere people, whose inheritance includes multiple linguistic, religious, and cultural identities, were cudgelled, usually with brute force, into speaking the same language, adopting the same dress, declaring their affinity with one religion, or otherwise rendering themselves into one species of human being, under one flag and one national anthem.

In the Indian sub-continent, the process of nation-state formation was accompanied not only by the ferocious blood-letting, mass migrations, the abduction and rape of women, and uprooting that are encompassed under the word 'partition', but since then by the vivisection of Pakistan in 1971—the memories of which for some victims and perpetrators alike are intertwined with the earlier holocaust—and even by the numerous secessionist, dissenting, and working-class movements that characterize the social and political landscape of Pakistan, Bangladesh, and India.[5] How the politics of cricket conspires with the politics of nation-state war mongering should be amply clear from the fact that *both* the Pakistani cricket team, after their abysmal loss to Australia, and the then Prime Minister Nawaz Sharif, after his meeting with Clinton in Washington at which he agreed to exercise his influence with the Mujahideen to withdraw to the Pakistani side of the Line of Control, dreaded returning home. One can scarcely doubt that a victory on the cricket field would have been followed by a tumultuous homecoming, just as an emphatic declaration by the United States of support for Pakistan, instead of the cold reception that awaited Nawaz Sharif, would have encouraged him to return home at once, where he would have basked in the warm glow of mass approbation. Instead, much like the airplanes that momentarily disappear from the radar scene, both the Pakistani team and Sharif vanished, as if in mute testimony to the famous Indian rope trick, and surfaced a few days later. The homes of the Pakistani cricket players were stoned, and effigies of

Nawaz Sharif were openly burned on the streets of Lahore and Islamabad: each form of disgrace spoke metonymically for the other loss, for the defeat of the nation-state. Let us recall, too, that in Bangladesh the earlier defeat of Pakistan on the cricket field at the hands of what was formerly its other, feminized half, was at once celebrated with the declaration of a national holiday, and Bangladesh's triumph in cricket was likened to the wresting of independence by East Pakistan from West Pakistan. The achievement of this cricketing triumph increasingly began to be trumpeted as Bangladesh's maturation, as something more than a rite of puberty.

No one should imagine, consequently, that Pakistan's defeat was welcomed by Indians only because of the small-scale war that was then going on in the heights of Kargil, and the feeling of betrayal experienced by many Indians at the aggression of Pakistan and Pakistani-supported forces. Pakistan's defeat on the cricket field in those days of conflict was doubtless sweeter to many Indians, but cricket has been a battlefield between the two since at least the late 1960s, and India's refusal to play a long-arranged test series in Pakistan in late 2000 owing to allegedly aggressive Pakistani designs on Kashmir suggests that the state of relations between the two countries can continue to be reliably gauged by their relations on the cricket field. Indeed, when the two countries met in an earlier qualifying match in the World Cup, Pakistanis and Indians imagined that this was the final. India handed Pakistan the defeat that least of all it can tolerate, and to some it no longer mattered if India reached the final: the World Cup had been played out, and the celebrations on the streets in Indian cities were on a grandiose scale. The last time sweets were publicly distributed to such fanfare was when India tested the nuclear bomb and so declared itself a nuclear power. It is a sign of our times that our sweets have now become so charged, vehicles—let us recall that sweets are conveyed from hand to hand—of masculine prowess and nation-state jingoism. Some Indian families do not announce the birth of a girl with sweets, but perhaps the government will now institute a national policy ensuring that sweets are only handed out when a boy is born. Boys of what the colonial regime described as the 'effeminate' races, such as Bengalis, the Hindus of the Gangetic Plains, and the rice-and-idli-eating Tamilians, will doubtless pose some tricky problems.

No longer are our sweets sweets, even our games are no longer games. The hard-edged professionalism that accompanies international sports rivalries, the sheer power play that so firmly characterizes professional sports, the ruthless competitive urge which sends players and fans alike into a frenzy, and the nation-state triumphalism that follows the return of each successful athlete to his or her country, have all taken the spirit of play out of the game. The millions, indeed billions, of 'dollars'—roubles, rupees, rupiahs, and even ringats are not the currency of international sport, any more than they are of world commerce—that are at stake in these sporting bonanzas,[6] from the World Cup (of soccer, that is) and the Olympics to the various self-aggrandizing American sporting events—the Super Bowl on Super Sunday in the 'greatest country on earth'—have transformed sports into a commercial venture that brings it into stiff competition with the armaments industry for the amount of revenue it generates. If the merchants of death can have no better sales pitch than to advertise their own fighter aircraft or artillery guns as the most effective destroyers of the enemy, the most eminent sportsmen and sportswomen of our times are those whose attraction resides in their power to vanquish their opponents. He who does not play to win, must face the opprobrium and humiliation of defeat. The modern world is particularly disdainful of losers. Yet, if one plays to win, then one is no longer playing a game; one is only making a statement, displaying one's might, acting on behalf of other interests, serving out an ideology, and allowing oneself to become a vehicle for the expression of debased expressions of national greatness.

In the interest of altering our conception of games, and from thence of politics and the meaning of the nation-state, it becomes necessary to step outside the established cognitive framework. To this end, I wish to suggest, and will shortly elaborate on the point, that it was a sad day for India when Pakistan went down to Australia in a crushing loss. Many Indians, particularly those who pride themselves on being modern, rational, and patriotic, will be outraged by this sentiment, and I will rattle their tunnelled nationalism and further disturb their sensibilities by stating that Indians were morally bound to lend their support to Pakistan, even while a battle may have raging between the two countries on the peaks of Kargil. No one believes any more that all the countries of the South will naturally gravitate towards each other, in a display of solidarity against imperial and neo-imperial powers, or that all of the women of the world will unite against patriarchy, so I hope that no one will mistake my plea as an instantiation of obdurate Third World nationalism. Let me also state at once that it is perfectly possible to adopt the view that the best side should win, though doubtless nationalist and cultural predilections will enter into any assessment of what counts for 'best', and that the playing field might well be changed, as it has often been, to ensure that the countries of the West remain the 'best'. It is even more reasonable to take the view that one should not support any side at all; not everyone is consumed by the passion for sport. This latter argument may appear to be more consistent with the argument that we should restore to sports the spirit of games, but this alleged neutrality is also consistent with the pretension, which advocates of sports hold with firmness, that politics and sports have nothing to do with each other. Quite to the contrary, if sports and politics are tied together in a blood wedding, as I have suggested, it becomes imperative to create a different political reading of sports, and to open it up to moral and cognitive spaces which would, in a manner of speaking, make a merry sport of sports. There is also the consideration that, as a matter of course, most people will invariably support one side rather than the other, and so it behooves us to consider what should be the basis for the political choices that we in effect make.

A Pakistani friend of mine, a prominent Muslim intellectual who has been settled in London for over thirty-five years, once told me that his son, then ten years old, asked him whether he should support Pakistan or England in a cricket match. His son was born in Britain, and like the greater majority of his peers, speaks English at home and otherwise 'identifies' with England. In reply, his father set up two scenarios, to which I have added a third. If England and Australia were playing each other, he advised his son that he should lend his support to the English team. England is the 'nation-state' to which the family now belongs, and one has obligations, as a citizen, as a moral subject, and as someone who claims rights and receives services, to the state to which one belongs. (Here, again, let me reiterate that neither my friend nor I am much beholden to the idea of 'loyalty', but it is the root of the existence of the nation-state; this concept may at least be granted some heuristic legitimacy.) But what if Pakistan and England were playing each other, his son asked, anticipating the second scenario.

His father explained that, in this case, he was bound to support Pakistan. England may well be the nation-state to which he and his son furnish their allegiance, but the 'nation' is an entity in which a human being is more comfortably and reasonably housed than in the 'state'. People surely commit violence in the name of the nation, though here the nation is usually inextricably intertwined with the notion of the nation-state, and it is also useful to remember that what makes a state a state is the monopoly it exercises in law over the right to use force. In common parlance, the nation-state speaks to us from the 'head', but the nation touches our 'heart'; the nation-state is disciplinary, but the nation is a site of communitas: thus nearly in every language and cultural tradition, though there are exceptions such as that of Germany, the nation is rendered as the 'motherland'. The state demands our political loyalties, but the nation *moves* us in myriad ways that affect our lives as social and cultural beings.

This brings me to the third scenario, which in my imagination was played out that evening in my friend's home. What if India and Pakistan were playing each other on the cricket field, whether in Britain or elsewhere? His son assumed, as would most people if similarly placed, that he ought to support Pakistan, but his father explained that the matter is more complex. Though Pakistanis lay claim to their own nation-state, civilizationally speaking they are Indians as much as those who live in India. (I have no doubt that some, particularly outside Sind and Punjab, will seek to refute this suggestion with the claim that Pakistan has more in common with Afghanistan and Central Asia than it does with India.) There is no such thing as a Pakistani civilization, and though Pakistanis might like to believe that their civilizational moorings are derived pre-eminently from Islam, they should apprise themselves of what middle-eastern Islam, which has set itself up—with the active encouragement of the West—as the true and authentic version of the faith, thinks of the Islam of South Asia. They might be shocked to learn that the most eminent scholars of Islam in the West and the Middle East, not to mention the journalists whose representations of Islam dominate the media, are likely to think of South Asian Islam as highly contaminated, as little better than the Hinduism with which it has lived in close proximity for over a millennium, and perhaps worse than Hinduism on account of its apostasy.[7] The true civilizational home of Pakistan is the Indic world, the culture of South Asia as a whole, but a recognition of this does not in the least strip Pakistanis of their Islam. It would, on the contrary, make them more confident of their Islam, and they might recognize that many of the greatest Muslim scholars and reformers since the nineteenth century, with notable exceptions such as Ali Shari'ati, have emanated from the Indian sub-continent. Likewise, the Hindus in India, if they were not so accustomed to thinking of India as a nation-state, might begin to think of Pakistan as an inextricable part of Indian civilization; they might even, however unthinkable it sounds, recognize in Islam a part of themselves.

Civilizational loyalties, howsoever hard to cultivate, should take precedence over the jejune attachment to the nation-state with which we are all so comfortable. The idea of 'civilizational loyalties' may not be so easy to grasp, and today the vast majority of the world's people, especially the young, have only grown up with no other idea but that of the nation-state and the hatreds that the nation-state system fosters. The word 'civilization' is likewise burdened by a lamentable past and the histrionics of history. Everywhere the march of the colonial powers was trumpeted with the resounding call of the 'civilizing mission'. The nineteenth century even instituted a 'civilizational scale', and where one stood on this scale, say at the top or the bottom, could have something to do with the shape of one's nose, or the contours of one's hair. But if people can kill in the name of God, religion, and humanity, it is scarcely surprising that oppressions should have been unleashed in the name of 'civilization'. That can, however, be no reason to abandon the idea of 'civilization', for civilizations, unlike modern states, have great resilience, and can entertain a plurality of often conflicting ideas. Though the nation-state, for example, is firmly tethered to discourses of history and science as it came to be shaped in the modern West, a civilization entertains a notion of the plurality of sciences, just as it is more hospitable to non-historicist and ahistoricist modes of comprehension and narration, whether construed as folktales, prophecy, oral literatures, proverbs, mythological tales, epics, puranas, or mother's wit. To grasp this idea of 'civilizational loyalties', consider further that among Pakistanis and Indians, the generation that lived at the time of the Partition still speaks fondly of the closeness of Hindu and Muslim relations, the manner in which 'Hindus' and 'Muslims' (when they were openly known, especially to children, to be such) partook of each other's festivals, and the almost imperceptible ways in which Muslims and Hindus shaded into each other. Among the younger generation, which was spared the pains of the Partition and migration, and which could have been expected to work towards healing the divisions, the hatred often runs much deeper.

There are certainly other, equally compelling, reasons why Indians should have been supportive of Pakistan in the final with Australia. Though my principal argument scarcely requires any props, Australia, a country which has seldom shown any interest in sharing the world-view of the South or signifying its affinity with the people of the formerly colonized world, cannot inspire hope among people who aspire for justice or equality. The architect of the Australian win, Shane Warne, has on more than one occasion shown his profoundly racist leanings, and a great many members of the Australian team are similarly afflicted with racist sentiments. Vivian Richards recalled in his autobiography that nowhere did he face such intense racist animosity as in Australia, and no one can forget the intense heckling that the Sri Lankan team encountered on its recent visit to this continent, which is barren in more than one way. Finding it difficult to play Muralitharan, the spin bowler who sent England reeling at the Oval in 1998 with a haul of sixteen wickets in one match, the Australians accused him of 'throwing' the ball, and the player had to suffer the indignity of having a laboratory test, where it was confirmed that a deformity accounted for the particular manner in which Muralitharan bowled. All of this transpired to the accompaniment of unabashedly racist pronouncements on television and in the print media; and though Muralitharan was cleared of the 'charges', and had his reputation restored to him, there was scarcely any apology from the fanatic Australian public. To have a country nurtured in the genocidal mentality lecture an ancient civilization on 'sportsmanlike' behaviour is an intolerable idea, but few Indians (or other South Asians) have given thought to this matter. Somehow Australians think that, having become 'multicultural' in the American fashion, pressing forth with a puerile conception of identity politics, they have become the very embodiment of pluralism.

Thus, there is in the tale of the misbegotten sweets a great many more tales to which we should be sensitive. Though it has not been my intent to furnish a semiotics of Indian sweets, such an exercise can alert us to the manner in which the most complex questions can arise from a consideration of seemingly little things. Far more germane for the present is the sobering thought that if we have reached that nadir where the gift and exchange of sweets is itself beginning to follow the contours of the debased nation-state system, our sweets should be treated like poison. We should call our games battles, fought with escalating venom and intensity, and perhaps we might find that on the battlefield of guns and mortar, even amidst the senseless artillery duels, there is an iota more of the common sense of humanity, a jot more of the spirit of games that has largely vanished from sports. Kargil awaits its Manto,[8] and in South Asia we should await the return of cricket to what passes for cricket in the World Cup.

Notes

1.   I would refer the reader to *Who are the Guilty*: *Report of a Joint Investigation into the Causes and Impact of Riots in Delhi from 31 October to 10 November*, jointly published by the PUDR (People's Union for Democratic Rights) and PUCL (People's Union for Civil Liberties) in 1984 at Delhi, as well as to *Delhi, 31 October to 4 November 1984: Report of the Citizens' Commission* (Delhi, 1984), where reference is made to the rumour of the distribution of sweets and its part in instigating the Hindus to violence.

2.   Some journalist friends have told me that the PUCL and PUDR were bound to dismiss stories of the distribution of sweets as just that, 'stories' without foundation, and that in some trans-Yamuna colonies, they themselves saw sweets being distributed. Luckily, my task here is not that of the investigative journalist, and the precise 'truth' of what transpired in the hours after Indira Gandhi's assassination is, from the perspective offered here, not entirely critical.

3.   Following Gandhi's assassination, his close associate and trusted follower, Sardar Patel, himself came under a cloud of suspicion. Whatever his sympathies for Hindu militants, and they appear to have been considerable, even Patel appears to have thought that the RSS had exceeded the bounds of decency in celebrating Gandhi's death. Writing to Golwalkar, the supreme ideologue of the RSS, on 11 September 1948, he stated: 'It was not necessary to spread poison in order to enthuse the Hindus and organize for their protection. As a final result of the poison, the country had to suffer the sacrifice of the invaluable life of Gandhiji. Even an iota of sympathy of the Government, or the people, no more remained for the RSS. In fact, opposition grew. Opposition turned more severe, when the RSS men expressed joy and distributed sweets after Gandhiji's death. Under these conditions it became inevitable for the

Government to take action against the RSS.'

4.   Sidney Mintz, *Sweetness and Power* (Baltimore: Johns Hopkins University Press, 1979); Ashis Nandy, 'Sugar in History: An Obituary of the Humble Jaggery', *Times of India* (16 July 1994).

5.   One set of thoughtful and nuanced perspectives on the violence that has engulfed much of South Asia is found in Veena Das, ed., *Mirrors of Violence: Communities, Riots and Survivors in South Asia* (Delhi: Oxford University Press, 1990).

6.   The scandal that engulfed the world of Indian cricket in 2000, where several players, who are nothing short of national icons, stood accused of match-fixing, and several—including the former captain of the Indian cricket team, Mohammed Azharruddin, were barred from the game for life—points to the ease with which money has influenced the game.

7.   The scholarship on Islam has become more subtle over the years, and venerated scholars such as Marshall Hodgson and Fazlur Rahman always understood the diversity of Islam; moreover, attacks on Orientalist scholarship have made at least some scholars more cautious about representing the Middle East as the 'true' home of Islam. Nonetheless, it is astonishing how far South Asian Islam is conspicuously missing from general histories of, and courses on, Islam. The fraternity of scholars in the West (especially in the Anglo-American world) who specialize in Indo-Islamic history is very small, even microscopic.

8.   Saadat Hasan Manto, well-known subcontinental fiction writer known for his stories on the trauma of the Partition.

INDEX